SolidWorks 2015
Part II - Advanced Techniques

Advanced Level Tutorials

**Parts, Surfaces, Sheet Metal, SimulationXpress,
Top-Down Assemblies, Core & Cavity Molds**

Written by: Sr. Certified SolidWorks Instructor

Paul Tran, CSWE, CSWI

SDC Publications
P.O. Box 1334
Mission, KS 66222
913-262-2664
www.SDCpublications.com
Publisher: Stephen Schroff

ISBN-13: 978-1-58503-928-9
ISBN-10: 1-58503-928-4

Printed and bound in the United States of America.

Acknowledgments

Thanks as always to my wife Vivian for always being there and providing support and honest feedback on all the chapters in the textbook.

I would like to give a special thanks to Karla Werner and Rachel Schroff for their editing and corrections. Additionally thanks to Kevin Douglas, Dave Worcester and Peter Douglas for writing the forewords.

I also have to thank SDC Publications and the staff for its continuing encouragement and support for this edition of **SolidWorks 2015 Part 2 Advanced Techniques**. Thanks also to Zach Werner for putting together such a beautiful cover design.

Finally, I would like to thank you, our readers, for your continued support. It is with your consistent feedback that we were able to create the lessons and exercises in this book with more detailed and useful information.

Foreword

For more than two decades, I have been fortunate to have worked in the fast-paced, highly dynamic world of mechanical product development providing computer-aided design and manufacturing solutions to thousands of designers, engineers and manufacturing experts in the western US. The organization where I began this career was US CAD in Orange County CA, one of the most successful SolidWorks Resellers in the world. My first several years were spent in the sales organization prior to moving into middle management and ultimately President of the firm. In the mid 1990's is when I met Paul Tran, a young, enthusiastic Instructor who had just joined our team.

Paul began teaching SolidWorks to engineers and designers of medical devices, automotive and aerospace products, high tech electronics, consumer goods, complex machinery and more. After a few months of watching him teach and interacting with students during and after class, it was becoming pretty clear – Paul not only loved to teach, but his students were the most excited with their learning experience than I could ever recall from previous years in the business. As the years began to pass and thousands of students had cycled through Paul's courses, what was eye opening was Paul's continued passion to educate as if it were his first class and students in every class, without exception, loved the course.

Great teachers not only love their subject, but they love to share that joy with students – this is what separates Paul from others in the world of SolidWorks Instruction. He always has gone well beyond learning the picks & clicks of using the software, to best practice approaches to creating intelligent, innovative and efficient designs that are easily grasped by his students. This effective approach to teaching SolidWorks has translated directly into Paul's many published books on the subject. His latest effort with SolidWorks 2015 is no different. Students that apply the practical lessons from basics to advanced concepts will not only learn how to apply SolidWorks to real world design challenges more quickly, but will gain a competitive edge over others that have followed more traditional approaches to learning this type of technology. As the pressure continues to rise on U.S. workers and their organizations to remain competitive in the global economy, raising not only education levels but technical skills are paramount to a successful professional career and business. Investing in a learning process towards the mastery of SolidWorks through the tutelage of the most accomplished and decorated educator and author in Paul Tran will provide a crucial competitive edge in this dynamic market space.

Kevin Douglas
Vice President Sales/Board of Advisors, GoEngineer

Foreword

I first met Paul Tran when I was busy creating another challenge in my life. I needed to take a vision from one man's mind, understand what the vision looked like, how it was going to work and comprehend the scale of his idea. My challenge was I was missing one very important ingredient, a tool that would create a picture with all the moving parts.

Research led me to discover a great tool, SolidWorks. It claimed to allow one to make 3D components, in picture quality, on a computer, add in all moving parts, assemble it and make it run, all before money was spent on bending steel and buying parts that may not fit together. I needed to design and build a product with thousands of parts, make them all fit and work in harmony with millimeters tolerance. The possible cost implications of failed experimentation were daunting.

To my good fortune, one company's marketing strategy of selling a product without an instruction manual and requiring one to attend an instructional class to get it, led me to meet a communicator who made it all seem so simple.

Paul Tran has worked with and taught SolidWorks as his profession for 30 years. Paul knows the SolidWorks product and manipulates it like a fine musical instrument. I watched Paul explain the unexplainable to baffled students with great skill and clarity. He taught me how to navigate the intricacies of the product so that I could use it as a communication tool with skilled engineers. *He teaches the teachers*.

I hired Paul as a design engineering consultant to create the thousands of parts for my company's product. Paul Tran's knowledge and teaching skill has added immeasurable value to my company. When I read through the pages of these manuals, I now have an "instant replay" of his communication skill with the clarity of having him looking over my shoulder - *continuously*. We can now design, prove and build our product and know it will always work and not fail. Most important of all, Paul Tran helped me turn a blind man's vision into reality and a monument to his dream.

Thanks Paul.

These books will make dreams come true and help visionaries change the world.

Peter J. Douglas

CEO, Cake Energy, LLC

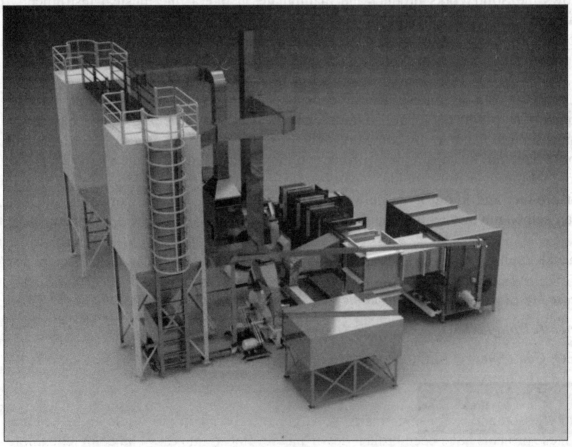

Images courtesy of C.A.K.E. Energy Corp., designed by Paul Tran

Preface

The modern world of engineering design and analysis requires an intense knowledge of Computer Aided Design (CAD) tools. To gain this deep understanding of unique CAD requirements one must commit the time, energy, and use of study guides. Paul Tran has invested countless hours and the wealth of his career to provide a path of easy to understand and follow instructional books. Each chapter is designed to build on the next and supplies users with the building blocks required to easily navigate SolidWorks 2015. I challenge you to find a finer educational tool whether you are new to this industry or a seasoned SolidWorks veteran.

I have been a part of the CAD industry for over twenty five years and read my share of instructional manuals. I can tell you Paul Tran's SolidWorks books do what most promise; however what others don't deliver. This book surpasses any CAD instructional tool I have used during my career. Paul's education and vast experience provides a finely tuned combination, producing instructional material that supports industry standards and most importantly, industry requirements.

Anyone interested in gaining the basics of SolidWorks to an in-depth approach should continue to engage the following chapters. All users at every level of SolidWorks knowledge will gain tremendous benefit from within these pages.

Dave Worcester
System Administer
Advanced Sterilization Products - A Johnson & Johnson Company

Author's Note

SolidWorks 2015 Basic Tools and Advanced Techniques are comprised of lessons and exercises based on the author's extensive knowledge on this software. Paul has 30 years of experience in the fields of mechanical and manufacturing engineering; 18 years were in teaching and supporting the SolidWorks software and its add-ins. As an active Sr. SolidWorks instructor and design engineer, Paul has worked and consulted with hundreds of reputable companies including; IBM, Intel, NASA, US- Navy, Boeing, Disneyland, Medtronic, Guidant, Terumo, Kingston and many more. Today, he has trained more than 8000 engineering professionals, and given guidance to nearly ½ of the number of Certified SolidWorks Professionals and Certified SolidWorks Expert (CSWP & CSWE) in the state of California.

Every lesson and exercise in this book was created based on real world projects. Each of these projects have been broken down and developed into easy and comprehendible steps for the reader. Learn the fundamentals of SolidWorks at your own pace, as you progress form simple to more complex design challenges. Furthermore, at the end of every chapter, there are self test questionnaires to ensure that the reader has gained sufficient knowledge from each section before moving on to more advanced lessons.

Paul believes that the most effective way to learn the "world's most sophisticated software" is to learn it inside and out, create everything from the beginning, and take it step by step. This is what the **SolidWorks 2015 Basic Tools & Advanced Techniques** manuals are all about.

About the Training Files

The files for this textbook are available for download on the publisher's website at **www.SDCpublications.com/downloads/978-1-58503-928-9**. They are organized by the chapter numbers and the file names that are normally mentioned at the beginning of each chapter or exercise. In the <u>Built Parts folder</u> you will also find copies of the parts, assemblies and drawings that were created for cross references or reviewing purposes.

It would be best to make a copy of the content to your local hard drive and work from these documents; you can always go back to the original training files location at anytime in the future, if needed.

Who this book is for

This book is for the mid-level user, who is already familiar with the SolidWorks program. It is also a great resource for the more CAD literate individuals who want to expand their knowledge of the different features that SolidWorks 2015 has to offer.

The organization of the book

The chapters in this book are organized in the logical order in which you would learn the SolidWorks 2015 program. Each chapter will guide you through some different tasks, from navigating through the user interface, to exploring the toolbars, from some simple 3D modeling and move on to more complex tasks that are common to all SolidWorks releases. There is also a self-test questionnaire at the end of each chapter to ensure that you have gained sufficient knowledge before moving on to the next chapter.

The conventions in this book

This book uses the following conventions to describe the actions you perform when using the keyboard and mouse to work in SolidWorks 2015:
Click: means to press and release the mouse button. A click of a mouse button is used to select a command or an item on the screen.

Double Click: means to quickly press and release the left mouse button twice. A double mouse click is used to open a program, or showing the dimensions of a feature.

Right Click: means to press and release the right mouse button. A right mouse click is used to display a list of commands, a list of shortcuts that is related to the selected item.

Click and Drag: means to position the mouse cursor over an item on the screen and then press and hold down the left mouse button; still holding down the left button, move the mouse to the new destination and release the mouse button. Drag and drop makes it easy to move things around within a SolidWorks document.

Bolded words: indicated the action items that you need to perform.

Italic words: Side notes and tips that give you additional information, or to explain special conditions that may occur during the course of the task.

Numbered Steps: indicates that you should follow these steps in order to successfully perform the task.

Icons: indicates the buttons or commands that you need to press.

SolidWorks 2015

SolidWorks 2015 is program suite, or a collection of engineering programs that can help you design better products faster. SolidWorks 2015 contains different combinations of programs; some of the programs used in this book may not be available in your suites.

Start and exit SolidWorks

SolidWorks allows you to start its program in several ways. You can either double click on its shortcut icon on the desktop, or go to the Start menu and select the following: All Programs / SolidWorks 2015 / SolidWorks, or drag a SolidWorks document and drop it on the SolidWorks shortcut icon.

Before exiting SolidWorks, be sure to save any open documents, and then click File / Exit; you can also click the X button on the top right of your screen to exit the program.

Using the Toolbars

You can use toolbars to select commands in SolidWorks rather than using the drop down menus. Using the toolbars is normally faster. The toolbars come with commonly used commands in SolidWorks, but they can be customized to help you work more efficiently.

To access the toolbars, either right click in an empty spot on the top right of your screen or select View / Toolbars.

To customize the toolbars, select Tools / Customize. When the dialog pops up, click on the Commands tab, select a Category, and then drag an icon out of the dialog box and drop it on a toolbar that you want to customize. To remove an icon from a toolbar, drag an icon out of the toolbar and drop it into the dialog box.

Using the task pane

The task pane is normally kept on the right side of your screen. It display various options like SolidWorks resources, Design library, File explorer, Search, View palette, Appearances and Scenes, Custom properties, Built-in libraries, Technical alerts and news, etc,.

The task pane provides quick access to any of the mentioned items by offering the drag and drop function to all of its contents. You can see a large preview of a SolidWorks document before opening it. New documents can be saved in the task pane at anytime, and existing documents can also be edited and re-saved. The task pane can be resized, close or move to different location on your screen if needed.

Table of Contents

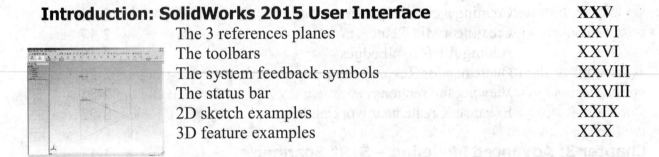
Advanced Modeling Topics

Sheet Metal Topics

Top-Down Assembly Topics

Introduction

SolidWorks User Interface

The SolidWorks 2015 User Interface

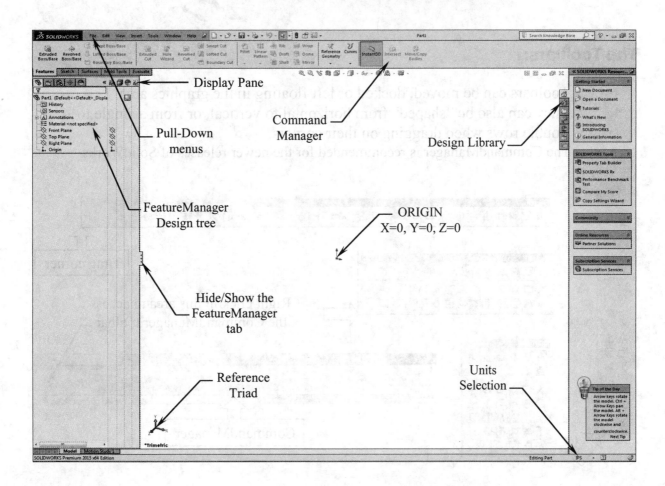

The 3 reference planes:

- The Front, Top and the Right plane are 90°apart. They share the same center point called the Origin.

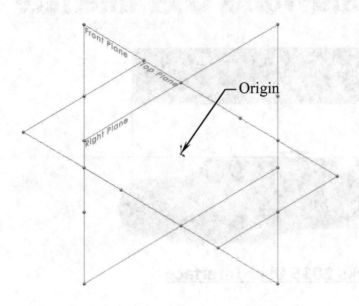

Origin

Y

Z

X

6 Degrees of Freedom

The Toolbars:

- Toolbars can be moved, docked or left floating in the graphics area.
- They can also be "shaped" from horizontal to vertical, or from a single to double rows when dragging on their corners.
- The CommandManager is recommended for the newer releases of SolidWorks.

Drag corner

Right click in this area to access the CommandManager toolbar

CommandManager

- If CommandManager is not used, toolbars can be docked or left floating.

- Toolbars can be toggled off or on by activating or de-activating their check boxes:

- Select **Tools / Customize / Toolbars** tab.

- The icons in the toolbars can be enlarged when its check box is selected

The View ports: You can view or work with SolidWorks model or an assembly using one, two or four view ports.

View Orientation

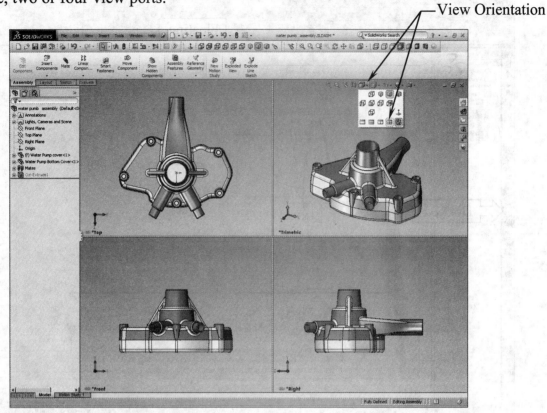

- Some of the **System Feedback symbols** (Inference pointers):

Snap to Vertex (endpoint)   Snap to Intersection

Snap to Edge (curve)   Horizontal Line

Snap to Mid-point   Vertical Line

The Status Bar: (View / Status Bar)

Displays the status of the sketch entity using different colors to indicate:

Green = Selected   **Blue** = Under defined
Black = Fully defined   **Red** = Over defined

2D Sketch examples:

Click-Drag-Release: Single entity.

(Click Point 1, hold the mouse button, drag to point 2 and release).

Click-Release: Continuous multiple entities.

(The Inference Lines appear when the sketch entities are Parallel, Perpendicular or Tangent with each other).

Click-Drag-Release: Single Rectangle

(Click point 1, hold the mouse button, and drag to Point 2 and release).

Click-Drag-Release: Single Centerpoint Arc

(Click point 1, hold the mouse button and drag to Point 2, release; then drag to Point 3 and release).

Click-Drag-Release: Single Circle

(Click point 1 [center of circle], hold the mouse button, drag to Point 2 [Radius] and release).

3D Feature examples:

2D sketch

Extrude

3D feature

2D sketch

Revolve

3D feature

2D sketch

Sweep

3D feature

2D sketch

Loft

3D feature

Box-Select: Use the Select Pointer to drag a selection box around items.

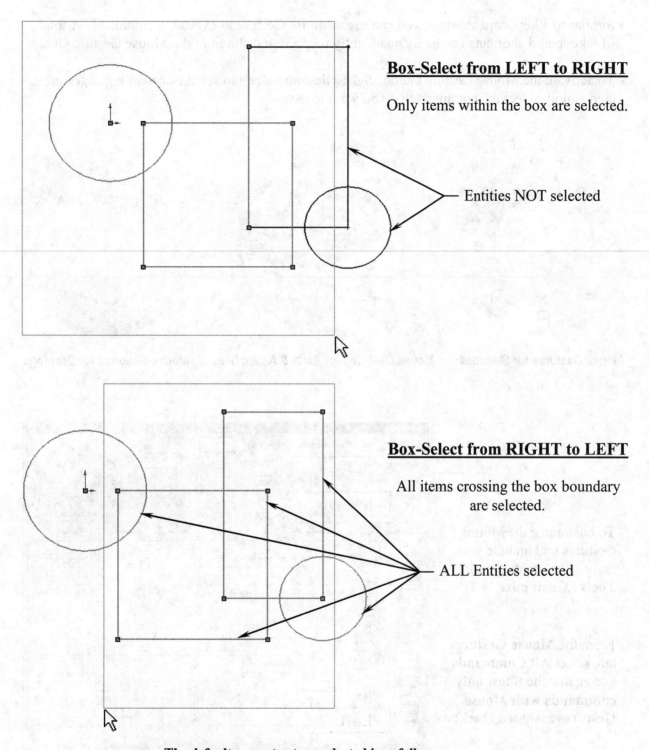

Box-Select from LEFT to RIGHT

Only items within the box are selected.

Entities NOT selected

Box-Select from RIGHT to LEFT

All items crossing the box boundary are selected.

ALL Entities selected

The default geometry type selected is as follows:

* Part documents – edges * Assembly documents – components * Drawing documents - sketch entities, dims & annotations. * To select multiple entities, hold the **Ctrl** while selecting after the first selection.

Exercise: 3D Sketch & Planes

A 3D sketch normally consists of lines and arcs in series, and splines. You can use a 3D sketch as a sweep path, as a guide curve for a loft or sweep, a centerline for a loft, or as one of the key entities in a routing system.

The following exercise demonstrates how several planes can be used to help define the directions of 3D Sketch Entities.

1. Sketching the reference Pivot lines:

- Select the <u>Top</u> plane and

  open a new sketch ✎ .

- Sketch **2 Centerlines** ┇

  and add Dimensions ⬦
  as shown.

4.000   4.000

2. Creating the 1st 45º Plane:

- Select **Insert/Reference Geometry/Planes** ⬧ .

- Click the **At Angle** option and enter **45** for Angle ⬦ .

- Select the **top** plane and the **vertical line** as noted.

Select the top plane
and the vertical line…

Plane

Message
Fully defined

First Reference

- Top Plane
- Parallel
- Perpendicular
- Coincident
- 45.00deg
  - ☐ Flip
- 1
- 0.100in
- Mid Plane

Second Reference

- Line1@Sketch1
- Perpendicular
- Coincident
- Project

- Click **OK** ✔ .

3. Creating the 2nd 45° Plane:

- Select **Insert/Reference Geometry/Planes** .

- Click the **At Angle** option and enter **45** for Angle .

- Select the **front** plane and the **horizontal line** as noted.

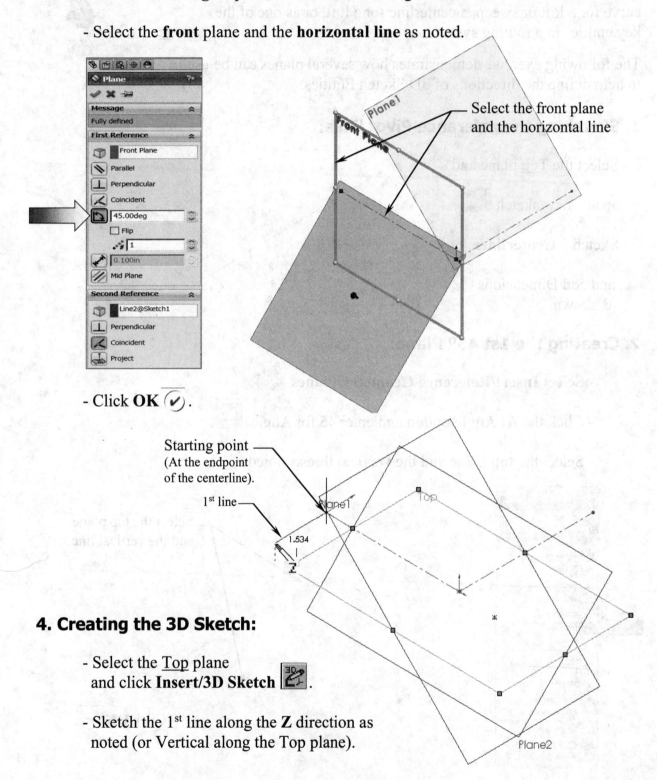

Select the front plane
and the horizontal line

- Click **OK** .

Starting point
(At the endpoint
of the centerline).

1st line

1.534

4. Creating the 3D Sketch:

- Select the Top plane
  and click **Insert/3D Sketch** .

- Sketch the 1st line along the **Z** direction as
  noted (or Vertical along the Top plane).

- Select the **Plane2** (45 deg.) from the Feature Manager tree and Sketch the 2nd line along the **Y** direction (watch the cursor feedback symbol).

> 💡 **Switching Planes**
>
> While sketching the lines, hold the **Control** key and click a plane to switch from one plane to another, or simply select them from the Feature tree each time.

1st line

- Sketch the rest of lines on the planes as labeled.

- For clarity, hide all the planes (select the **View** menu and click off **Planes**). We will select the planes from the FeatureManager tree when needed.

Top View (Ctrl + 5)   Right View (Ctrl + 4)

- Add Dimensions 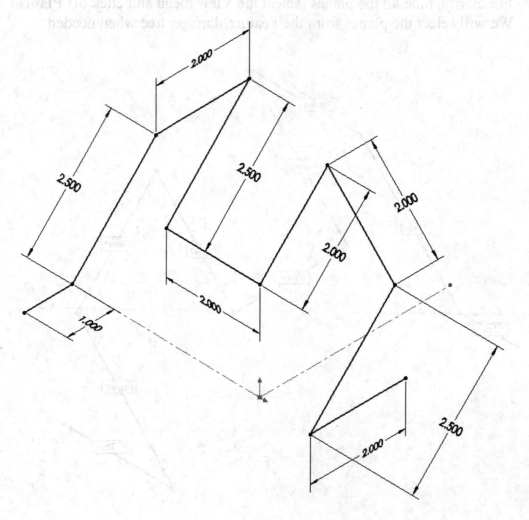 to fully define the sketch.

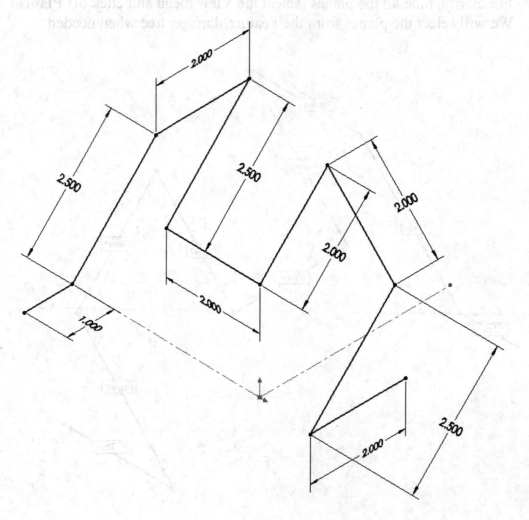

- Add **Sketch Fillets** of **.500 in.** to all corners.

Fillet Parameters

0.500in

☑ Keep constrained corners
☐ Dimension each fillet

- **Exit** the 3D Sketch or press **Ctrl+Q**.

5. Creating a Perpendicular plane:

- Select **Insert/Reference Geometry/Plane**.

- Select the **line** and its **endpoint** approximately as shown.

- The **Perpendicular** option should be selected by default.

Plane

Message
Fully defined

First Reference
Line2@3DSketch1
⊥ Perpendicular
☐ Set origin on curve
Coincident
Project

Second Reference
Point5@3DSketch1
Coincident
Project

Click here

- A new plane normal to the selected line is created.

- Click **OK**.

6. Sketching the Sweep Profile:

- Select the <u>new plane</u>
  (Plane3) and open a new sketch .

- Sketch **2 Circles**
  on the same center and
  add the dimensions as
  shown to fully define
  the sketch.

7. Sweeping the Profile along the 3D Path:

- Click 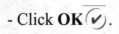 or Select **Insert/Boss Base/Sweep**

- Select the **Circles** as the Sweep Profile .

- Select the **3D Sketch** as the Sweep Path .

- Click **OK** .

- The resulting Swept feature.

8. Hiding the Planes:

- From the menu, select **View/Planes**.

- The planes are temporarily put away
  from the scene.

9. Saving your work:

- Click **File/Save As:**
  3D Sketch_Planes.

- Click **Save**.

Exercise: 3D Sketch & Composite Curve

A 3D sketch normally consists of lines and arcs in series and Splines. You can use a 3D sketch as a sweep path, as a guide curve for a loft or sweep, a centerline for a loft, or as one of the key entities in a routing system.

The following exercise demonstrates how several 3D Sketches can be created, combined into 1 continuous Composite Curve, and used as a Sweep Path.

1. Creating a 2D sketch:

- Select <u>Top</u> plane and sketch

    a **1.00" dia**. **Circle** ⊙

    and 2 Centerlines ⋮ .

2. Creating a Helix:

- Select **Insert/Curve/**

    Helix-Spiral 🐍 .

- Pitch: **.250 in**.

- Revolution: **10**.

- Starting Angle: **0 deg**.

- Click **OK** ✓ .

Helix/Spiral

Defined By:
Pitch and Revolution

Parameters
- Constant Pitch
- Variable Pitch

Pitch:
0.250in

☐ Reverse direction

Revolutions:
10

Start angle:
0.00deg

- Clockwise
- Counterclockwise

☐ **Taper Helix**
0.00deg
☐ Taper outward

3. Creating the 1st 3D sketch:

- Select **Insert/3D Sketch**

- Select the **Line** command
  and sketch the 1st line
  along the X direction.

On-Plane relation
(End point & Right plane)

- Add other lines in the directions as labeled.

- Add Dimensions to fully define the sketch.

- Add Sketch Fillets
  of **.250 in**. to all corners.

- **Exit** the 3D Sketch or press **Ctrl + Q**.

4. Creating the 2nd 3D sketch:

- Select **Insert/3D Sketch** .

- Select the **Line** command and sketch the 1st line along the X direction.

- Sketch the rest of the lines following their direction shown below.

On-Plane relation
(End point & Right plane)

- Add Dimensions
  to fully define the sketch.

- Add **Sketch Fillets** of **.250 in**.
  to all corners.

1.500
2.500
3.000
R.250
R.250
R.250
.750
(2.500)
(3.000)
(1.500)

- **Exit** the 3D Sketch or press **Ctrl+Q**.

5. Combining the 3 sketches into 1 curve:

- Select **Insert/Curve/Composite** or select it from the Curves button on the Features toolbar.

- Select the 3 Sketches either from the Feature Manager tree or directly from the graphics area.

- Click **OK** .

- The sketches are now combined into 1 continuous curve called a Composite Curve.

6. Creating a new work plane:

- Select **Insert/Reference Geometry/Plane** .

- Select the **edge** and **endpoint** as noted, the Perpendicular should be selected.

Select the Curve and the Endpoint

- Click **OK** .

7. Sketching the Sweep Profile:

- Select the <u>new plane</u> (Plane1) and open a new sketch .

- Sketch a **Circle** and add a **.165** dia. dimension .

Pierce Relation

- Add a **Pierce** relation between the center of the circle and the curve.

Ø.165

- **Exit** the Sketch .

8. Sweeping the Profile along the Path:

- Select **Insert/Boss Base/ Sweep** .

- Select the **Circle** as the Sweep Profile .

- Select the **Composite Curve** as the Sweep Path .

- Click **OK** (✓).

9. Saving your work:

- Click **File/Save As**.

- Enter **3D Sketch_ Composite Curve**.

- Click **Save**.

CHAPTER 2

Plane Creation

Planes
Advanced Topics

- In SolidWorks, planes are not only used to sketch geometry, but also used to create section views of a model or an assembly. Planes are also used as the end conditions to extrude features and as neutral planes to define the draft angles, etc.

- There are several options to create planes:

 Parallel Plane.   At Angle Plane.

 Perpendicular Plane.   Offset Distance Plane.

 Coincident Plane.   Mid Plane.

 Project Plane.

- Each plane requires slightly different types of references, some of them may require only one and some others may require two or three.

- This chapter discusses how planes are created using sketch geometry and other features that are available in the model, as references.

Plane Creation

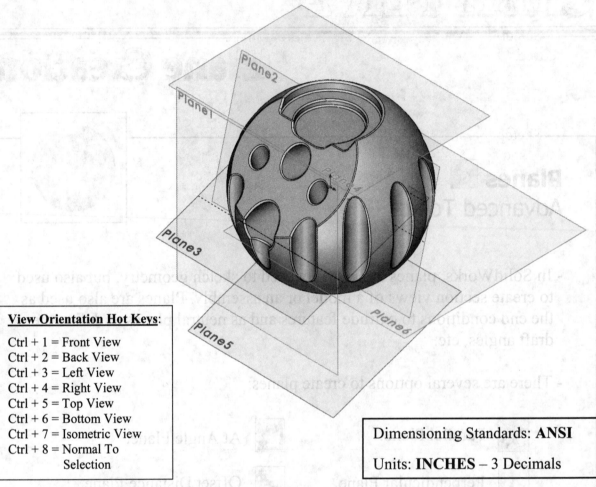

Dimensioning Standards: **ANSI**

Units: **INCHES** – 3 Decimals

Tools Needed:

Insert Sketch	Rectangle	Circle
Planes	Add Geometric Relations	Dimension
Sketch Mirror	Offset Entities	Boss/Base Revolve
Circular Pattern	Extruded Cut	Fillet/Round

1. Starting with a new Part document:

- Select **File / New / Part** and click **OK**.

- Select the <u>Front</u> plane from the FeatureManager tree.

- Click 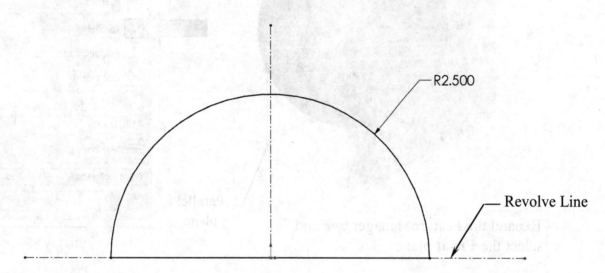 or select **Insert / Sketch**.

- Sketch the profile below and add dimensions
as shown. (It might be easier to sketch a circle, instead of a centerpoint arc, add
the 2 centerlines, and then trim away the bottom half of the circle).

R2.500

Revolve Line

2. Revolving the Base:

- Click or select **Insert / Boss Base / Revolve**.

- Set Revolve Type to: **Blind**.

- Set Revolve Angle to: **360 deg.**

- Click **OK**.

- *Note: Drag the Direction arrow to
see the preview of the rotate angle.*

Direction
arrow

R2.500

3. Creating a Tangent plane: (Requires a cylindrical face and a parallel plane).

- Click or select: **Insert / Reference Geometry / Plane**.

- Click the **face** of the sphere.

Cylindrical face

Parallel plane

- Expand the FeatureManager tree and select the **Front** plane.

- The **Tangent** option is selected automatically.

- Click the **Parallel** option in the Second Reference section.

- Click **OK** ✓.

4. Adding a Center hole:

- Select the new plane (Plane1) and open a new sketch.

- Sketch a **Circle** centered on the origin.

- Add a **1.000"** diameter dimension.

- The circle should be fully defined at this point.

Ø1.000

- Click or select:
Insert / Cut / Extrude.

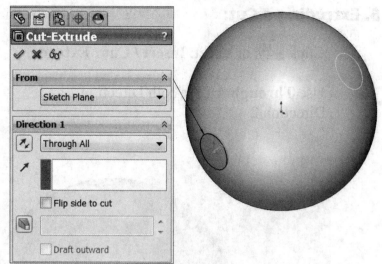

- Select **Through All** for
Direction 1.

- Click **OK** ✅.

5. Creating a flat surface:

- This step will demonstrate the use of geometric relations to fully define the sketch
without using dimensions.

- Select the <u>Right</u> plane from the FeatureManager tree.

- Click ✏️ or select **Insert / Sketch** and switch to the right view (Ctrl+4).

- Sketch a **Line** and add the Relations ⊥ as shown.

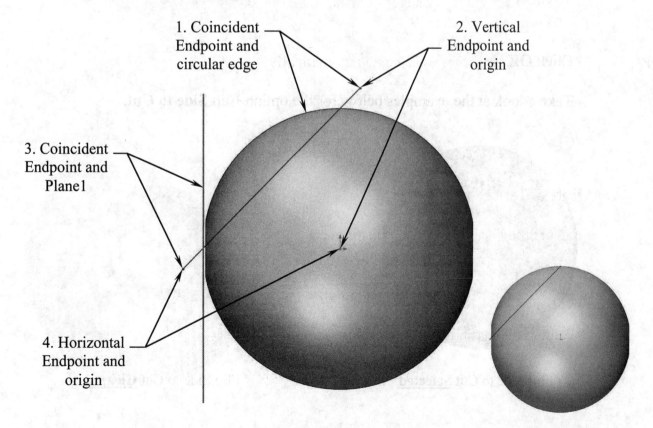

1. Coincident Endpoint and circular edge

2. Vertical Endpoint and origin

3. Coincident Endpoint and Plane1

4. Horizontal Endpoint and origin

6. Extruding a Cut:

- Click or select: **Insert / Cut / Extrude**.

- Use **Through All** for both Direction 1 <u>and</u> Direction 2.

- Click **OK** ✓.

- Take a look at the examples below for the option **Flip Side to Cut**.

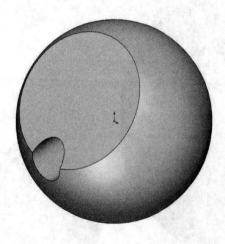

Flip Side to Cut <u>**Selected**</u>

Flip Side to Cut <u>**Cleared**</u>

7. Creating an At-Angle plane: (Requires a Reference Plane, a Reference Axis, and an Angular Dimension).

    - Select the **Front** plane from FeatureManager tree.

    - Click or select **Insert / Reference Geometry / Plane**.

    - Select the **horizontal centerline** as ref. axis.

    - Select the **At Angle** option.

    - Enter **15 deg**. in the dialog box and click **Flip**.

    - Click **OK** ✅.

> 💡 **Show Sketch** 👓
>
> Right click on *Sketch1* (on the FeatureManager tree, below the **Revolve1**) and select **Show**.

Reference Axis

8. Creating a Ø.750 hole:

- Select the <u>new plane</u> (Plane2).

- Click or select **Insert / Sketch**.

- Sketch a **Circle** ⊕ and add the dimensions and a vertical relation as shown.

.950

Ø.750

Add a ref. centerline to use later in step 10.

Vertical

- Click or select **Insert / Cut / Extrude**.

- Direction 1: **Through All**.

- Direction 2: **Through All**.

- Click **OK** ✓.

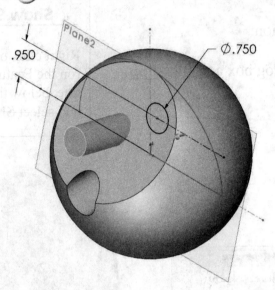

9. Showing the Sketches:

- On the FeatureManager tree expand the Cut-Extrude1 (click the + symbol),
  right click on **Sketch2**, and select **Show**.

- Expand the Cut-Extrude2 (click the + symbol), right-click on **Sketch3**, and
  select **Show**, also Hide the Sketch1.

10. Creating a Coincident plane: (Requires a Reference Line and a Sketch Point or a Vertex).

- Click or select **Insert / Reference Geometry / Plane**.

- Select the **Centerline** and the **Endpoint** as indicated.

- The **Coincident** option should be selected automatically.

- Click **OK** ✅.

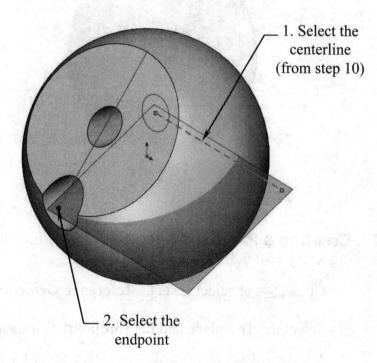

1. Select the centerline (from step 10)

2. Select the endpoint

11. Creating the Ø.500 holes:

- Select the <u>new plane</u> (Plane3).

- Click ✏ or select **Insert / Sketch**.

- Sketch a **Circle** ⊕ and Mirror it ⚠ (Use either Dynamic Mirror or Mirror Entity to mirror the circles).

- Add Dimensions ✎ as shown to fully define the sketch.

Mirror Centerline

1.000

1.000

Ø.500

- Click or select **Insert / Cut / Extrude**.

- Direction 1: **Through All**.

- Direction 2: **Through All**.

- Click **OK** ✓.

12. Creating a Parallel plane: (Requires a Reference Plane and Reference Point).

- Click or select **Insert / Reference Geometry / Plane**.

- Select the **Top** plane and the **Endpoint** as indicated.

- Based on the selection, the system selects the **Parallel** and **Coincident** options.

- Click **OK** ✓.

2. Select the Endpoint

1. Select the TOP plane

13. Creating the Ø2.500 Recess:

- Select the <u>new Plane</u> (Plane4) and insert a new sketch .

- Sketch a **Circle** ⊕ and add Dimension ◈ .

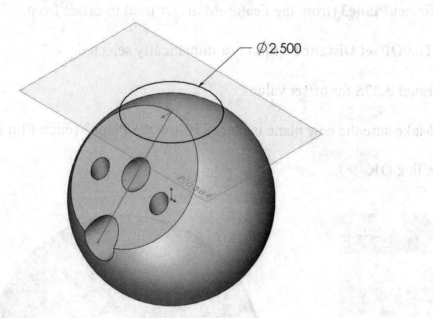

Ø2.500

- Click 📇 or select **Insert / Cut / Extrude**.

- End Condition: **Blind**.

- Extrude Depth: **.625** in.

- Click **OK** ✅ .

Ø2.500

- Hide 🔗 the Sketch2, Sketch3 and all planes.

1. Opening the Spanner sketch document:

- From the Training Files folder, locate and <u>open</u> the document named: **Spanner Sketch**.

- <u>Edit</u> the **Sketch1**. This is the open end of the spanner.

Symmetry centerline

Maximum Arc Condition

Tangent Relations

⊥ with the 10° centerline

💡 Arc Conditions

The 1.375 dimension is measured from the outer tangents of the arcs, this is called: Maximum Arc Conditions*

* There are two options to create the Max/Min Arc condition dimensions:

Option 1: Select the Smart Dimension tool, click on the 2 arcs, and place the dimension anywhere.
    - Select the Leaders tab from the tree (circled).
    - Select the Max options for both arcs (Circled).

Option 2: Hold down the SHIFT key and click on the 2 arcs, the dimension's leader lines will snap to the arc tangents automatically.

2. Extruding the base feature:

- Click or select **Insert / Boss-Base / Extrude**.

- End Condition: **Mid Plane**.

- Extrude Depth: **.250 in**.

- Click **OK** ✅.

Renaming Features

Slow double click on each feature's name (or press F2) and rename them to something more descriptive like: Open-End, Transition-Body, Closed-End, etc...

3. Creating the transition sketch:

- Select <u>Top</u> plane from the FeatureManager tree.

- Click 📝 or select **Insert / Sketch**.

- Sketch the profile below using Lines ╲.

Note: only add the Sketch Fillets after the sketch is fully defined.

- Add dimensions ✏ or Relations ⊥ as needed.

4. Extruding the Transition feature:

- Click or select **Insert / Boss-Base / Extrude**.

- End Condition: **Mid Plane**

- Extrude Depth: **.175 in**.

- Click **OK** ✅.

5. Adding the reference geometry:

- Select the <u>face</u> as indicated.

- Click 🖉 or select **Insert / Sketch**.

- Sketch a Centerline ⋮ at the mid-point of the two vertical edges.

Sketch Face

Mid-point

- Exit the Sketch 🖉 or select **Insert / Sketch**.

6. Creating a new work plane: Plane at Angle

- Click or select **Insert / Reference Geometry / Plane**.

- For Reference Entities ▣ Select the **Sketch4** (centerline) and the **upper face** of the Transition.

- Enter **10 deg**. (arrow), click **Flip** (if needed) to place the plane on the bottom.

Reference Face

Reference Centerline

- Click **OK** ✓.

- SolidWorks creates a plane that starts from the reference face and pivots around the centerline.

- The preview of the new 10 degrees plane.

Pivots from the center of the thickness

7. Creating the Closed-End sketch:

- Select the new **10° plane** from the FeatureManager tree.

- Click or select **Insert / Sketch**.

- Sketch a circle and add dimensions as shown.

Vertical

8. Extruding the Closed-end feature:

- Click or select **Insert / Boss-Base / Extrude**.

- **Direction 1:** **Blind**.

- Extrude Depth: **.200 in**.

- **Direction 2:** **Blind**.

- Extrude Depth: **.130 in**.

- Click **OK**.

9. Adding a 12-Sided polygonal hole:

- Select the <u>face</u> indicated as sketch plane.

- Click or select **Insert / Sketch**.

- Sketch a Polygon ⊕ with **12 sides** Ⓝ (arrow).

- Add a **.625 Dia**. Dimension ◇ to the inside construction circle.

- Add a **Concentric** relation ⏚ between the construction circle and the circular edge.

Sketch
Face

Concentric

Add a Horizontal
relation to 1 line.

Ø.625

10. Extruding a cut:

- Click 🔲 or select **Insert / Cut / Extrude**.

- End Condition: **Through All**.

- Click **OK** ✓.

Ø.625

11. Creating the Recess profile:

- Select the <u>face</u> indicated as sketch plane.

- Click or select **Insert / Sketch**.

- Sketch the profile shown below using the **Straight-Slot** command.

- Add Dimensions and Relations to fully define the sketch.

12. Extruding the Recessed feature:

- Click or select **Insert / Cut / Extrude**.

- End Condition: **Blind**.

- Extrude Depth: **.030 in**.

- Click **OK**.

13. Mirroring the Recessed feature:

- Hold the **Control** key, select the <u>Top</u> reference plane, and the Recessed feature from the FeatureManager tree.

- Click or select **Insert / Pattern Mirror** menu, then select **Mirror**.

- Click **OK** .

- Rotate the model to verify the results.

14. Adding the .030" fillets:

- Click or select **Insert / Features / Fillet/Round**.

- Enter **.030 in**. for Radius.

- Select the edges as shown for Edges to fillet.

- Tangent Propagation: **Enabled**.

- Click **OK** .

Select these edges
on both sides...

Radius: 0.03in

15. Adding the .050" fillets:

- Repeat step 14 and add a **.050"** fillet to the 4 edges shown below.

Radius: 0.05in

Select 4 edges

16. Adding the .015" fillets:

- Click and add a **.015"** fillet to the edges and faces shown below.

Select the **Edges** on both sides...

Select the **Faces** on both sides...

- Click **OK** ✅.

- Verify your fillets with the model shown below.

17. Adding text:

- Select the <u>face</u> indicated as sketch plane.

- Click or select **Insert / Sketch**.

- Click and type **5/8** in the text dialog box.

- Click **OK** .

- Add dimensions to position the text.

Sketch Face

Manipulator Point

.075

1.325

- Clear Use document's font check box .

- Change Width factor to **150%** .

- Leave Spacing at **100%** .

- Font: **Century Gothic** .

- Style: **Regular** - Points size: **14 pt**.

<u>NOTE:</u>
Use the Curves option when you want your sketch letters to wrap along a curve.

It will work better if the curve is created in the same sketch, as construction geometry.

> **Positioning Text**
>
> Each set of sketch text comes with a Manipulator Point, dimensions can be added from this point to position the text.

18. Extruding the text:

- Click or select **Insert / Boss-Base / Extrude**.

- End Condition: **Blind**.

- Extrude Depth: **.015 in**.

- Click **OK**.

Extrude4

From

Sketch Plane

Direction 1

Blind

0.015in

☑ Merge result

☐ Draft outward

💡 Extruding Text

Text or letters can be used as a normal sketch and extruded with drafts.

Text can also be extruded as a boss or a cut feature.

.075

1.325

19. Adding more text:

- Select the indicated face as sketch plane.

- Click or select **Insert / Sketch**.

- Click and type SPANNER in the Text dialog box.

- Add dimensions to fully position the text.

Sketch Face

.075

5/8   SPANNER

2.750

More Settings

- Clear Use document's font check box .

- Change Width factor to **150%** .

- Keep Spacing at **100%** .

- Font: **Century Gothic** Font... .

- Style: **Regular**.

- Points size: **14 pt**.

- Click **OK** .

20. Extruding the text:

- Click or select **Insert / Boss-base / Extrude**.

- End Condition: **Blind**.

- Extrude Depth: **.015 in**.

- Click **OK** .

Text Color

To change the color of extruded text: Right click the extruded feature (text) from the Feature tree, select Appearances and choose a different color.

21. Saving your work:

- Select **File / Save as / Spanner / Save**.

22. Optional:

- To add the same text on the opposite side of the part, repeat from step 17 through step 20.

- Since the mirror option will not work correctly for text, you can either copy the sketch of the text, edit it, re-position, and extrude it again - OR - copy and paste the extruded text and then edit it's sketch to reposition.

Questions for Review

Advanced Modeling

1. The Min / Max conditions can be selected from the dimensions properties, under the Leaders tab.
    a. True
    b. False

2. The Mid-Plane extrude type protrudes the sketch profile to both directions equally.
    a. True
    b. False

3. It is sufficient to create a plane at an angle with a surface and an angular dimension.
    a. True
    b. False

4. When sketching a polygon, the number of sides can be changed on the Properties tree.
    a. True
    b. False

5. A 3D solid feature can be mirrored using a centerline as the center of mirror.
    a. True
    b. False

6. Text cannot be used to extrude as a boss or a cut feature.
    a. True
    b. False

7. Extruded text can be mirrored just like any other 3D features.
    a. True
    b. False

8. Text in a sketch can be extruded with drafts, inward or outward.
    a. True
    b. False

7. TRUE   8. TRUE
5. FALSE   6. FALSE
3. FALSE   4. TRUE
1. TRUE   2. TRUE

von Mises (psi)
6.095e+004
5.587e+004
5.079e+004
4.572e+004
4.064e+004
3.556e+004
3.049e+004
2.541e+004
2.033e+004
1.525e+004
1.018e+004
5.101e+003
2.476e+001

<u>Exercise:</u> Circular Text Wraps

1. Opening a part file:

- From the Training Files folder, open an existing part named: **Text Wrap**.

2. Adding Text:

- Select the <u>Top</u> plane and open a new sketch.

- Sketch a circle at Ø**5.500"** and convert it into construction geometry.

- Sketch the other centerlines, trim, then add the dimensions and relations as indicated.

- Click the **Text** command.

- Enter the word: **SolidWorks**.

Symmetric relation (both top and bottom) between the endpoints and the centerlines

- Select the upper construction curve to bend the text around it.

Select these options

- Click the **Font** button and set the size to **72 points.**

Select this curve

- Select all other options as noted to align the text.

3. Repeating:

- Still working in the same
  sketch, repeat step 2 and
  add the number:
  2015.

- Add a Symmetric relation
  between the endpoints of
  the construction curve
  and the vertical
  centerline.

Symmetric

- Use the same text settings
  as the last text.

4. Extruding the text:

- Click **Extruded
  Boss-Base**.

- Change Direction 1
  to **Offset From
  Surface**.

- Enter **.030"** and
  click **Reverse Offset**.

- Select the **face** as
  indicated.

- Click **OK** ✓.

Select this face

5. Saving your work:

- Click **File / Save As**.

- Enter **Circular Text Wrap**.

- Press **Save**.

CHAPTER 4

Sweep with Composite Curves

Sweep ⊏ with Composite Curves

Unlike extruded or revolved shapes, the sweep option offers a more advanced way of creating complex geometry, where a single profile can be swept along 2D guide paths or 3D curves to define the shape.

To create a sweep feature the Sweep Path gets created first, then a single closed sketch Profile.

The Profile will be related to the Sweep Path with a Pierce or a coincident relation.

When the Profile is swept, the Sweep Path and Guide Curves help control the shape and its behaviors such as twisting, tangencies, etc.

The Composite Curve ⟋ option allows multiple sketches or model edges to be jointed into one continuous path for use in sweep features. (The sketches must be connecting with one another in order for the composite curve to work.)

This lesson will guide you through the creation of a helical extension spring; where several 2D sketches will be combined with a 3D helix to create one continuous curve.
This curve is called: **Composite Curve**.

Ø.080

Helical Extension Spring
Sweep with Composite Curves

Dimensioning Standards: **ANSI**

Units: **INCHES** – 3 Decimals

Tools Needed:

Insert Sketch	Line	Circle
Tangent Arc	3 Point Arc	Add Geometric Relations
Dimension	Composite Curve	Sweep

1. Sketching the first profile:

- Select the <u>Front</u> plane from the FeatureManager Tree.

- Click 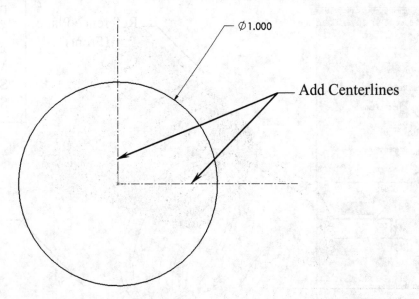 or **Insert / Sketch**.

- Sketch a **Circle** and two centerlines then add the dimension as shown.

Ø1.000

Add Centerlines

2. Converting the circle into a Helix:

- Select **Insert / Curve / Helix / Spiral**.

Defined by:	**Pitch and Revolution**
Pitch:	**.100**
Revolution:	**10**
Starting angle:	**0°**
Taper helix:	**Enabled**
Taper angle:	**10°**

- Click **OK**.

3. Creating a 2-degree plane:

- Show the previous sketch (Sketch1).

- Click or select **Insert/Reference Geometry/ Plane**.

Reference Plane (Front)

Pivot Line

> **Show Sketch**
>
> - Sketches can be made visible for use with other operations, such as Convert Entities, Sweep Path, Loft Profiles, new Plane creation, etc…
> - From the Feature-Manager Tree, click the Sketch1 and select SHOW.

- Select the **Horizontal Centerline** as the Pivot Line.

- Select the **at Angle** option 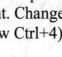.

- Enter **2.00deg.** for Angle.

- Enable the **Flip** option. (Make sure the new plane leans to the right. Change to the Right view Ctrl+4).

- Click **OK** ✓.

- Hide the Sketch1.

Plane1

2° Plane

4. Sketching the large loop:

- Select the <u>Plane1</u> from the FeatureManager Tree.

- Click ![icon] or select **Insert / Sketch**.

- Sketch a **3-point Arc** ![icon] and add dimension as shown:

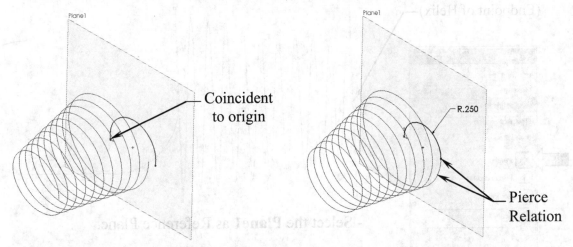

Coincident to origin

R.250

Pierce Relation

- Add a **Pierce** relation between the end point of the Arc and the Helix.

- **Exit** the sketch ![icon] or select **Insert / Sketch**.

5. Sketching the large hook:

- Select the <u>Right</u> plane from the FeatureManager Tree.

- Click ![icon] or select **Insert / Sketch**.

- Sketch the profile and add dimension and relations as shown below:

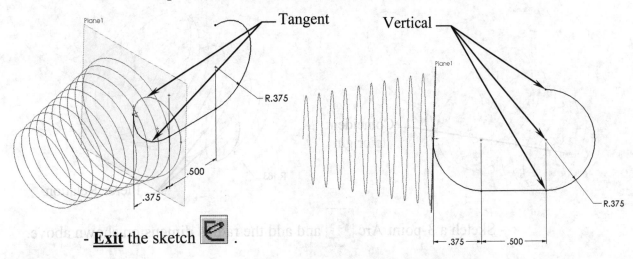

Tangent

Vertical

R.375

.500

.375

R.375

.375

.500

- **Exit** the sketch ![icon] .

6. Creating a Parallel plane:

- Select the Plane1 from the FeatureManager Tree.

- Click or **Insert / Reference Geometry / Plane**.

Reference Point
(Endpoint of Helix)

Reference Plane
(Plane1)

- Select the **Plane1** as Reference Plane.

- Click the left **Endpoint** of the helix as Reference Point.

- Select the **Parallel** option.

- Click **OK**.

7. Adding the small loop:

- Select the new plane (Plane2) from the FeatureManager Tree.

- Click or **Insert / Sketch**.

Coincident
to origin

R.163

Pierce Relation

- Sketch a 3-point Arc and add the radius dimension shown above.

- Add a **Pierce** relation 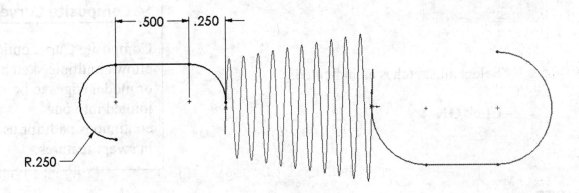 between the endpoint of the Arc and the Helix.

- **Exit** the sketch or **Insert / Sketch**.

8. Creating a small hook:

- Select the <u>Right</u> plane from the FeatureManager Tree.

- Click or **Insert / Sketch**.

- Sketch the profile and add the dimensions shown.

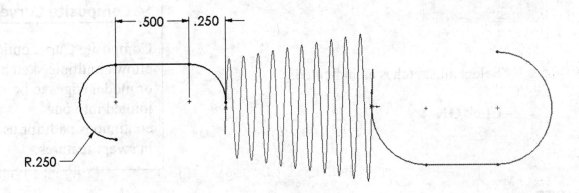

- Add the relations Vertical and Tangent to the indicated entities.

- **Exit** the sketch or click **Insert / Sketch**.

9. Creating a Composite Curve:

- Click under the Curves button or select: **Insert / Curve / Composite**.

- Select all sketches as indicated.

- Click **OK** ✅.

> 💡 **Composite Curve**
>
> Composite Curve option allows multiple sketches or model edges to be jointed into one continuous path for use in swept features.

NOTE:

- *The transitions sketch between the <u>helix</u> and the sketch of the <u>hook</u> are not perfectly tangent. Since we cannot add a fillet between the helix (3D) and the hook (2D) we will try another approach called **Fit Spline** to smooth out any tangency problem in the model.*

No Tangent

No Tangent

10. Converting to 3D sketch:

- The Fit Spline command can only be used with sketch entities, not 3D curves.
So the next step is to convert the composite curve to a 3D sketch.

- Click **3D Sketch** under the Sketch drop down menu (arrow).

- Select the Composite Curve and click **Convert Entities** .

Curve to 3D sketch

- The composite curve is converted to a 3D sketch.

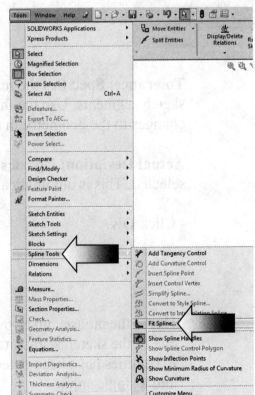

- Box-select the entire 3D sketch and click:
  Tools / Spline Tools / Fit Spline .

- Select / enter the following:

    * **Constraint.**
    * **Tolerance: .003in.**
    * **Inflection Points.**
    * **Minimum Radius.**
    * **Curvature Comb.**

> ☀ **Fit Spline tool** ⌊
>
> The Fit Spline tool to fit sketch segments to a spline. Fit splines are parametrically linked to underlying geometry so that changes to the geometry update the spline.

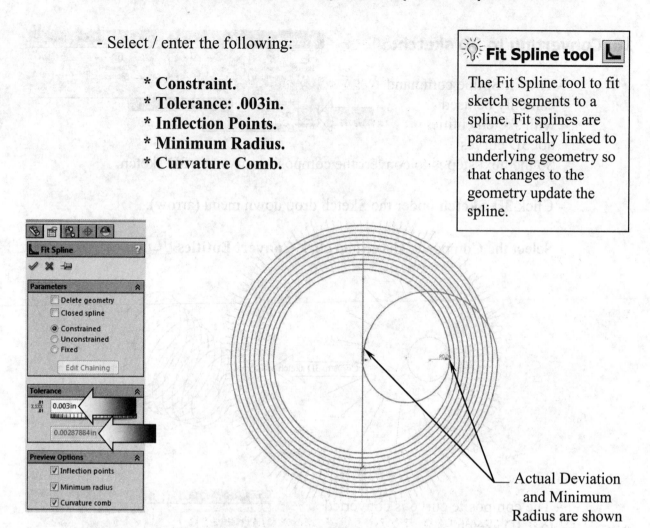

Actual Deviation and Minimum Radius are shown

Tolerance: Specifies the maximum deviation allowed from the original sketch segments. Use the thumbwheel to adjust the tolerance so you can see changes to the geometry in the graphics area.

Actual Deviation: Updates based on the Tolerance value and the geometry selected. This is automatically calculated.

- Click **OK**.

- Hover the mouse cursor over one of the sketch segments. All entities have been fitted into a <u>single spline</u>.

11. Creating a Perpendicular plane:

- Click 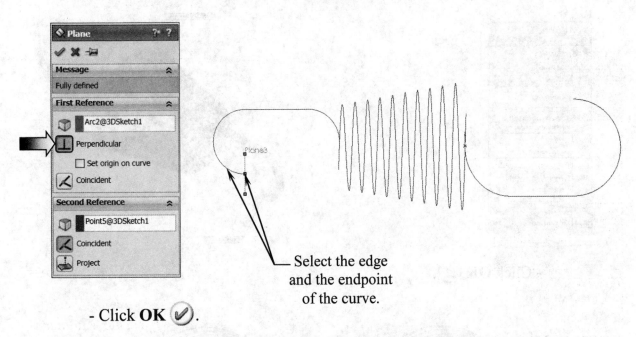 or **Insert / Reference Geometry / Plane**.

- Click the **edge** and the **endpoint** as noted.

- Select the **Perpendicular** option ⊥.

Select the edge
and the endpoint
of the curve.

- Click **OK** ✓.

12. Sketching the sweep profile (the wire diameter):

- Select the new plane (**Plane3**) from the FeatureManager Tree.

- Click 🖊 or select: **Insert / Sketch**.

- Sketch a **Circle** ⊕ at the end of the hook.

- Add a **Piece** Relation ⊥ to fully define the sketch.

- **Exit** the sketch 🖊 or **Insert / Sketch**.

Pierce relation
between the center
of the circle and
the helix

Ø.080

13. Sweeping the profile along the path:

- Click on the Features toolbar or select: **Insert / Boss-Base / Sweep**.

- Select the **small circle** as sweep profile .

- Select the **composite curve** as sweep path .

- Click **OK** ✔.

Before Fit Spline

After Fit Spline

14. Saving your work:

- Click **File / Save As /**

- Enter **Helical Extension Spring** for the file name and click **Save**.

<u>Other Examples:</u>

<u>Conical Spring</u>

<u>V-Shaped - 1 Rev. Closed</u>

<u>Ground-End</u>

<u>Closed-End</u>

<u>Circular Expanded</u>

<u>V-Shape - 3 Rev. Open</u>

Questions for Review

Sweep with Composite Curve

1. Beside the Pitch and Revolution option, a helix can be defined with Pitch and Height.
   a. True
   b. False

2. It is sufficient to create an Offset Distance plane using a reference plane and a distance.
   a. True
   b. False

3. The sweep profile should have a Pierce relation with the sweep path.
   a. True
   b. False

4. Several sketches or model edges can be combined to make a Composite curve.
   a. True
   b. False

5. A Composite curve cannot be used as a sweep path.
   a. True
   b. False

6. The composite curve combines all sketches and model edges into one continuous curve, even if they are not connected.
   a. True
   b. False

7. In a sweep feature, SolidWorks allows only one sweep path, but multiple guide curves can be used.
   a. True
   b. False

8. Several sketch profiles can be used to sweep along a path.
   a. True
   b. False

7. TRUE   8. FALSE
5. FALSE   6. FALSE
3. TRUE   4. TRUE
1. TRUE   2. TRUE

<u>Exercise</u>: Circular Spring – 180deg.

Front Plane

R3.000

Origin

1. Sketching the Sweep Path:

- Select the <u>Front</u> plane and open a new sketch.

- Sketch an **Arc** as shown and add a Horizontal relation between the left and the right endpoints; then add a radius dimension.

- **Exit** the sketch.

Right Plane

.250

2. Sketching the Sweep Profile:

- Select the <u>Right</u> plane and open a new sketch.

- Sketch a horizontal **Line** towards the right.

- Add a **.250 in**. dimension.

- **Exit** the sketch.

3. Creating a Swept <u>Surface</u>:

- Click or select **Insert / Surface / Sweep**.

- Select the horizontal **Line** to use as the Sweep Profile.

- Select the **Arc** as the Sweep Path.

Surface-Sweep1

Profile and Path

Sketch2

Sketch1

Options

Orientation/twist type:

Twist Along Path

Define by:

Turns

30.000

☑ Show preview

- Expand the **Options** dialog box.

- Select **Twist Along Path**, under Orientation / Twist Type.

- For Define By: Select **Turns**.

- For number of Turns: Enter **30**.

- Click **OK** .

4. Sketching the Wire-Diameter:

- Select the <u>Right</u> plane and open a new sketch.

- Sketch a **Circle** at the right end of the swept surface.

- Add a **Ø.125 in**. diameter dimension.

- **Exit** the sketch.

5. Creating a Swept Boss-Base: (Solid)

- Click or select **Insert / Bose-Base / Sweep**.

- Select the **Circle** to use as the Sweep Profile.

- For Sweep Path, select the **Edge** of the Swept-Surface.

- Click **OK** .

Right click
& HIDE

6. Hide the Swept-Surface:

- Right click over the Swept-Surface

  and select Hide .

7. Save your work:

- Select **File / Save As.**

- For file name, enter **Expanded Circular Spring**.

- Click **Save**.

CHAPTER 4 (cont.)

Using Variable Pitch

Sweep with Variable Pitch Helix

- In a Sweep feature, there is only one Sweep Profile, one Sweep Path, and one or more Guide Curves.

- The Sweep Profile describes the feature's cross-section; the Sweep Path helps control the twisting and how the Sweep Profile moves along the path.

- The Sweep path can either be a 2D or a 3D sketch, the edges of the part, or a Composite Curve.

- Beside the Pitch and Revolution option, the Helix and Spiral command offer other options to create more advanced curves such as:

  * Height and Revolutions.
  * Height and Pitch.
  * Spiral.
  * Constant Pitch.
  * Variable Pitch.

Region parameters:

	P	Rev	H	Dia
1	0.115in	0	0in	1in
2	0.115in	1.5	0.1725	1in
3	0.375in	6.5	1.3975	1in
4	0.25in	11.5	2.96in	1in
5	0.115in	12.5	3.1425	1in
6	0.115in	14	3.315i	1in
7	.			

- We will take a look at the Variable Pitch option in this lesson and learn how a helix with multiple pitch is created using a table, to help control the changes of the dimensions.

- To create the flat ground ends, an extruded cut feature is added at the end of the process.

Multi-Pitch Spring with Closed Ends
Using Variable Pitch

| Dimensioning Standards: **ANSI** |
| Units: **INCHES** – 3 Decimals |

Tools Needed:

Insert Sketch	Helix / Spiral	Add Geometric Relations
Dimension	Base/Boss Sweep	Extruded Cut

1. Creating the base sketch:

- Select the <u>Front</u> plane from the FeatureManager tree.

- Click or select: **Insert / Sketch**.

- Sketch a **Circle** ⊕ centered on the origin.

- Add a diameter dimension of **1.000"**.

Ø1.000

2. Creating a helix using Variable Pitch:

- Click 🗲 or select **Insert / Curve / Helix-Spiral**.

- Under Define By, select: **Pitch and Revolution**.

- Under Parameter, select: **Variable Pitch**.

- Under Region Parameters, enter the values for the **Pitch**, **Revolutions**, and **Diameters**. (Ignore the Height column, SolidWorks will fill in the values automatically).

- Set Angle to **0deg** and **Clockwise** direction.

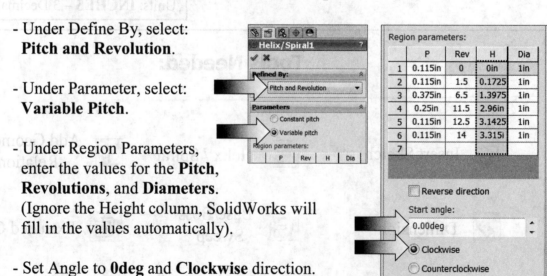

Region parameters:

	P	Rev	H	Dia
1	0.115in	0	0in	1in
2	0.115in	1.5	0.1725	1in
3	0.375in	6.5	1.3975	1in
4	0.25in	11.5	2.96in	1in
5	0.115in	12.5	3.1425	1in
6	0.115in	14	3.315i	1in
7				

☐ Reverse direction

Start angle:

0.00deg

◉ Clockwise

○ Counterclockwise

- Your Variable Pitch helix should look like the image shown below.

- Click **OK** ✅.

3. Sketching the sweep profile (the wire diameter):

- Select the <u>Top</u> plane and open a new sketch 📝 .

- Sketch a **Circle** ⊕ near the right end of the helix.

- Add a **Pierce** relation between the center
  of the circle and the helix.

Pierce the
centerpoint to
the helix

Ø.100

Ø.100

- **<u>Exit</u>** the sketch. The Sweep command isn't available while the sketch is active.

4. Sweeping the profile along the path:

- Click or select: **Insert / Bose-Base / Sweep**.

- Select the **small circle** for sweep profile .

- Select the **helix** for sweep path .

- Click **OK** .

- The resulting Swept feature.

5. Creating a trimmed sketch:

- Select the <u>Top</u> plane from the Feature-Manager tree and open a new sketch.

- Sketch a **Rectangle** and add a **Midpoint** relation between the line on top and the origin.

- Add a width and a height dimensions. The sketch should now be fully defined.

6. Extruding a cut:

- Click or select: **Insert / Cut / Extrude**.

- Set the Direction 1 to **Through All**.

- Set the Direction 2 to **Through All**.

- Enable the **Flip Side to Cut** checkbox.

- Click **OK**.

7. Saving your work:

- Click **File / Save As / Variable Pitch Spring / Save**.

Questions for Review

Sweep with Composite Curve

1. Multiple Sweep Profiles can be used in a sweep feature.
   a. True
   b. False

2. Multiple Sweep Paths can be used in a sweep feature.
   a. True
   b. False

3. Only one Sweep Profile and one Sweep Path can be used in a sweep.
   a. True
   b. False

4. A Helix can be defined by:
   a. Pitch and Revolution
   b. Height and Revolution
   c. Height and Pitch
   d. Spiral
   e. All of the above

5. Several connected Helixes can be combined into one single Composite Curve.
   a. True
   b. False

6. The Sweep Profile sketch should be related to the Sweep Path using the relation:
   a. Perpendicular
   b. Parallel
   c. Coincident
   d. Pierce

7. The Sweep Path controls the twisting and how the Sweep Profile moves along.
   a. True
   b. False

8. The Edges of the part can also be used as the Sweep Path.
   a. True
   b. False

7. TRUE
8. TRUE
5. TRUE
6. D
3. TRUE
4. E
1. FLASE
2. FALSE

<u>Exercise:</u> Projected Curve & Composite Curve

1. Create the part based on the drawing as shown.
2. Dimensions are in inches, 3 decimal places.
3. Focus on Projected Curve & Composite Curve options.

Ø.172 THRU

Ø.980

A

A

(15°)

B

(32°)

SECTION A-A

.058

.212

1.75 REVOLUTION
.073 PTICH

.595

.356

.015

.073

.029

R.029

DETAIL B

4. Follow the instructions on the following pages, if needed.

1. Opening a part document:

- From the Training Files folder, locate and open the part document named:
Project and Composite Curves.

- This is an actual die to form the shape of a catheter. We will create the groove that wraps around this die, using the Project and Composite Curve options.

2. Creating a helix:

- Select the <u>Top</u> plane and open a new sketch.

- Select the **bottom edge** (for clarity) and press **Convert- Entity**.

- Click or select:
Insert / Curve / Helix-Spiral.

Convert the edge into a circle

- Enter the following:

   * **Constant Pitch**.

   * Pitch: **.073"**

   * **Reverse Direction**.

   * Revolutions: **1.75**

   * Start Angle: **15deg**.

   * **Counterclockwise**.

- Click **OK** .

- Notice the helix starts at a 15° angle? This way the end of the helix will match up with the bend radius in the next step.

3. Sketching the upper transition:

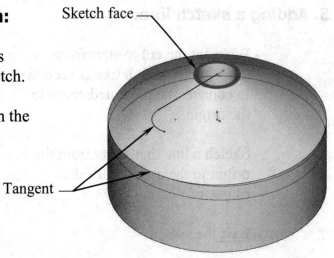

Sketch face

- Select the small <u>upper face</u> as indicated and open a new sketch.

- Sketch a **Line** that starts from the origin and connects with a **Tangent Arc**.

Tangent

- Add a **Tangent** relation between the arc and the circular edge of the part.

- Sketch a **centerline** that starts from the origin and connects to the right endpoint of the arc.

- Add a **Coincident** relation between the right endpoint of the arc and the circular edge of the part, then add a **15°** angular dimension.

Coincident

15.00°

- The sketch should be fully defined at this point. **Exit** the sketch.

4. Creating a projected Curve:

- Click 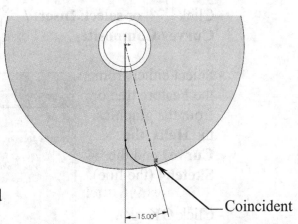 or select: **Insert / Curve / Projected**.

Select 2 faces

- Select the **Sketch on Faces** option.

- For Sketch to Project, select the **Sketch3**.

- For Projection Faces, select the **2 faces** as noted.

- Click **OK** .

5. Adding a sketch line:

- We want the cut to start from the origin, a sketch line is needed to connect the projected curve to the origin.

- Sketch a line that starts from the origin to the endpoint of the projected curve.

- **Exit** the sketch.

Sketch face

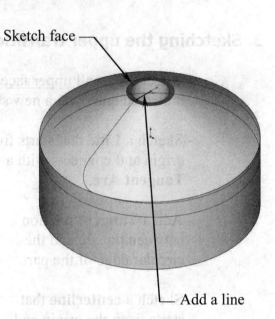

Add a line

6. Creating a Composite Curve:

- Click or select: **Insert / Curve / Composite**.

- Select either from the Feature tree or from the graphics: the **Helix**, the **Curve1** and the **Sketch4** (the line).

- Click **OK** .

Select the Helix the Curve1 and the Sketch line

7. Sketching the sweep profile:

- Sketch a small circle on the **Front** plane and add the dimension/relation shown.

Pierce relation

Ø.058

Ø.058

- **Exit** the sketch.

8. Creating a swept cut:

- Click or select: **Insert / Cut / Sweep**.

- For Sweep Profile, select the **circle**.

- For Sweep Path, select the **composite curve**.

- Click **OK** ✓.

9. Removing the undercut:

Sketch face

- **If** the swept feature stopped short, we'll need to clean it up. Select the face as noted and open a new sketch.

Convert entities

- Convert the face into a sketch.

- Click or select: **Insert / Cut / Extrude**.

- Set Direction 1 to: **Through All**.

- Click **OK** ✓.

10. Saving your work:

- Click **File / Save As**.

- Enter **Project and Composite Curves** for the name of the file.

- Press **Save**.

CHAPTER 5

Advanced Modeling with Sweep & Loft

Advanced Modeling with Sweep & Loft

- The Sweep option creates a solid, thin, or surface feature by moving a single sketch profile along a path and guiding with one or more guide curves.

- In order to create a sweep feature properly, a set of rules should be taken into consideration:

  o The Sweep option uses only one sketch profile and it must be a closed non-intersecting contour for a **solid** feature.
  o The sketch profile can be either closed or open for a **surface** feature.
  o Only one path is used in a sweep and it can be open or closed.
  o One or more guide-curves can be used to guide the sketch profile.
  o The sketch profile must be drawn on a new plane starting at the end point of the path.

- The Loft option creates a solid, thin, or surface feature by making a transition between the sketch profiles.

- Keep in mind the following requirements when creating a loft feature:

  o The Loft option uses multiple sketch profiles that must be closed, and non-intersecting for a **solid** feature.
  o The sketch profiles can be either closed or open, for a **surface** feature.
  o Use the Centerline Parameter option to guide the profiles from the inside.
  o Use Guide Curves option to guide the sketch profiles from the outside.
  o The Guide Curves can be either a 2D or a 3D sketch.

Water Pump Housing
Advanced Modeling with Sweep & Loft

View Orientation Hot Keys:

Ctrl + 1 = Front View
Ctrl + 2 = Back View
Ctrl + 3 = Left View
Ctrl + 4 = Right View
Ctrl + 5 = Top View
Ctrl + 6 = Bottom View
Ctrl + 7 = Isometric View
Ctrl + 8 = Normal To
       Selection

Dimensioning Standards: **ANSI**

Units: **INCHES** – 3 Decimals

Tools Needed:

 Insert Sketch   Split Entities   Add Geometric Relations

 Rib   Plane   Revolved Boss/Base

 Extruded Boss/Base   Swept Boss/Base   Lofted Boss/Base

Understanding the Draft Options

- Drafts are normally required in most plastic injection molded
  parts to ensure proper part removal from the mold halves.
- The Draft option in SolidWorks adds tapers to the faces using
  the angles specified by the user.
- Drafts can be inserted in an existing part or added to a feature
  while being extruded.
- Drafts can be applied to solid parts as well as the surface models.
- There are several types of draft available:

  * Neutral Plane
  * Parting Line
  * Step Draft

Neutral Plane Draft

Split Line Draft

Step Draft

1. Opening a part document:

- From the Training Files folder, locate and <u>open</u> the part document named: **Water Pump Sketch**.

- The sketch was created ahead of time to help focus on the key features of this lesson: Sweep and Loft.

- **Edit** the Sketch1.

2. Extruding the Base with Draft:

- Click **Extruded Boss/Base.**

- End Condition: **Blind.**

- Depth: **1.00 in**.

- Draft: **7 deg. inward**.

- Click **OK** ✔.

3. Sketching the upper Inlet Port:

- Select the <u>Front</u> plane and open a new sketch.

- Sketch the profile as shown.

- Add the dimensions and relations as indicated.

- Add a **vertical Centerline** from the Origin and use it as the center of the revolve in the next step.

4. Revolving the upper Inlet Port:

- Click **Revolve Boss/Base** or Select: **Insert / Features / Boss-Base / Revolve** from the drop down menus.

- The vertical centerline should be selected automatically to use as the Axis of Revolution.

- Revolve Direction: **Blind**.

- Revolve Angle: **360 deg**.

- Click **OK**.

5. Adding the .500" Fillets:

- Click **Fillet** or select **In
  Features / Fillet-Round.**

- Enter **.500 in.** for radius valı

- Select the **7 edges** as shown

Select
7 edges

- Click **OK** ✅.

6. Adding the .275" Fillets:

- Click **Fillet** or select **Insert / Features /
  Fillet-Round.**

- Enter **.275 in.** for radius value.

- Select the **upper edge** of the
  base.

- Make sure the option:
  Tangent Propagation is
  Enabled so that the fillet
  can propagate itself to all
  connecting edges.

- Click **OK** ✅.

Select the
Upper edge

7. Creating the 1st Offset-Distance Plane:

- Click **Plane** or select **Insert / Reference Geometry / Plane.**

- From the Flyout FeatureManager tree, select the **Front** plane to offset from.

- Enter **3.000 in**. for distance.

- Place the new plane on the **right side**.

- Click **OK** ✔.

Click here to bring out the FeatureManager tree (Flyout)

8. Creating the 2nd Offset-Distance Plane:

- Click **Plane** or select **Insert / Reference Geometry / Plane.**

- Select the <u>Front</u> plane again from the Flyout FeatureManager tree to offset from.

- Enter **5.000 in**. for offset distance.

- Place the new plane also on the **right side**.

- Click **OK** ✔.

9. Creating the 3rd Offset-Distance Plane:

- Click **Plane** or select **Insert / Reference Geometry / Plane.**

- Select the <u>Front</u> plane once again from the Flyout FeatureManager tree to offset from.

- Enter **6.000 in**. for offset distance.

- Place the new plane also on the **right side**.

- Click **OK** ✓.

10. Sketching the 1st loft profile:

- Select the <u>Front</u> plane and open a new sketch.

- Sketch a **Rectangle** that's just **.125 in**. above the bottom edge of the part.

- Add the dimensions and relations as shown to fully define the sketch.

Symmetric relation

1.750

2.500

.125

- <u>**Exit**</u> the sketch.

11. Sketching the 2nd loft profile:

- Select the <u>Plane1</u> and open a new sketch .

- Sketch another **Rectangle** as shown.

- Add the dimensions and relations
  needed to fully define the
  sketch.

- **<u>Exit</u>** the sketch.

12. Sketching the 3rd loft profile:

- Select the <u>Plane2</u> and open a new sketch .

- Sketch a **Circle** just above the Origin as shown below.

- Use the **Split-Entities** command and split the circle into **4 segments**.

- Add Vertical and Horizontal relations between the
  split points.

- The Split Entities
  command is used to
  split the entities in
  each sketch to an even
  number of connecting points
  for use within a loft feature.

- Add the dimensions and
  relations needed to fully
  define the sketch.

- **<u>Exit</u>** the sketch.

13. Sketching the 4th loft profile:

- Select the Plane3 and open a new sketch .

- Convert the circle from the previous sketch, this creates an On-Edge relation between the 2 circles and they will update at the same time when the first circle is changed.

Convert from the previous sketch...

- **Exit** the sketch.

Plane3

14. Creating a loft feature:

- Click Loft or select: **Insert / Boss-Base / Loft** from the drop down menus.

- Select the **4 sketch profiles** in the graphics area.

(Since there are no guide curves to help control the loft, the profiles should be selected from the same side each time to prevent them from twisting.)

- For clarity, right click in the yellow shaded area and select the following options:

  • Opaque
  • Clear Mesh Faces

- Click **OK** .

Select the 4 sketch profiles, use the same connecting point of each profile...

Profile(Sketch6)

15. Creating the mounting bosses:

- Select the <u>bottom face</u> and open a new sketch.

- Sketch **5 Circles** as shown.

- <u>Avoid</u> the hidden entities. (When sketching, your circles may snap to some of the hidden edges of the model causing over defined when adding the dimensions. To overcome this, hold the control key every time a hidden edge highlights, this will cancel the Auto-Relation snapping).

- Add a **Tangent** relation for each circle, to the outer edge of the part.

- Add an **Equal** relation to all 5 circles.

- Add dimensions to fully position the 5 circles.

16. Extruding the 5 mounting bosses:

- Click **Extrude Boss-Base** or select: **Insert / Extrude / Boss-Base**, from the drop down menus.

- Set the following:

    - End Condition: **Blind**

    - Depth: **1.250 in**.

    - Draft: **1 deg. Inward.**

- Click **OK** .

17. Sketching the rear Inlet Port:

- Select the <u>upper face</u> and open a new sketch.

- Sketch the profile of the Inlet at a **30° angle**, one end of the profile is locked onto the Origin.

- Add dimensions and other relations to fully position the sketch.

- There are more than one centerlines in this sketch, select the 30° centerline before clicking the Revolve command.

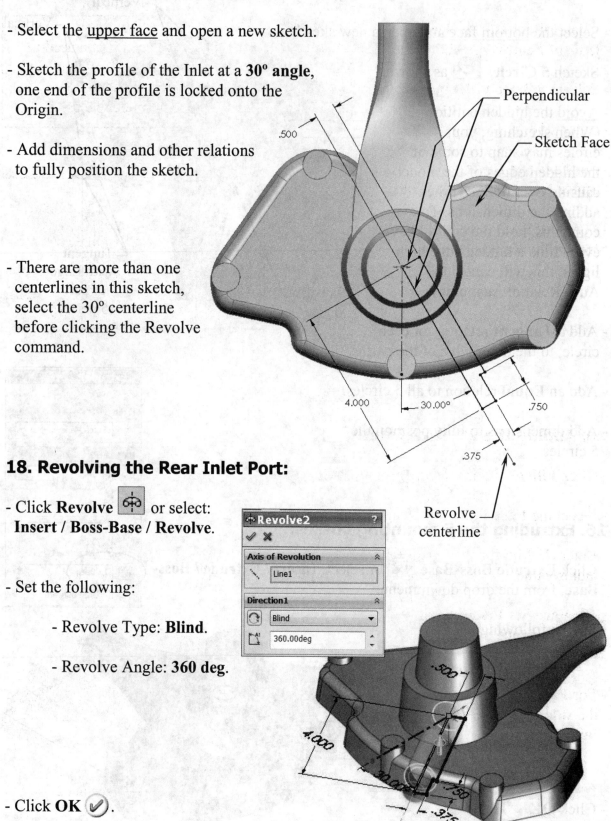

Perpendicular

Sketch Face

.500

4.000   30.00°   .750   .375

Revolve centerline

18. Revolving the Rear Inlet Port:

- Click **Revolve** or select:
  Insert / Boss-Base / Revolve.

- Set the following:

  - Revolve Type: **Blind**.

  - Revolve Angle: **360 deg**.

Revolve2

Axis of Revolution
Line1

Direction1
Blind
360.00deg

- Click **OK**.

19. Adding the 1st Face Fillet:

- Click **Fillet** or select:
Insert / Features / Fillet-Round.

- Select the **Face Fillet** button.

- Enter **.250 in.** for radius value.

- For **Face Set 1**, select the
upper face of the lofted feature.

- For **Face Set 2**, select the **side
face** of the lofted feature.

- Click **OK** ✅.

> 💡 **Face Fillet**
>
> A Face Fillet a used to
> create a blend between
> non-adjacent, non-
> continuous faces.

Face Set 1

Face Set 2

Face Set 2

20. Adding the 2nd Face Fillet:

- Click **Fillet** or select: **Insert / Features / Fillet-Round.**

- Select the **Face Fillet** button again.

- Enter **.250 in.** for
radius value.

- For **Face Set 1**, select
the **upper face** of the
lofted feature.

- For **Face Set 2**, select
the **side face** of the
lofted feature.

- Click **OK** ✅.

Face Set 1

Face Set 1: 0.25in

Face Set 2

Face Set 2

21. Adding the 3rd Face Fillet:

- Click **Fillet** or select:
Insert / Features / Fillet-Round.

- Click **Face Fillet**.

- Enter **.150 in.** for radius value.

- For **Face Set 1**, select the **lower face** of the lofted feature.

- For **Face Set 2**, select the **side face** of the lofted feature.

- Click **OK**.

Face Set 1

Face Set 2

22. Adding the 4th Face Fillet:

- Click **Fillet** or select:
Insert / Features / Fillet-Round.

- Click **Face Fillet**.

- Enter **.150 in.** for radius value.

- For **Face Set 1**, select the **lower face** of the lofted feature.

- For **Face Set 2**, select the **Side face** of the lofted feature.

- Click **OK**.

Face Set 1

Face Set 2

23. Mirroring the rear Inlet Port:

- Click **Mirror** or select:
Insert / Pattern Mirror / Mirror.

- For Mirror Face/Plane, select
the **Right** plane from the
flyout FeatureManager tree.

- For Features to Mirror, select
the **Rear Inlet Port** either
from the Graphics area or
from the Feature tree.

- Click **OK** .

24. Adding the .175" Fillets:

- Click **Fillet** or select: **Insert / Features / Fillet-Round.**

- Select the **Constant Size** fillet option (arrow)

- Enter **.175 in.** for radius
value.

- Select the edges as noted
to add the fillets.

Select edges
to fillet

- The option Tangent-
Propagation should be
on by default.

- Click **OK** .

25. Shelling the part:

- Click **Shell** or select:
  Insert / Features / Shell.

- Under the Parameters
  section, enter **.080 in**. for
  wall thickness.

- Select a total of **10 faces**
  to remove.

- Click **OK** ✅.

10 faces to remove

26. Adding the .0625" Fillets:

- Click **Fillet** 🔘 or select:
  Insert / Features / Fillet-Round.

- Enter **.0625 in**. for
  radius value.

- Select the **edges** as
  shown to add the
  fillets.

- Click **OK** ✅.

Edges to fillet
(outer edges)

27. Adding a Rib:

- Select the <u>Front</u> plane from the FeatureManager tree

  and open a new sketch .

- Sketch a **Line** as shown.

- Add Coincident relations between the
  endpoints of the line and the
  edges of the part.

> **Rib Features**
>
> A rib is an extruded
> feature which adds
> material of a specified
> thickness in a specified
> direction. Drafts can
> also be added to the
> faces of the rib.

Coincident
with edges

3.500

2.500

28. Extruding the Rib:

- Click **Rib** or select: **Insert / Features / Rib.**

- Select **Both Directions** under the Thickness section.

- Enter **.275 in**. for the
  thickness of the rib.

- Enable the **Draft** option
  and enter **1.00 deg**.

- Enable the **Draft
  Outward** check box.

- Click **OK** .

29. Creating a Full-Round fillet:

- A Full-Round creates fillets that are tangent to three adjacent face sets.

- Click **Fillet** or select: **Insert / Features / Fillet-Round.**

- Select the **Full Round** fillet option.

- For Face 1, select the **left surface** of the Rib.

- For Face 2, select the **middle surface** of the Rib.

- For Face 3, select the **right surface** of the Rib.

- Click **OK**.

Face 1 – Left Side of Rib

Face 3 – Middle of Rib

Face 2 – Right Side of Rib

30. Mirroring the Rib:

- Click **Mirror** or select: **Insert / Pattern Mirror / Mirror.**

- For Mirror Face/Plane, select the **Right** plane.

- For Features to Mirror, select the **Rib** and its **fillet**.

- Click **OK**.

31. Adding the .025" fillets:

- Click **Fillet** or select: **Insert / Features / Fillet- Round.**

- Select the **Constant Radius** fillet option.

- Enter **.025 in**. for radius value.

- Select the edges as indicated to add the fillets.

- Enable the Tangent-Propagation checkbox.

- Click **OK** .

Select edges
(Inner Edges)

32. Adding the .175" fillets:

- Click **Fillet** or select: **Insert / Features / Fillet-Round.**

- Click **Constant Radius**.

- Enter **.175 in**. for radius value.

- Select the **edges** of the 2 ribs as shown.

- Click **OK** .

Select the edges of
the Rib to add fillets

33. Saving your work:

- Click **File / Save As**.

- Enter **Water Pump Cover** as the name of the file.

- Click **Save.**

CHAPTER 6

Loft vs. Sweep

Loft vs. Sweep

- The Loft and the Sweep commands are normally used to create advanced, complex shapes. The differences between the two are:

  • Sweep uses a single sketched profile to sweep along a path and is controlled by one or more guide curves.

Sweep uses one profile, one path and multiple guide curves

  • Loft uses multiple sketched profiles to loft between the sections and is controlled by 1 or more guide curves or 1 Centerline Parameter.

Loft uses multiple profiles, one centerline parameter, or multiple guide curves

- In order to create a solid feature, each sketch profile must be a single, closed, and non-intersecting shape.

- The guide curves can be either a 2D sketch or a 3D curve.

- The sweep path and guide curves must be related to the sketch profiles with either a Coincident or Pierce relation.

- The loft profiles should have the same number of entities or segments. The Split-Entities ✎ commands can be used to split the sketch entities and add the necessary connectors to helps control the loft more accurately.

Water Meter Housing
Loft vs. Sweep

Dimensioning Standards: **ANSI**

Units: **INCHES** – 3 Decimals

Tools Needed:

	Insert Sketch		Line		Split Entities
	Sketch Fillet		Mirror		Add Geometric Relations
	Dimension		Base/Boss Extrude		Extruded Cut
	Plane		Base/Boss Sweep		Base/Boss Loft

1. Sketching the 1st Loft Profile:

- Select the <u>Top</u> plane from the FeatureManager tree.

- Click ![sketch icon] or select **Insert / Sketch**.

- Sketch a **rectangle** centered on the Origin and add the dimensions as shown.

Mid-Point relation

- **Exit** the sketch.

2. Creating a new plane:

- Click ![plane icon] or select **Insert / Reference Geometry / Plane**.

- Select the <u>Top</u> reference plane from the FeatureManager tree.

- Select **Offset Distance** option and enter **3.000** in.

- Click **OK** ![ok icon].

New Plane

3. Sketching the 2ⁿᵈ Loft Profile:

- Select the <u>new plane</u> (**Plane1**) and open a new sketch 🖉 .

- Sketch a Circle ⊙ and add dimensions 🔷 and Relations ⊥ as needed.

- Select the **Split Entities** command under: **Tools / Sketch Tools**.

Split the circle ✎ into 8 segments, and add the vertical & horizontal relations to the points.

Ø7.000

Vertical

Horizontal

(Click the 3 points as noted to create the angle dim).

- <u>**Exit**</u> the Sketch 🖉 .

4. Creating the Lofted Base feature:

- Click 🝔 or select **Insert / Boss-Base / Loft**.

- Profiles: Select the **2 sketches** as indicated.

| SelectionManager |
| Select Other |
| Zoom/Pan/Rotate |
| ✓ OK |
| ✗ Cancel |
| Merge Tangent Faces |
| Close Loft |
| Show All Connectors |
| Reset Connectors |
| Mesh Preview |
| Zebra Stripes Preview |

Show All Connectors

- Click **OK** ✅ .

5. Constructing the Inlet's 1st Loft Profile:

- Select the <u>Front</u> plane and open a new sketch .

- Sketch a **Rectangle**, add Dimensions, and Sketch Fillets.

6. Creating an Offset Distance plane at 5.500":

- Click or select **Insert / Reference Geometry / Plane**.

- Select the **Front** reference plane from the FeatureManager tree.

- Select **Offset Distance** option and enter **5.500 in**. for distance.

- Click **OK**.

New Plane

- **Exit** the Sketch.

7. Constructing the Inlet's 2nd Loft Profile:

- Select the <u>Plane2</u> and open a new sketch

- Sketch a **Circle** and add Dimensions to fully define.

- Click **Split Entities** and split the circle into 8 segments.

Split the circle into 8 segments and add the vertical & horizontal relations between the points.

⌀2.000

Plane2

1.500

90.00°

135.00°

⌀2.000

Plane2

90.00°

135.00°

1.500

- **Exit** the Sketch .

8. Creating the Inlet feature:

- Click or select **Insert / Boss-Base / Loft**.

Loft2

Profiles
- Sketch3
- Sketch4

Start/End Constraints

Guide Curves

Centerline Parameters

Sketch Tools

Drag Sketch

Options
- ☑ Merge tangent faces
- ☐ Close loft
- ☑ Show preview
- ☑ Merge result

- For profiles: Select the **2 sketches** from the graphics area.

- Show all connector points to ensure a smooth transition between the 2 profiles. Enable the **Merge Tangent Faces** option.

- Click **OK** .

Right click & Show-All-Connectors

Profile(Sketch4)

9. Creating an Offset Distance plane from the Right:

- Click or select **Insert / Reference Geometry / Plane.**

- Select the **Right** reference plane from the FeatureManager tree.

- Select **Offset Distance** option and enter **4.000 in**. for distance.

- Click **OK** ✅.

New Plane

10. Constructing the Outlet's 1ˢᵗ Loft profile:

- Select the <u>new plane</u> (Plane3) and open a new sketch.

- Sketch a **Circle** ⊕ split it 〰 into 8 segments. Add dimensions ✎ as noted.

Split the circle 〰 into 8 segments and add the
vertical & horizontal relations to the split points.

Ø2.000

75.00°

1.500

120.00°

6.000

- Add the Vertical and Horizontal relations to the endpoints of the arcs to fully define them.

- **Exit** the Sketch.

11. "Re-Using" the previous sketch*:

- Expand the feature **Loft2** from the FeatureManager tree (click the **+** sign).

- Locate the sketch of the Rectangle (**sketch3**), Right click and select **SHOW**.

— Show Sketch*

* The previous sketch is made visible in the graphics area to be used again in the next loft operation.

12. Creating a plane Parallel:

- Click or select **Insert / Reference Geometry / Plane**.

- Select the **Top** reference plane from the FeatureManager tree.

- Select the **Parallel** plane option.

- Click the **Center Point** of the Circle.

- Click **OK** ✓.

Reference Point

New Plane

Reference Plane
(TOP)

- The new plane is created (Plane4).

13. Constructing the Centerline Parameter:

- Select the <u>new plane</u> (Plane4) and open a new sketch .

- Switch to the Top view orientation (Ctrl+5) .

- Sketch the profile as shown below.

- Add Dimensions and Sketch Fillet as shown.

R3.000

Pierce Relation

Pierce Relation

- Make sure the end of each line
  is either coincident or pierced
  to the circle and the rectangle.

- **Exit** the Sketch .

R3.000

Plane4

14. Creating the Outlet loft feature:

- Click or select **Insert / Boss / Loft**.

- Select the **2 Sketch Profiles** (Rectangle and Circle) from the graphics area.

- Expand the **Centerline Parameters** option and select **Sketch6** from either the graphics area or from the FeatureManager tree.

- Using the Centerline Parameter to guide the loft will cause the sketch planes of all the intermediate sections to be normal to the centerline.

- After the preview appears, check the connectors to ensure a proper loft transition.

- Click **OK**.

> **Centerline Parameters**
>
> If the number of entities in each sketch is the same, a "Centerline Parameter Sketch" can be used instead of the guide curves.

Centerline Parameter

Centerline(Sketch6)   Profile(Sketch5)

Loft Profiles

Right click on one of the connectors and select: Show All Connectors

Centerline(Sketch6)   Profile(Sketch5)

15. Adding .250" fillet to the Bottom:

- Click or select **Insert / Features / Fillet-Round**.

- Enter **.250 in**. for radius value and select the **bottom edges** as indicated.

- Click **OK** ✓.

Edges to fillet

16. Add .175" fillets to the lofts:

- Click or select **Insert / Features / Fillet-Round**.

- Enter **.175 in**. for Radius and select <u>all</u> side edges as noted.

- Click **OK** ✓.

Select all edges

Radius: 0.175in

17. Shelling the part:

- Click or select **Insert / Features / Shell**.

- Enter **.175 in.** for wall thickness and select the **3 faces** as noted.

- Click **OK** ✓.

Select 3 faces

18. Creating the 1st Mounting bracket:

- Select the <u>Face</u> as noted and open a new sketch ✏️ .

- Sketch the profile as shown below, use Convert Entities 🔲 where applicable.

- Add Dimensions ◇ and Relations ⊥ needed to fully define the sketch.

R.750

R1.375

Convert
Circle

Ø.500

5.000

The center of R1.375
is coincident with the
center of the circle.

Sketch
Face

19. Extruding the Left bracket:

- Click or select **Insert / Boss-Base / Extrude**.

- End Condition: **Blind**   - Depth: **.500 in**.

- Click **OK**.

20. Creating the 2nd Mounting bracket:

- Select the <u>Face</u> as noted and open a new sketch .

- Either copy the previous sketch – or – recreate the same sketch again on the right side.

- Add Dimensions and Relations needed to fully define the sketch.

21. Extruding the Right bracket:

- Click or select **Insert / Boss-Base / Extrude**.

- End Condition: **Blind**.   - Depth: **.500 in**.

- Click **OK** ✓.

22. Constructing the Upper Ring:

- Select the <u>Face</u> as indicated and open a new sketch.

- Sketch the profile below, use Convert Entities where needed.

- The centers of the Ø.250 Circles are coincident with the Ø7.375 bolt-circle.

23. Extruding the Upper Ring:

- Click or select **Insert / Boss-Base / Extrude**.

- End Condition: **Blind**. - Depth: **.400 in**. (upward)

- Click **OK** ✓.

24. Adding a Seal-Ring bore:

- Select the <u>Face</u> as noted and open a new sketch.

- Select the **inside circular edge** and click **Offset Entities**.

- Enter **.150 in**. for Offset Value (larger diameter).

- Click **OK** ✓.

25. Extruding Cut the Seal Ring bore:

- Click or select **Insert / Cut / Extrude**.

- End Condition: **Blind**.

- Depth: **.250 in**.

- Click **OK** ✅.

26. Adding fillets:

- Click or select **Insert / Features / Fillet-Round**.

- Enter **.0625 in**. for radius value.

- Select the 7 edges as noted.

- Click **OK** ✅.

Edges to fillet

27. Adding Chamfers:

- Click or select **Insert / Features / Chamfer**.

- Enter **.060 in**. for Depth.

- Enter **45 deg**. for Angle.

- Select the **edges** of the 6 holes.

- Click **OK** .

Select the
front & back
Edges of the
holes, on
both sides.

28. Saving your work:

- Select **File / Save As / Water Meter Housing / Save**.

Questions for Review

Loft Vs. Sweep

1. In a new part mode, when the Sketch Pencil is selected first, SolidWorks will prompt you to select a sketch plane.
   - a. True
   - b. False

2. It is sufficient to create a Parallel-Plane-At-Point with a Reference Plane and a Reference Point.
   - a. True
   - b. False

3. A loft feature uses multiple sketch profiles to define its shape.
   - a. True
   - b. False

4. Only one guide curve can be used in each loft feature.
   - a. True
   - b. False

5. Multiple guide curves can be used to connect and control the loft feature.
   - a. True
   - b. False

6. The guide curves can be either a 2D sketch or a 3D curve.
   - a. True
   - b. False

7. The loft profiles and the guide curves should be related with Coincident or Pierce relations.
   - a. True
   - b. False

8. The loft profiles should be created before the guide curves.
   - a. True
   - b. False

7. TRUE   8. TRUE
5. TRUE   6. TRUE
3. TRUE   4. FALSE
1. TRUE   2. TRUE

Exercise: Loft

There are several different ways to model this part; but this exercise focuses on the Loft technique.

1. Create the part below, using the Loft and the Circular Pattern features.

5.000

1.000

.750

1.500

3.500

Edge flush with OD.

4X 1.000

Edge flush with OD.

2. Use the instructions on the following pages, if needed.

1. Starting with the base sketch:

- Select the <u>Front</u> plane and open a new sketch.

- Sketch the profile shown.

- Add the dimensions to fully define the sketch.

2. Revolving the base:

- Click or select **Insert / Boss-Base / Revolve**.

- Direction 1: **Blind**.

- Revolve Angle: **360deg**.

- Click **OK** ✅.

3. Creating the 1st loft profile:

- Select the <u>face</u> indicated and open a new sketch.

- Sketch the profile shown by converting the 2 circular edges then add 2 vertical lines.

- Trim the circles to form one continuous profile.

- <u>**Exit**</u> the sketch.

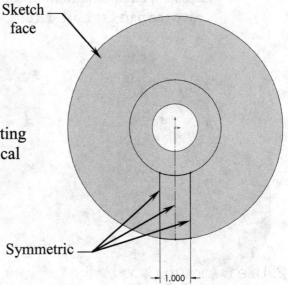

Sketch face

Symmetric

4. Creating the 2nd loft profile:

- Select the <u>upper face</u> as indicated and open a new sketch.

- Using the same techniques as in the previous sketch, construct this new sketch the same way.

- Add the Collinear relations to both sides, between the 2 sketches.

- **Exit** the sketch.

Sketch face

Collinear both sides

5. Creating the 1st loft feature:

- Click or select: **Insert / Boss-Base / Loft**.

- Select the outer corner of the 1st sketch profile.

- To prevent the loft from twisting, select the outer corner of 2nd loft profile, also from the same side as the 1st.

- Click **OK** ✅.

6. Pattern and save:

- Create a circular pattern of the lofted feature with a total of 4 instances, then save the part as: **Loft_Exe**.

CHAPTER 7

Loft with Guide Curves

Loft with Guide Curves

- This lesson demonstrates the creation of a waved washer using the loft technique, where 4 sketch profiles and a single 3D guide curve are used.

- A loft feature normally contains several sections, one centerline parameter and one or more guide curves.

- In this case study, four identical sketches will be used as the loft profiles and a single guide curve will be used to connect the sections.

- Since the loft profiles are identical, the derived-sketch option will be used to show how the sketches can be derived or copied.

- A derived sketch is driven by the original sketch. It can only be positioned with relations or dimensions, but its sketched entities cannot be changed.

- When the Original sketch is changed, the derived-sketch will be updated automatically; however the derived sketches can be Un-derived to break their associations with the Original sketch.

- The loft profiles are connected with a 3D curve; the 3D curve will be generated through some reference points called: Curve-Through-Reference-Points, and Pierced to the loft profiles.

- The Curve-Through-Reference-Points will be used to guide and control the transition between the loft profiles.

Waved Washer
Loft with Guide Curves

Dimensioning Standards: **ANSI**

Units: **INCHES** – 3 Decimals

Tools Needed:

 Insert Sketch   Line   Circle

 Sketch Point   Add Geometric Relations   Dimension

 Derived Sketch   Curve Through Reference Points   Base/Boss Loft

1. Creating the 1ˢᵗ Construction profile:

- Select the <u>Top</u> plane from the FeatureManager tree.

- Click or select **Insert / Sketch**.

- Sketch a **Circle** and convert it into a construction circle.

Options
☑ For construction

- Add **8 sketch points** ✳ approximately as shown.

Vertical

Horizontal
top & bottom

Horizontal

Vertical
left &
right

2. Fully defining the sketch:

- Select the dimension tool and add dimensions to the sketch points.

- Add a vertical and a horizontal relation as indicated.

Point 2

45.00°

Point 3

Point 1

⌀2.000

> ### 3-Point Angle Dimension
>
> To create the 45° dimension, select the Smart Dimension tool and click on the 3 points (starting at the origin), as indicated.

- <u>**Exit**</u> the Sketch.

3. Creating an Offset Distance plane:

- Click or select **Insert / Reference Geometry / Plane**.

- Select the **Top** plane as Reference Entities.

- Select **Offset Distance** option and enter **.150 in**.

- Click **OK** ✅.

New Plane

4. Creating the 2nd construction profile using Derived Sketch:

- Hold the **Control** key, select the **new Plane** (plane1) and the **Sketch1** from FeatureManager tree.

- Click **Insert / Derived Sketch**.

Derived Sketch

5. Positioning the Derived Sketch:

- Add a Vertical & Coincident relation between the indicated points.

Vertical

Coincident

- **Exit** the Sketch or select **Insert / Sketch**.

6. Creating a Curve through Reference Points

- Click or select **Insert / Curve / Curve-Through-Reference-Points**.

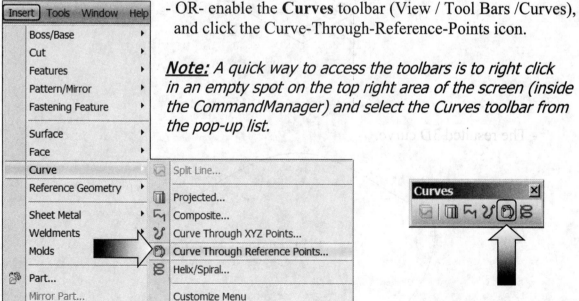

- OR- enable the **Curves** toolbar (View / Tool Bars /Curves), and click the Curve-Through-Reference-Points icon.

Note: A quick way to access the toolbars is to right click in an empty spot on the top right area of the screen (inside the CommandManager) and select the Curves toolbar from the pop-up list.

Curve Though Reference Points

- Select the sketch points in the order as shown (required for this lesson only). (Point 1 is on top, point 2 is on the bottom, 3 top, 4 bottom, and so on).

- Click [✓ Closed curve] to close the curve.

- Click **OK** ✅.

- The resulted 3D curve.

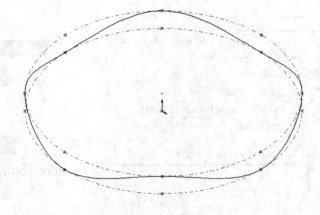

7. Sketching the 1st loft section:

- Select the <u>Front</u> plane from the FeatureManager tree.

- Sketch a **Rectangle** ☐ add Dimensions ◈ and Relations ⊥ as shown.

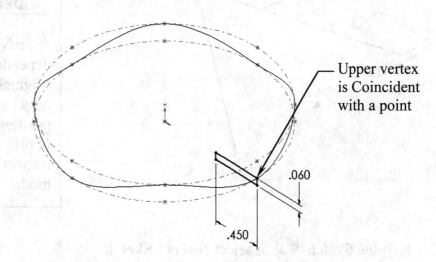

Upper vertex is Coincident with a point

.060

.450

- <u>**Exit**</u> the sketch ✐ or select **Insert / Sketch**.

8. Creating the 2nd loft section using Derived-Sketch:

- Hold the **Control** key, select the **Front** plane and the sketch of the **rectangle** from the Feature tree.

- Select **Insert / Derived Sketch**.

- The derived sketch is created and placed on top of the original sketch; drag it to the left side and then add a coincident relation to the point on the bottom as noted.

Coincident

9. Fully defining the Derived Sketch:

- Add a **Collinear** relation 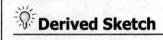 between the 2 lines as indicated.

Collinear

> 💡 **Derived Sketch**
>
> A derived sketch is a dependent copy of the original sketch. It can only be moved or positioned on the same or different plane with respect to the same model.

- **Exit** the Sketch or select **Insert / Sketch**.

10. Sketching the 3rd loft section: (or use the Derived Sketch option)

- Select the <u>Right</u> plane from the FeatureManager tree.

- Sketch a **Rectangle** (or copy and paste the previous sketch).

- Add Dimensions and Relations needed to fully define the sketch.

Coincident with Top plane
(from the right view orientation)

.060

.450

Coincident with
the bottom point

- **Exit** the Sketch or select **Insert / Sketch**.

11. Creating the 4th loft section using Derived-Sketch:

- Hold the **Control** key, select the **Right** plane <u>and</u> the sketch of the 3rd **rectangle**, from the FeatureManager tree.

- Select **Insert / Derived Sketch**.

Coincident

12. Constraining the Derived sketch:

- Add a **Collinear** relation between the 2 lines as shown.

Collinear

- <u>**Exit**</u> the Sketch or select **Insert / Sketch**.

13. Creating a Loft with Guide curve:

- Click or select **Insert / Boss-Base / Loft**.

- Select the <u>four</u> rectangular sketches as Loft Profiles.

Profile(Sketch6)

- Select the <u>3D curve</u> as Guide Curve.

- Click **Close Loft** ☑ Close loft under Options (arrow).

Guide Curve(Curve1)

Profile(Sketch6)

- Click **OK** ✓.

- The completed Waved Washer (with the construction sketches still visible).

14. Hiding the construction sketches:

- Right click on the construction sketches and select **Hide** .

Hide sketch ⟍

15. Saving your work:

- Select **File / Save As / Waved-Washer / Save**.

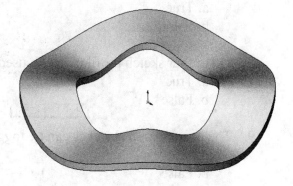

Questions for Review

Loft with Guide Curves

1. A sketch profile can be copied onto another plane or a planar surface.
   a. True
   b. False

2. Sketch points can be added in any sketch to help define the sketch geometry or locations.
   a. True
   b. False

3. If a derived sketch is driven by the original sketch, its entities cannot be changed.
   a. True
   b. False

4. A 3D curve can be created using the reference points in the sketches or model's vertices.
   a. True
   b. False

5. The loft sections should either be Pierced or Coincident with the guide curves.
   a. True
   b. False

6. The guide curves can also be used to control the loft sections from twisting.
   a. True
   b. False

7. Only two guide curves can be used in each loft feature.
   a. True
   b. False

8. Up to four sketch profiles can be used in a loft feature.
   a. True
   b. False

9. The construction sketches can be toggled (Show/Hide) at any time.
   a. True
   b. False

9. TRUE
7. FALSE   8. FALSE
5. TRUE   6. TRUE
3. TRUE   4. TRUE
1. TRUE   2. TRUE

Exercise: V-Shaped – 3 revolutions

1. Creating the Base sketch:

- From the Top plane sketch a **circle**, centered on the origin.

- Add a diameter dimension of **.100"**.

2. Activating the Surfaces toolbar:

- Right click on the **Sketch Tab** and click click on the **Surfaces** tab to enable it.

Ø.100

3. Extruding a **surface**:

- From the Surfaces toolbar click: **Extruded Surface**.

- Use the **Blind** type and enter **.060"** for extrude depth.

- Click **OK** .

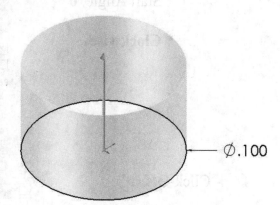

Ø.100

4. Creating a helix:

- Select the <u>Top</u> plane and open a new sketch.

- Select the **bottom edge** of the extruded surface and press **Convert Entities**.

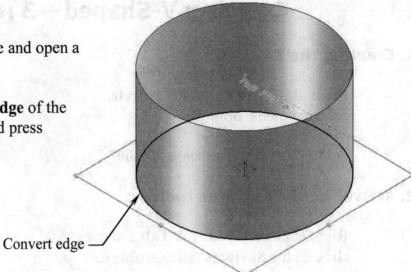

Convert edge

- From the Features toolbar click: **Curves / Helix and Spiral**.

- Enter the following:

    * Defined by: **Pitch and Revolution**

    * **Constant Pitch**

    * Pitch: **0.020"**

    * Revolutions: **3**

    * Start Angle: **0**

    * **Clockwise**

- Click **OK** ✓.

5. Creating a surface profile:

- Select the <u>Top</u> plane and open a new sketch.

- Sketch a **vertical line** and add a **.010"** linear dimension.

- Add a **Pierce** relation between the endpoint of the line and the helix.

Pierce relation ——

.010

- Switch to the **Surfaces** toolbar and click **Extruded Surface**.

- For extrude type, use the default **Blind** type.

- Enter **.020"** for extrude depth.

- Click **OK** ✓.

.010

6. Creating a Curve Driven Pattern:

- From the Features toolbar and click:
Linear Pattern / Curve Driven Pattern.

- For Direction 1, select the **Helix** (Edge 1).

- Enter **61** for Instances.

- Enable **Equal Spacing** checkbox.

- Under Curve Method select:
Transform Curve.

- Under Alignment-Method select:
Tangent to Curve.

- Under Face Normal Select:
the **Cylindrical surface** of the cylinder.

Face Normal

Bodies to Pattern

Direction 1

Direction 1	
Equal spacing:	0.100in
Instances:	61

- Expand the **Bodies to Pattern** section and select the **Extruded Surface** in step 5.

- Click **OK** ✓.

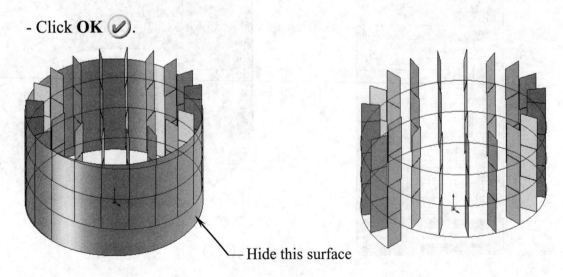

Hide this surface

7. Creating a Curve Through Reference Points:

- From the Features toolbar select:
Curves / Curve Through Reference points.

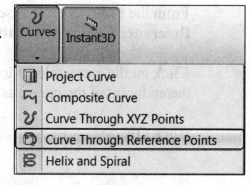

- Click the starting point (point 1) at the end of the helix and go clockwise to point 2, then point 3 as indicated.

Point 2 —⎯ ⎯— Point 1

- Continue going around and select all connecting points. Simply delete any mistakes from the Through Points dialog box.

- Be sure to **uncheck** the Close Curve checkbox since the two ends of this curve are not supposed to connect.

- Click **OK** ✅.

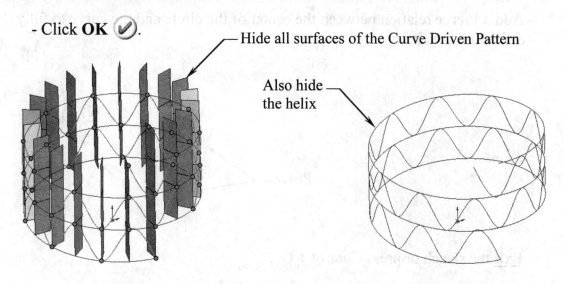

— Hide all surfaces of the Curve Driven Pattern

Also hide — the helix

8. Creating a Perpendicular plane:

- From the Features toolbar select:
  Reference Geometry / Planes.

- Click on the curve (closer to the end) <u>and</u> also click
  the endpoint of the curve, as noted.

- Click **OK** .

Select two
references

9. Sketching the sweep profile:

- Select the <u>new plane</u> and open a new sketch.

- Sketch a **small circle** next to the curve and add a diameter dimension of **.002"**.

- Add a **Pierce** relation between the center of the circle and the curve to fully
  define the sketch.

∅.002

Pierce

- <u>**Exit**</u> the sketch or press Control + Q.

10. Creating the final sweep:

- Switch to the Features toolbar and click: **Swept Boss Base**.

- Select the **small circle** to use as the sweep Profile.

- Select the **3D curve** as the sweep path.

- Click **OK** ✅.

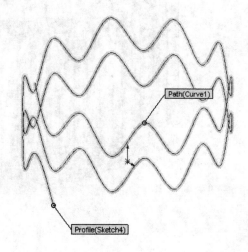

11. Saving your work:

- Click **File / Save As**.

- Enter **V-Shape Spring** for the name of the file.

- Click **Save**.

CHAPTER 7 (cont.)

Advanced Sweep - Wire Form

Advanced Sweep
Wire Form

- This second half of the chapter discusses one of the advanced techniques on creating a continuous wrapped wire around a coil.

- There will be two separate sweep features created in this design. The first sweep feature is the coil, shapes like a spring; the sweep profile is made tangent to the sweep path. To achieve this, a couple of construction lines are used to help locating one of its quadrant points on the path.

- The second sweep feature, due to its complex shape, is done by using a 3D sketch as a sweep path. It is going to wrap around the first sweep feature in a unique way that makes 3D sketch is one of the few options to create it with.

- The method in this lesson demonstrates the use of locating points created in two different sketches to guide a 3D sketch. The lines in the 3D sketch are connected to the pre-defined endpoints of the lines, and the shape of the wire, or the sweep path is formed.

- To ensure the point locations are identical between the two sketches, the option Derived-Sketch is used. That way if one of the endpoints in the original sketch is moved, the same point in the derived sketch will also moved.

- The entities in the derived sketch are driven by the original sketch. Changes done to original sketch are reflected in the derived sketch. To break the link between the derived sketch and its parent sketch, right click the derived sketch from the FeatureManager tree and select **Underived**. (After the link is broken, the derived sketch will no longer update when the original sketch is changed).

Wire Form
Advanced Sweep

Dimensioning Standards: **ANSI**

Units: **INCHES** – 3 Decimals

Tools Needed:

Insert Sketch	3D Sketch	Line
Add Geometric Relations	Sketch Fillet	Circle
Dimension	Centerline	Fillet/Round
Sketch Circular Pattern	Helix/Spiral	Sweep Boss/Base

1. Staring a new part document:

- Go to **File / New / Part**.

- Set the Drafting Standard to **ANSI** and the Units to **Inches, 3 decimals**.

- Select the <u>Top</u> plane and open a new sketch .

- Sketch a **Circle** centered on the origin as shown

- Add a diameter of **Ø2.000"** to fully define the sketch.

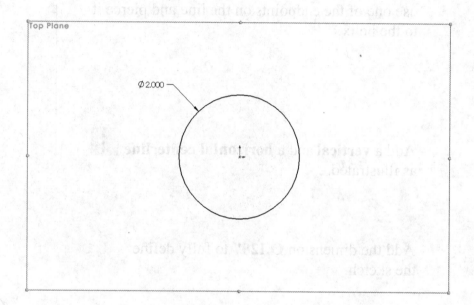

2. Creating the sweep path:

- Click the **Helix / Spiral** command on the Curves drop down menu, or select: **Insert / Curve Helix-Spiral**.

- Set the following:

  * **Constant Pitch**
  * Pitch = **.125"**
  * Revolutions: **8**
  * Start Angle = **0deg**
  * **Clockwise**

- Click **OK** ✓.

3. Creating the sweep profile:

- Select the <u>Right</u> plane and open a new sketch 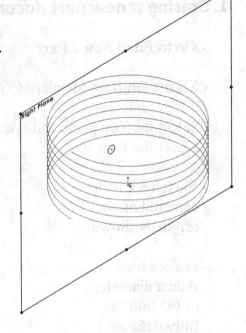.

- Sketch a **Circle** ⊕ on this plane.
  The lower quadrant point of the circle must
  be pierced to the helix, and one way to achieve
  that is to create a couple of centerlines and then
  use one of the endpoints on the line and pierce it
  to the helix.

- Add a **vertical** and a **horizontal centerline**
  as illustrated.

⌀.120

- Add the dimension **Ø.120"** to fully define
  the sketch.

Add a Vertical and a
Horizontal centerline

- Add a **Pierce** relation between the
  endpoint of the vertical centerline
  and the helix.

⌀.120

⌀.120

Pierce relation

Add Relations	⫸
⊗ Pierce	

4. Creating the sweep feature:

- Switch to the **Features** tool tab.

- Click the ⬚ **Swept Boss / Base** command.

- Select the **Helix** to use as the Sweep Path.

- Select the small **Circle** to use as the Sweep Profile.

- Leave all other parameters at their default settings.

- Click **OK** ✓.

5. Creating the 1st offset plane:

- From the Features tool tab, click **Reference Geometry / Plane** ⬚ or select: **Insert / Reference Geometry / Plane**.

- For the First Reference select the **Top** plane from the FeatureManager tree.

- Under Offset Distance enter: **1.150"**.

- Place the new plane <u>above</u> the Top reference plane.

- Click **OK** ✓.

6. Creating the 2nd offset plane:

- Click the **Plane** command once again.

- Select the **Top** plane for First Reference.

- Enter **.045"** for Offset Distance.

- Place the new plane <u>under</u> the Top reference plane.

- Click **OK**.

7. Sketching on the 1st offset plane:

- Select the **Plane1** and open a new sketch.

- Sketch **2 Circles** that are centered on the origin.

- Sketch a vertical **Line** and ensure that both ends of the line are coincident with the upper quadrant points of the two circles.

- Add the two diameter dimensions shown.

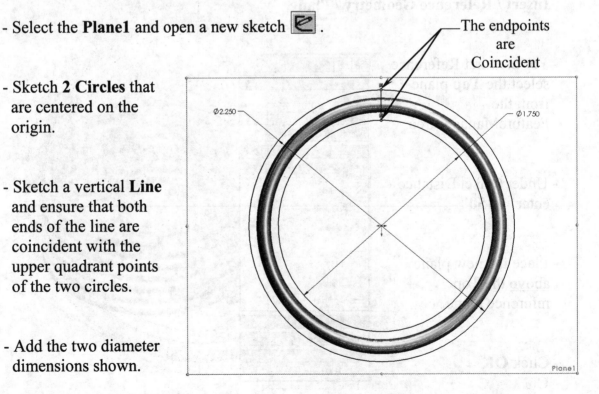

The endpoints are Coincident

Ø2.250

Ø1.750

Plane1

- Hold the **Control** key and
  select both circles.

- Release the control key and
  enable the **For Construction**
  checkbox on the Property tree.

- This option
  toggles the
  selected entities
  back and forth
  between a line and a construction line.

Convert to
construction
lines

8. Creating a Circular Sketch pattern:

- Select the vertical line (Entity to Pattern) and
  click the **Circular Sketch Pattern** command 🎲 .

Entity to pattern

- The origin is
  automatically
  selected as the
  center of the pattern.

- Enable the **Equal-
  Spacing** checkbox.

- Enter **32** for the
  number of instances.

- Click **OK** ✅ .

- The pattern is still under defined at this point.

- Hold the **Control** key and select the 3 points as noted.

- Select the **Horizontal** relation from the Property tree.

Horizontal relation between 3 points

- The sketch turns black to indicate a Fully Defined status. Click **OK** to exit the Property tree.

9. Converting to construction geometry:

- Since we only need the endpoints of each line to help locate the lines in the next sketch, we will need to convert all the lines into construction lines at this point.

- Either hold the Control key and select **all the lines**, or press Control+A to select all entities then hold the control key and un-select the 2 circles.

Convert <u>all</u> lines to construction

- Enable the **For Construction** checkbox on the Property tree

- **<u>Exit</u>** the sketch.

10. Creating a derived sketch:

- Hold the **Control** key and select the **Plane2** and the **Sketch3** from the feature tree.

- Click **Insert / Derived Sketch** (arrow).

- A copy of the sketch is created on the selected plane.

Coincident relation

Add Relations
— Horizontal
∣ Vertical
✕ Coincident

- Add a **Coincident** relation between the 2 center points as noted.

- Add a **Collinear** relation
  between the <u>horizontal line</u>
  on the right and the <u>Front plane</u>
  as indicated.

- All entities in the sketch should
  change to the black color at this
  point.

- **Exit** the sketch.

Collinear relation

11. Creating a 3D sketch:

- The endpoints on the lines will help us in creating the 3D sketch a little easier
  and also more accurate. Make sure both of the sketches are visible.

- From the Sketch tool tab, click
  the drop down arrow
  and select **3D Sketch** .

- Select the **Line** tool from
  the 3D Sketch toolbar.

- Sketch a line that starts at
  one of the endpoints on top
  and connect it to one of the
  endpoints down below.

- The feature Swept1 is hidden for
  Clarity.

(Use the Click + Release technique
to create multiple lines, while the
Click +Hold + Drag creates only
1 line each time).

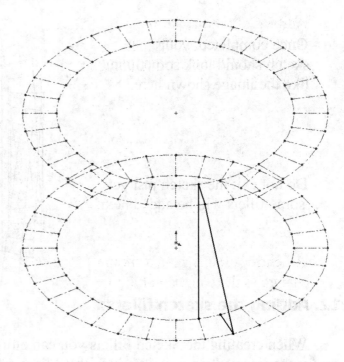

- Add 3 more lines as shown.
  Be sure to snap to each
  existing endpoint when
  sketching the lines.

- Continue to add the other lines as shown below. If you run into an error, simply
  press Escape and start sketching the lines again.

- It is maybe a little easier if you
  could change the orientation
  of the view after a few lines.

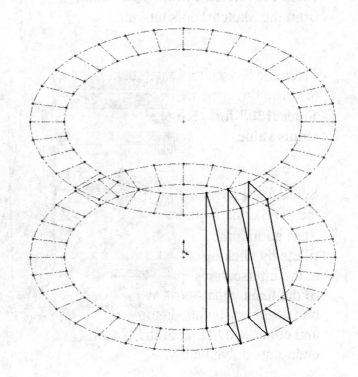

- While in the middle of the line
  mode you can press and hold
  the scroll-wheel to rotate
  slightly to a different angle,
  then continue with your sketch.

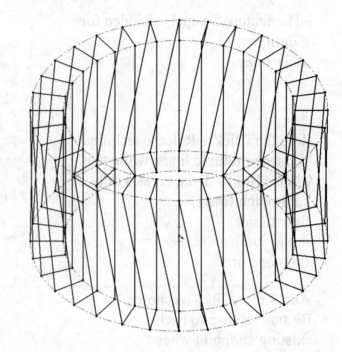

- Once completed, your
sketch should look something
like the image shown here.

- Do not exit the sketch just yet,
some fillets will be added next.

12. Adding the sketch fillets:

- When creating the Sketch Fillets you can either select the 2 lines, or click directly
at the intersection point between the 2 lines to add the fillets. If a fillet gets
deleted its sharp corner will reappear.

- Click the **Sketch Fillet** command
from the Sketch Tools tool tab.

- Enter **.120"** for
radius value.

- Start adding the
fillets by clicking
at the intersections
of the lines.

- Continue to add the same fillet to the other lines.

- It does not really matter which direction (clockwise or counter clockwise when adding the fillets, but it does make it a little easier to go around 1 direction and not to jump back and forth as you may miss one or more vertices.

- After completed, your sketch should look like the image shown below. This 3D sketch will be used as the sweep path in the next few steps.

13. Creating a new plane:

- Click the **Plane** command or select: **Insert / Reference Geometry / Plane**.

- Select the <u>Top</u> plane for the First Reference.

- Select one of the <u>upper endpoints</u> of any line for the Second Reference.

Select the Top plane and an Endpoint of a line

- Click **OK** .

14. Sketching the sweep profile:

- Select the <u>new plane</u> and open a new sketch 🖉 .

- Sketch a **Circle** that is coincident to the endpoints of the same line, and add the diameter dimension **Ø.080"**.

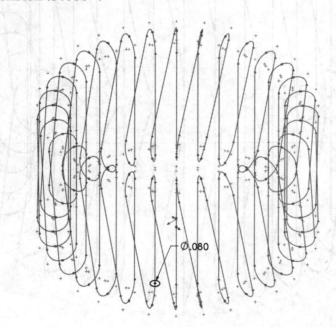

Ø.080

- The sketch should be fully defined at this point.

- **Exit** the 3D sketch or press Control + Q.

- Show the Swept1 feature.

15. Creating the sweep feature:

- Switch to the **Features** tool tab.

- Select the **Swept Boss/Base** command .

- For Sweep Path, select the **3D Sketch**.

- For Sweep Profile, select the small **Circle**.

- Enable the **Merge Tangent Faces** checkbox.

- The preview in yellow color indicates the sweep can be created successfully.

- Click **OK** .

- The result of the second swept feature.

16. Saving your work:

- Click **File / Save As**.

- For the file name, enter: **Advanced Sweep_Wire Form**.

- Select a location to save the file and click **Save**.

Exercise: Using Curve Through Reference Points

1. Creating the Base sketch:

- From the <u>Top</u> plane sketch a circle and a horizontal Centerline then convert them to Construction lines.

- Add a diameter dimension of **.100"**.

- Select the Horizontal Centerline and click **Circular Sketch Pattern**.

- Enter **16** instances, **Equal Spacing**.

Coincident

- Add a couple of Coincident relations between the endpoints of any of the instances and the circle, to fully define the sketch.

- <u>**Exit**</u> the sketch (or press **Control +Q**).

2. Creating an offset plane:

- Create a new plane that is **.020"** <u>above</u> the **Top** plane.

- Click **OK** ✓.

3. Creating a Derived sketch:

- Hold the **Control** key and select the **Sketch1** and the **Plane1**.

- Click **Insert / Derived Sketch**.

- Add a coincident relation between the centers of the 2 circles and a vertical relation between any 2 endpoints.

- **Exit** the sketch.

Coincident

Vertical

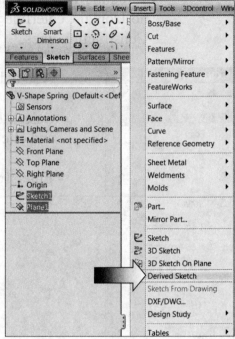

4. Creating a Curve Through Reference Points:

- From the **Features** toolbar, click:
Curves / Curve Through Reference Points.

- Click the starting point (point 1), move clockwise and click point 2, then point 3 so on. Continue around.

Point 3 (upper)

Point 2 (lower)

Point 1 (upper)

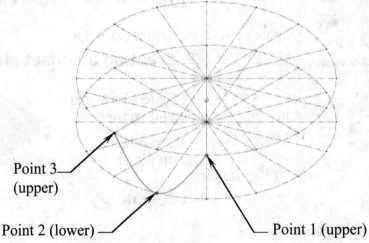

- Continue going around a full revolution and select all the connecting points in the 2 sketches.

- At the end of the path, do not click point 1 again as the **Closed Curve** option will joins the 2 ends together automatically.

- Enable the **Closed Curve** checkbox.

- Click **OK** ✅.

Stop here ―

5. Sketching the sweep profile:

- Select the <u>Front</u> plane and open a new sketch.

- Sketch a circle and add a diameter dimension of **.003"**.

- Add a **Pierce** relation between the center of the circle and the 3D curve.

- **Exit** the sketch.

Ø.003

Pierce relation

6. Creating a swept feature:

- From the **Features** toolbar, click **Swept Boss Base**.

- Click the small circle as the Sweep profile.

- Select the 3D curve as the Sweep path.

- Click **OK** .

7. Saving your work:

- Click **File / Save as**:

- Enter: **Curve Through Reference Points** for the name of the file.

- Click **Save**.

CHAPTER 8

Using Surfaces

Advanced Modeling - Using Surfaces

- Surfaces are a type of geometry that can be used to create solid features.

- The surface options are used to form complex free-form shapes and to manipulate files imported from other Cad formats.

- Unlike solid models, surfaces can be opened, overlapped, and have no thickness. Each surface can be constructed individually and then knitted together. A solid feature is created by thickening the surfaces that have been knit into a closed volume.

- Surfaces can be modeled in any shape and their sketches can either be extruded, revolved, swept, or lofted into a surface. These surfaces can also be replaced and filled with other surfaces.

- Edges of the surfaces can be extended and trimmed. Surfaces can be moved, rotated, and copied.

- The angle between the faces of a surface can be calculated using the Draft-Analysis tool; Positive Drafts, Negative Drafts, and Required Drafts are reported on screen.

- This 1st half of the chapter discusses the use of some surfacing tools in the newer releases of SolidWorks.

Advanced Modeling
Using Surfaces

Dimensioning Standards: **ANSI**

Units: **INCHES** – 3 Decimals

Tools Needed:

Insert Sketch	3 Point Arc	Ellipse
Dimension	Add Geometric Relations	Split Line
Plane	Lofted Surface	Surface Thicken

1. Constructing a new work plane:

- Select the <u>Front</u> plane from the FeatureManager tree.

- Click or select **Insert / Reference Geometry / Plane**.

- Select the **Front** plane and click the **Offset Distance** button.

- Enter **3.000 in**. and enable the **Flip** check box to reverse the direction.

- Click **OK**.

2. Sketching the 1st profile:

- Select the <u>new plane</u> (Plane1).

- Click or select **Insert / Sketch**.

- Sketch a **3-Point-Arc** and add the dimensions as shown.

- Add a **Vertical** relation between the center of the arc and the origin point.

- **Exit** the Sketch.

3. Sketching the 2nd profile:

- Select the <u>Front</u> plane from the FeatureManager tree.

- Click 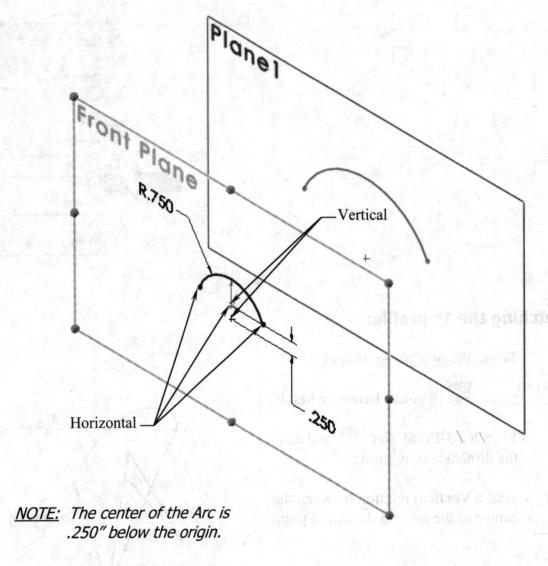 or select **Insert / Sketch**.

- Sketch a **3-Point-Arc** as shown.

- Add a **.750** radius dimension to the arc.

- Add a Horizontal and a Vertical relation as indicated.

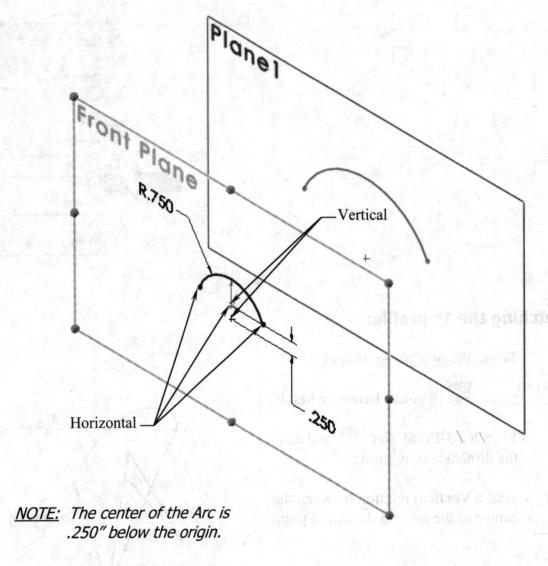

Plane1

Front Plane

R.750

Vertical

Horizontal

.250

<u>NOTE:</u> *The center of the Arc is
.250" below the origin.*

- **Exit** the sketch .

4. Sketching the Guide Curve:

- Select the <u>Right</u> plane from the FeatureManager tree and open a new sketch.

- Sketch a **3-Point-Arc** and add a **4.00** in. dimension .

- Add the **Pierce** relations as noted .

Pierce relation

Right Plane

R4.000

Pierce relation

- **Exit** the sketch .

__Activating the Surfaces toolbar:__ Right-click on one of the tabs (Features, Sketch, etc.) and select Surfaces. The new Surfaces toolbar appears next to the other tabs.

5. Creating a Surface-Loft:

- Click 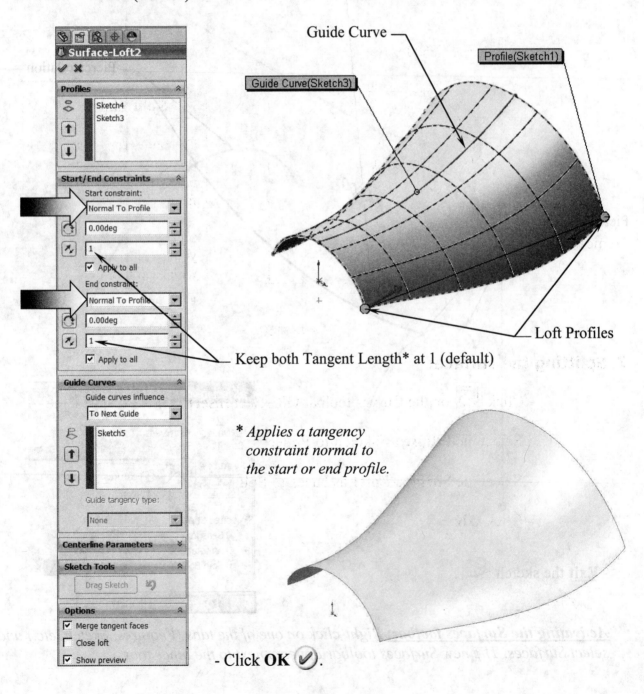 or **Insert / Surface / Loft**.

- Select the **2 Sketched Profiles** by clicking on their *right-most endpoints*.

- Expand the Guide-Curve section and select the **Sketched Arc** as noted.

- Set <u>both</u> *Start/End Constraints* to *Normal-To-Profile*. Set both Tangent Length to 1 (default).

Guide Curve

Profile(Sketch1)

Guide Curve(Sketch3)

Loft Profiles

Keep both Tangent Length* at 1 (default)

*Applies a tangency
constraint normal to
the start or end profile.*

- Click **OK** ✓.

6. Sketching the Split profile:

- Select the <u>Top</u> plane from the FeatureManager tree.

- Click or **Insert / Sketch**.

- Change to Top view orientation .

- Sketch an **Ellipse** and add Dimensions/Relations as shown.

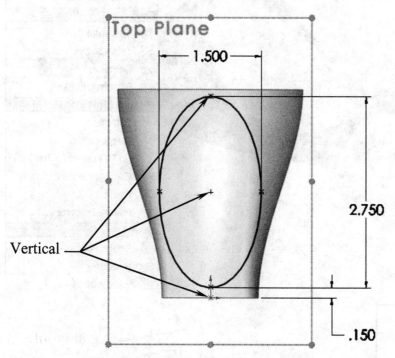

Top Plane

1.500

2.750

.150

Vertical

> :bulb: **Split Lines**
>
> The Split Lines command projects a sketch entity onto a face (or a set of faces) and divides a selected face into multiple separate faces, enabling you to select and work with each face.

7. Splitting the surface:

- Click on the Curves toolbar OR select **Insert / Curve / Split Line**.

- Select the **Ellipse** as Sketch-to-Project .

- Select the **Surface-Loft1** as Faces-to-Split .

- Click **OK** .

8. Deleting Surfaces:

- Right click on the **outer portion** of the surface.

- Select **Face** / **Delete** from the menu.

- Click **Delete** under Options (circled).

- Click **OK**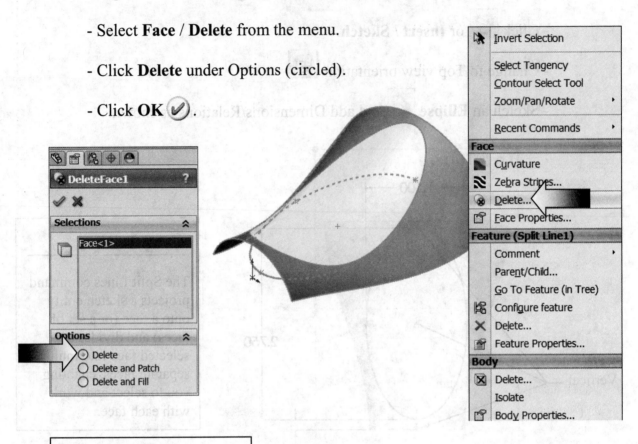

DeleteFace1

Selections

Face<1>

Options
- Delete
- Delete and Patch
- Delete and Fill

Face
- Curvature
- Zebra Stripes...
- Delete...
- Face Properties...

Feature (Split Line1)
- Comment
- Parent/Child...
- Go To Feature (in Tree)
- Configure feature
- Delete...
- Feature Properties...

Body
- Delete...
- Isolate
- Body Properties...

Invert Selection
Select Tangency
Contour Select Tool
Zoom/Pan/Rotate
Recent Commands

💡 **Delete Face**

This command deletes one
or more faces from a surface
or solid body.

Other options are:
* Delete and Patch, which
  automatically patches and
  trims the body.
* Delete and Fill, which
  generates and fills any gap.

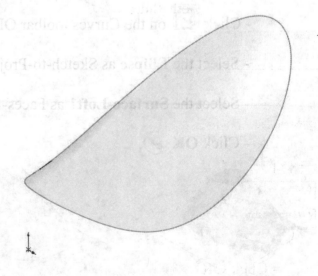

- The resulting surface.

9. Thickening the surface:

- Click 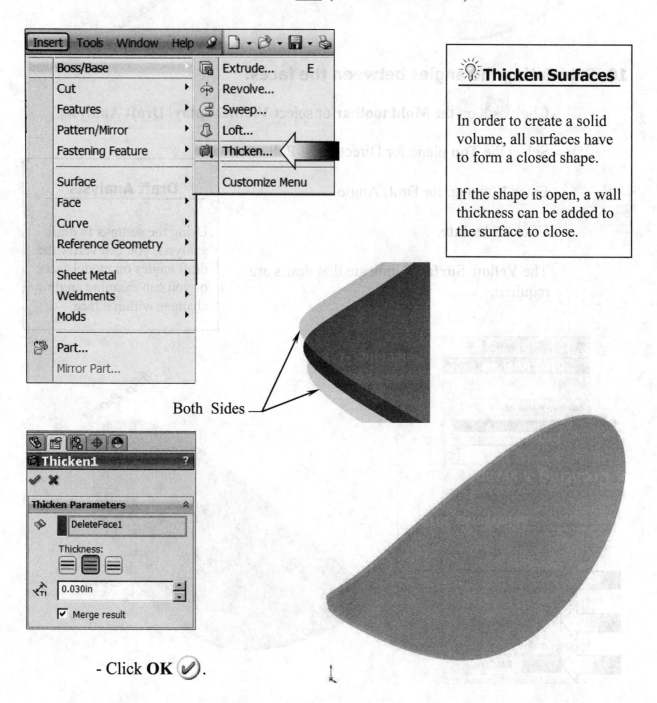 or select **Insert / Boss-Base / Thicken**.

- Click on the **surface** as Surface-To-Thicken .

- Choose **Thicken Both Sides** option .

- Enter **.030** in. as Thickness (.060 total thickness).

> **Thicken Surfaces**
>
> In order to create a solid volume, all surfaces have to form a closed shape.
>
> If the shape is open, a wall thickness can be added to the surface to close.

Both Sides

- Click **OK** .

- The surface turns into a solid model.

10. Calculating the angles between the faces:

- Click on the **Mold toolbar** or select **View/Display/ Draft Analysis**.

- Select the **Top** plane for Direction of Pull.

- Enter **1.00** deg. for Draft Angle.

- Click **Calculate**.

- The **Yellow Surfaces** indicate that drafts are required.

> 💡 **Draft Analysis**
>
> Using the settings in draft analysis, you can verify the draft angles on model faces or you can examine angle changes within a face.

Draft Analysis

The **Draft Analysis** is a tool to check the correct application of draft to the faces of each part. With draft analysis, you can verify draft angles, examine angle changes within a face, as well as locate parting lines, injection, and ejection surfaces in parts.

Draft analysis results listed under Color Settings are grouped into four categories, when you specify Face classification:

<u>**Positive draft:**</u> Displays any faces with a positive draft based on the reference draft angle you specified. A positive draft means the angle of the face, with respect to the direction of pull, is more than the reference angle.

<u>**Negative draft:**</u> Displays any faces with a negative draft based on the reference draft angle you specified. A negative draft means the angle of the face, with respect to the direction of the pull, is less than the negative reference angle.

<u>**Draft required:**</u> Displays any faces that require correction. These are faces with an angle greater than the negative reference angle and less than the positive reference angle.

<u>**Straddle faces:**</u> Displays any faces that contain both positive and negative types of draft. Typically, these are faces that require you to create a split line.

*Note: When analyzing the draft for surfaces, an additional **Face classification** criterion is added: **Surface faces with draft**. Since a surface includes an inside and an outside face, surface faces are not added to the numerical part of the classification (**Positive draft** and **Negative draft**). **Surface faces with draft** lists all positive and negative surfaces that include draft.*

- Mouse cursor over the upper surface to see the read out draft angle for that particular area.

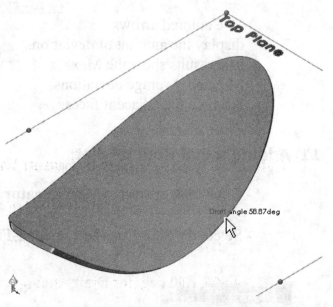

- Position the mouse cursor over the yellow areas (required drafts) and check the draft angles to see if they meet your draft requirements.

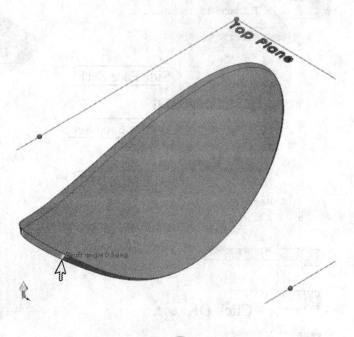

- Click **OK** ✔.

- The option Deviation-
Analysis can be used to
diagnose and calculate
the angle between faces.

- The colored arrows
display the amount of deviation.
The results show the Max,
Min and Average deviations
between the adjacent faces.

11. Adding a Full Round Fillet:

- Click 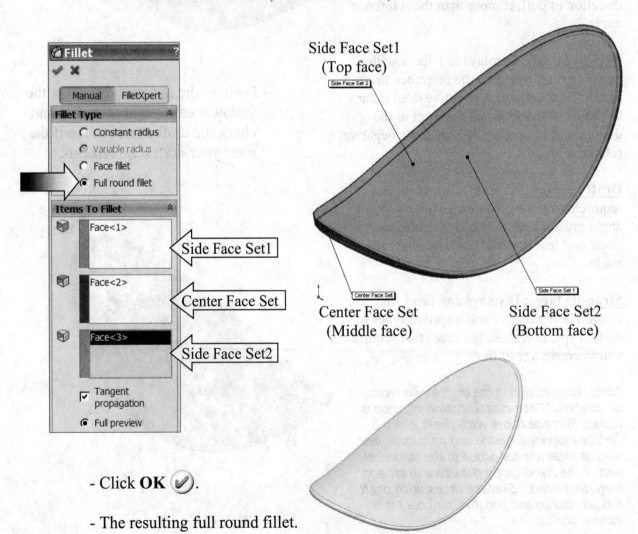 or select **Insert / Features / Fillet-Round**.

- Select the Side-Face-Set1, Center-Face-Set, and Side-Face-Set2 as noted.

Side Face Set1
(Top face)

Center Face Set
(Middle face)

Side Face Set2
(Bottom face)

- Click **OK**.

- The resulting full round fillet.

12. Creating an Offset Distance plane:

- Select the <u>Top</u> plane from the FeatureManager tree and click , or select **Insert / Reference Geometry / Plane**.

- Enter **.850 in**. for Distance and place the new plane <u>above</u> the Top plane.

- Click **OK** .

13. Sketching the Slot Contours:

- Select the new plane (**Plane2**) and open a new sketch.

- Create the sketch using either **Mirror** or **Offset** options.

- Sketch the profile as shown, add dimensions to fully position the sketch.

- Create an offset of **.0625** in. from the 2 sketch lines, using the settings below.

(Add the corner radius after the sketch is fully defined).

- Trim the inner intersections and create a second offset as shown.

- Clean up the corners and add the .031 radius as indicated.

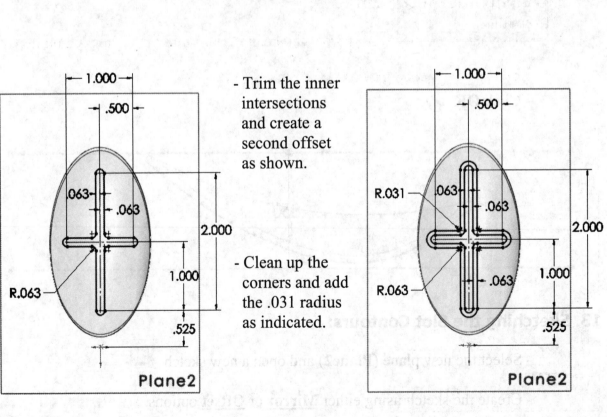

14. Extruding Cut the 1st Contour:

- Click or select **Insert / Cut / Extrude**.

- Expand the Selected Contour section and select one of the **Outer Lines** (Outer Contour)

- Use **Offset From Surface** end condition.

- Enter **.030 in**. for Depth.

- Click the **Top face** of the model.

- Enable **Reverse Offset** check box.

- The Slot is cut, following the contours of the upper face.

- Click **OK** ✓.

Select one of the outer lines (contour)

Offset from this face

15. Extruding Cut the 2nd Contour:

- Expand the Cut-Extrude1 from the FeatureManager tree, right click on the

Sketch5 and select **SHOW** .

- Hover over one of the <u>inner lines</u> and select the entire contour when it highlights.

- Click or select **Insert / Cut / Extrude**.

- Select **Though All** for end condition.

- Click **OK** .

Select all
inner entities

- Hide the Sketch5 when finished.

16. Saving your work:

- Select **File / Save As / Lofted-Surface / Save**.

Questions for Review

Using Surfaces - Advanced Modeling

1. Surfaces are a type of geometry that can be used to create complex shapes.
   a. True
   b. False

2. Surfaces can be opened, overlapped, and have no thickness.
   a. True
   b. False

3. Surfaces can be modeled into any shape and can be extruded, revolved, swept, or lofted.
   a. True
   b. False

4. The split line option can be used to "divide" a surface into two or more surfaces.
   a. True
   b. False

5. Several surfaces can be lofted together to form a solid feature.
   a. True
   b. False

6. Surfaces cannot be moved or copied in a part document.
   a. True
   b. False

7. Each surface can be created individually and then knitted together as one surface.
   a. True
   b. False

8. The same Sketched profile can be Re-used to create different extruded contours.
   a. True
   b. False

9. Offset From Surface (extrude option) only works with surfaces, not solid features.
   a. True
   b. False

1. TRUE	2. TRUE
3. TRUE	4. TRUE
5. TRUE	6. FALSE
7. TRUE	8. TRUE
9. FALSE	

CHAPTER 8 (cont.)

Lofted Surface

Let's take a look at a couple of techniques when modeling advanced shapes.

We will start out by creating some surfaces using various surfacing tools. These surfaces will get knitted into one surface; this surface will then get thickened into a solid part. Finally the part is split into two halves and gets assembled in an assembly document.

1. Creating new offset planes:

- Select the <u>Front</u> plane from the FeatureManager tree.

- Click or select **Insert / Reference Geometry / Plane**.

- Choose **Offset Distance** and enter **4.00 in**.

- Use **Flip** direction if needed to place the new plane on the **back side**.

- Enter **2** for number of instances.

- Click **OK** ✅.

2. Sketch the first profile: (the front section)

- Select the <u>Front</u> plane from the FeatureManager tree.

- Click or select **Insert / Sketch**.

- Sketch the profile and add the dimensions shown.

- <u>Exit</u> the Sketch or select **Insert / Sketch**.

3. Sketching the second profile: (the middle section)

- Select the <u>Plane1</u> from FeatureManager tree.

- Click or select **Insert / Sketch**.

- Sketch the profile and add the dimensions shown.

- <u>Exit</u> the Sketch or select **Insert / Sketch**.

💡 Copy & Paste

The 1st profile can be copied and pasted to make the next 2 sketches. The dimensions will then be adjusted to size.

4. Sketching the third profile: (the end section)

- Select the <u>Plane2</u> from the FeatureManager tree.

- Click or select **Insert / Sketch**.

- Sketch the profile and add dimensions as shown.

- **Exit** the Sketch or select **Insert / Sketch**.

5. Selecting the loft profiles:

> ### ◌̇ Lofted Surface
>
> Lofted Surface creates a surface by making transitions between the sketch profiles.
>
> Two or more profiles are needed to create a loft.

- To prevent the loft feature from being twisted, it is recommended that all sketch profiles should be selected from the same side.

Twisted – Profiles selected from different sides…

Correct – Profiles selected from the same sides…

6. Lofting between the profiles:

- Click or select **Insert / Surface / Loft**.

- Select the **upper-right vertex** of each profile .

- Enable **Merge Tangent Faces**.

- Click **OK** .

> 💡 **Merge Tangent Faces**
>
> Select Merge tangent faces to cause the corresponding surfaces in the resulting loft to be tangent if the corresponding lofting segments are tangent.

Select the upper vertex of each profile

- The resulting Surface-Loft.

7. Creating a Revolved sketch:

- Select the <u>Top</u> plane from the FeatureManager tree.

- Click or select **Insert / Sketch**.

- Sketch the revolve profile and add dimensions as shown.

R4.000

Coincident

4.750

8. Revolving the Spherical surface:

- Click or select **Insert / Surface / Revolve**.

- Revolve Type: **Blind**.

- Revolve Angle: **360 deg**.

> ### Revolved Surface
>
> Revolved Surface creates a surface by rotating a sketch profile around a centerline (or the Axis of Revolution).

- Clear the Merge-Result checkbox.

- Click **OK**.

- The Revolved Surface.

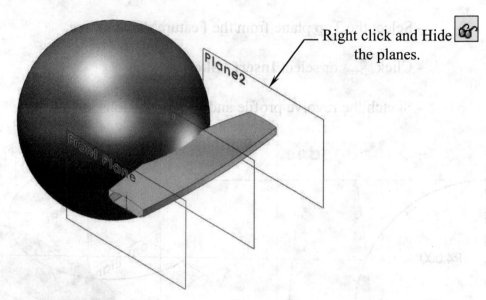

Right click and Hide the planes.

9. Copying the Revolved Surface:

- Click or select **Insert / Surface / Move/Copy**.

- Select the **Surface-Revolve1** under Surfaces to Move/Copy.

- Enable the **Copy** check box.

- Enter **1** for Number of Copies.

- Enter **9.500** in the **Delta X** distance box.

- Click **OK**.

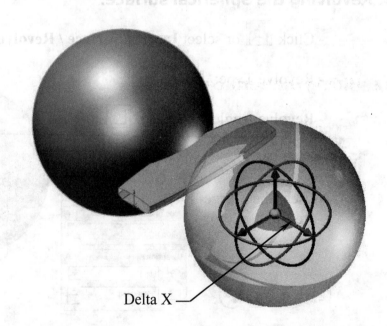

Delta X

10. Trimming the Base part:

- Click or select **Insert / Surface / Trim**.

- For Trim-Type, click **Mutual Trim** .

- For **Trimming-Surfaces**, select all **3 surfaces** .

- For **Keep Selection**, select the Surface-Loft1 .

- Click **OK** .

> 💡 **Trim Surface**
>
> A surface or a sketch can be used as a trim tool to trim the intersecting surfaces.

Keep Selection

Trimming Surfaces

11. Hiding the surfaces:

- Right click over the two revolved surfaces and select **Hide.**

12. Filling the openings with Surface-Fill:

- For Patch Boundary: select the **6 edges** as shown ⬚ .

- For Curvature Control use: **Contact** `Contact` ▾ .

- <u>Enable</u> **Apply to all edges**.

- <u>Clear</u> the **Optimize Surface** option.

- Click **OK** ✅ .

> 💡 **Filled Surface**
>
> Filled surface constructs a surface patch to fill a non-planar opening in a model.

Select 6 edges

Contact - S0 - Boundary

- The right side cutout is filled with a new surface (Surface-Fill1).

<u>Exercise</u>: Advanced Surfaces

1. Opening an Existing file:

- Go to the Training Files folder.

- Open the document named:
  Advanced Surfaces Exercise.

4 Loft Profiles

Profile(Loft Profile4-Contour)

2. Creating the Loft body:

- Create a **Solid Loft** from the **4 profiles** as indicated.

- Use the **2 bottom Guide Curves** to control the sides.

- Use the top **Guide-Curve** to control the upper curvatures.

2 Bottom
Guide Curves

1 Top Guide Curve

Guide Curve(Top Guide Curve-Contour)

3. Adding Fillets:

- Add a **.500 in**. fillet to the upper edges, and a **.250 in**. fillet to the edges on the end, as indicated.

* By adding the fillets in the sketches the tangent lines can be eliminated using the Merge-Tangent-Faces in the loft options.

R.500*

R.250

4. Creating the Split Lines & Lofted-Cuts:

- Use the 2 sketches named: **Circular-Split** and **Side-Split** to create 2 split surfaces.

- Create 2 lofted-cuts at **.093** in. deep, using either the **Offset** or **Ruled** surface options.

5. Adding the Nose and Fillets:

- Add the Nose feature that measured between **1.250 in**. to **1.500 in**. from the front face.

- Remove all sharp edges with **.040 in**. fillets.

6. Saving your work:

- Save the exercise as:
Advanced_Surfaces_Exe.

Exercise: Advanced Surfacing Techniques

- Surfaces are a type of geometry that can be used to create solid features. Surfaces can be created in a variety of different ways; from a sketch or multiple sketches, a surface can be made by extruding, revolving, sweeping and lofting.
- Surfaces are normally created individually and knitted together so that an enclosed volume or a solid feature, can be generated afterwards.
- This exercise discusses some advanced techniques on surfacing such as: Lofted Surface, Boundary Surface, Trimmed Surface, Offset Surface, Extrude From, and variable fillets.

1. Opening the existing document named:

Advanced Surfacing Techniques from the Training Files folder. <u>Rollback</u> below the sketch: 1st Loft Guide-Curves.

2. Creating the 1st Lofted Surface:

- Click or select:
Insert / Surface / Loft.

- Select the **2 Loft Profiles** and the **2 Guide Curves** as indicated.

- Click **OK** .

Loft Profile 2

Guide Curve 1

Guide Curve 2

Loft Profile 1

Lofted-Surface creates a feature by making transitions between two or more profiles. A loft can either be a surface or solid and one or more Guide Curves can be used to guide the transitions between the profiles.

3. Creating the 2nd Lofted Surface:

- Click or select: **Insert / Surface / Loft**.

- Select the **3 Loft Profiles** and the **4 Guide Curves** as indicated.

- Click OK after each selection of profile and guide curves.

3 Loft Profiles

4 Guide Curves

3 Loft Profiles

4 Guide Curves

<u>Note</u>: Click ✔ after each selection

Select Open Loop
Select Closed Loop
Select Region
Select Group

- Click **OK** ✔.

4. Creating the Boundary-Surfaces:

- Click [ ] or select **Insert / Surface / Boundary-Surface**.

- For **Direction 1**, select the **2 edges** as shown (Blue tags).

> **Boundary-Surface** creates a new surface from a set of 2D or 3D sketch entities.
> The Boundary Surface can be tangent or curvature-continuous in both directions (all sides of the surface).
> This option offers a higher quality result than the Loft.

Direction 1:
Select 2 edges
(Light Blue Tags)
May need to select twice.

Light Blue ➤

- For **Direction 2**, select the **3 Arcs** in the Boundary Sketch as shown (Purple tags).

Direction 2:
Select 3 Arcs
(Purple tags)
May need to click twice to get a response.

Purple ➤

- Click **OK** [✓].

Note: Click [✓] after each selection

5. Repeating:

- Repeat step number 4 and create another Boundary-Surface on the opposite side.

6. Creating an Extruded-Surface:

- Select the **Eyes Sketch** from the FeatureManager tree and Click or select: **Insert / Surface / Extrude**.

- Change the option **Extrude From** to **Surface/Face/Plane** (Arrow).

- Select the surface as indicated, to extrude.

> **Extruded-Surface** creates a new surface from a 2D or 3D sketch, which protrudes normal to the sketch plane.

- Change **Direction 1** to **Mid Plane** (Arrow).

- Enter **.410"** for Extrude Depth.

- Click **OK** ✓.

7. Creating a Trimmed Surface:

- Click or select **Insert / Surface / Trim**.

> **Trimmed-Surface** uses a plane, a surface, or a sketch as a trim tool to trim the intersecting surfaces.

- Select **Mutual** under Trim Type (Arrow).

- For **Trimming Surfaces**, select **all surfaces** of the model.

- For **Pieces To Remove**, select the **5 Faces** as shown (Arrow).

Pieces to Remove

Select Mutual

Trimming Surfaces

Remove Sel.

Pieces to Remove

8. Creating another Extruded Surface:

- Select the **Thunder Sketch** and click or select **Insert / Surface /Extrude**.

- Set the **Direction 1** to **Blind** and click **Reverse Direction**.

- Set **Extrude Depth** to: **1.250"**.

- Click **OK**.

9. Creating an Offset-Surface:

- Click or select **Insert / Surface / Offset**.

- Select the **2 surfaces** as shown (Arrow).

- Enter **.100"** for **Offset Distance**.

- Place the copy on the **bottom** of the original.

- *Note: Create 2 offset surfaces separately if the next trim failed.*

- Click **OK** ☑.

> **Offset-Surface** creates a copy of a surface in either direction, and is parallel to the selected surface(s). The offset distance can be zero or any other value.

Select 2 surfaces to offset…

Offset Surface .100in. below…

10. Creating a Mutual Trimmed Surface:

- Click or select **Insert / Surface / Trim***.

- Select **Mutual** under Trim Type (Arrow).

- For **Trimming Surfaces**, select **all surfaces** of the Thunder Sketch and the Offset Surfaces.

Trimming Surfaces

Trimming Surfaces

* *Note: Trim one feature each time would also work well.*

- For **Remove Selection**, select the following:

   * The **surfaces** of the **Thunder Sketch**,
     Keep the inside faces as noted.

   * The **2 Offset Surfaces**.

Keep the inside surfaces…

Remove Sel.

- Hide all trimmed surfaces when done.

- Click **OK** .

11. Creating an Extruded Surface:

- Select the **Corner Radius Trim** Sketch
  and click or select **Insert / Surface / Extrude**.

- Set the **Direction 1** to **Blind**
  and click **Reverse Direction**.

- Set Depth to **2.000"**.

- Click **OK** .

(These new surfaces will be used to trim-off the 4 corners).

12. Creating a corner Trimmed Surface:

- Click or select **Insert / Surface / Trim**.

- Select **Mutual** under Trim Type (Arrow).

- For **Trimming Surfaces**, select the following:

* The **4 extruded faces** and the **4 corner pieces**.

* The **2 left/right faces** of the model.

Trimming Surfaces

Pieces to Keep

Surface-Trim4

Trim Type
- Standard
- Mutual ← Select Mutual

Selections
Surfaces:
- Surface-Extrude3
- Surface-Extrude3
- Surface-Trim2
- Surface-Trim3
- Surface-Extrude3
- Surface-Extrude3
- Keep selections ← Keep Selections
- Remove selections

Surface-Trim2-Trim1
Surface-Trim3-Trim1

Surface Split Options
- Split all
- Natural
- Linear

- For **Pieces to Keep**, select the **Left and Right Faces** of the model.

- Click **OK**.

Hide the Corner Trim surface when finished

13. Creating a Knit-Surface:

- Click or select **Insert / Surface / Knit**.

- Select **all surfaces** either from the FeatureManager tree or from the graphics area.

- Click off the Gap Control.

- Click **OK**.

Knit Surface

Selections
- Boundary-Surface2
- Surface-Trim4[2]
- Surface-Trim3[1]
- Surface-Trim3[3]
- Surface-Trim3[5]
- Surface-Trim3[4]
- Try to form solid
- Merge entities

Gap Control

14. Adding a Variable Fillet:

- Click or select **Insert / Features / Fillet-Round**.

- Select the **2 edges** shown.

- Use the **Call-out tags** and enter the radius values as noted.

- Click **OK** ✓.

15. Adding a Constant Fillet:

- Click or select **Insert / Features / Fillet-Round**.

- Select the **2 edges** as shown.

- Enter **.200"** for Radius values.

- Click **OK** ✓.

16. <u>Optional</u>: Adding texture

- From the **Appearances** folder, select the **Rubber/Texture** folder.

- Drag & Drop the **Textured Rubber** onto the part, select the <u>Apply to Part</u> option.

Rubber Textured

17. Saving your work:

- Click **File / Save As**.

- Enter **Advanced Surfacing Techniques** for the name of the file.

- Click **Save**.

CHAPTER 9 (cont.)

Using the Deform Feature

There are 3 options in deform: Deform with a Point, Curve-To-Curve deform, and Surface Push. Curve to curve deform is a more precise option to deform a complex shape. You deform the part by starting with an initial curve to a set of target curves.

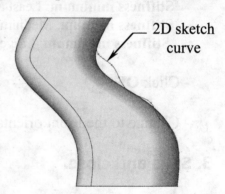

We will take a look at the Curve-To-Curve option and learn to deform a solid and a surface body, using a 2D sketch curve to control the deform shape.

1. Opening a part document:

- From the training CD, locate and open the document named: **Deform Solid**. Click **NO** to bypass the Feature Recognition options.

- This part document comes with a 2D sketch curve. Change to the Front view orientation (Control+1).

2D sketch curve

2. Creating a Curve-to-Curve deform:

- Click **Insert / Features / Deform**.

- Click the **Curve to Curve** option.

- For Initial Curve, click the **right edge** of the part as shown.

- For Target Curve, select the **2D curve sketch** as noted.

(more on next page…)

Initial Curve

Target Curve

- Click in the **Anchor** section.

- Select the **10 edges** as indicated (the curved edges on top and bottom are touching the Target-Curve and cannot be used as the fixed edges).

- The 10 selected edges will remained fixed, they will not be affected by the deform feature.

- Under the **Shape Options*** section, drag the Accuracy slider all the way to the right.

Select 10 edges

    *Stiffness: Controls the rigidity of the deform shape in the deformation process.
    *Stiffness minimum: Least amount of rigidity.
    *Stiffness medium: Medium amount of rigidity.
    *Stiffness maximum: Largest amount of rigidity

- Click **OK** ✅.

- Change to the Front orientation to examine the results (Cntrl+1).

3. Save and close.

1. Opening a part document:

- For the 2nd half of this deform exercise, open a part document named: **Deform Surface**.

- Click <u>NO</u> to bypass the Feature Recognition options.

- This document contains 1 half of the surface body part. After it is deformed, we will mirror it to make a complete surface body part.

2. Creating a Curve to Curve deform:

- Select **Insert / Features / Deform**.

- Click the **Curve to Curve** option, if not yet selected.

- Change to the Front orientation (Cntrl+1).

2D sketch curve

- For Initial Curve, select the **right edge** of the part as indicated.

- For Target Curve, select the **2D curve sketch** as noted.

(more on next page...)

Initial Curve

Target Curve

- Click in the **Anchor** section.

- Select the **3 edges** as indicated to keep fixed.

- Under the Shape Options drag the Accuracy slider all the way to the right.

    (Note: Increasing the surface accuracy decreases the computer performance).

- Click **OK** ✅.

Select 3 edges

Shape accuracy: Controls the surface quality.
Weight: Controls the degree of influence between two options: Fixed Edges and Moving Curves.
Maintain boundary: Ensures that boundaries selected for fixed curves/edges/faces are fixed.
Surface tangent: Matches target edges of faces and surfaces with a smooth transition.
Curve direction: Matches Target curves by mapping Initial curves to Target curves using the normal of the Target curves to shape the deform.

3. Mirroring a surface body:

- Click 🔳 from the Features toolbar or select: **Insert / Features / Mirror**.

- For Mirror Face / Plane, select: the **Front** plane from the FeatureManager tree.

- Expand the **Bodies to Mirror** section and click the surface body either from the graphics area or from the FeatureManager tree.

- Click **OK** ✅.

4. Save and close.

CHAPTER 10

Using Filled Surfaces

Using Filled Surfaces
Curvature Controls

- Use Filled Surface and Planar Surface commands to fill or patch a surface boundary with any number of sides.

- The boundary can be a set of existing model edges, sketches, or curves, including composite curves. The boundary should be closed for the patch to work properly.

- There are several options to help you control the curvatures when patching a surface boundary such as: Contact, Tangent, and Curvature. These options are explained later in the lesson.

- Other than the Curvature Control options the Apply-to-All-Edges check box enables you to apply the <u>same</u> curvature control to all edges. If you select the function after applying both **Contact** and **Tangent** to different edges, it applies the current selection to <u>all</u> edges.

- If your surface model has two or four-sided surfaces try using the **Optimize surface** option. The Optimize surface option applies a simplified surface patch that is similar to a lofted surface. Potential advantages of the optimized surface patch include faster build times, and increased stability when used in conjunction with other features in the model.

- This lesson will teach us the use of the Filled Surface and Planar Surface commands.

Using Filled Surfaces
Patch with Curvature Controls

View Orientation Hot Keys:

Ctrl + 1 = Front View
Ctrl + 2 = Back View
Ctrl + 3 = Left View
Ctrl + 4 = Right View
Ctrl + 5 = Top View
Ctrl + 6 = Bottom View
Ctrl + 7 = Isometric View
Ctrl + 8 = Normal To
       Selection

Dimensioning Standards: **ANSI**

Units: **INCHES** – 3 Decimals

Tools Needed:

    Planar Surface   Filled Surface   Knit Surface

1. Opening a part document:

- Click **File / Open**.

- Browse to the Training Files folder,
  open the part document named:
  Filled Surfaces.

- This part document was previously
  created in another CAD software. There is
  no feature history available on the FeatureManager tree.

- There are three openings in the part that we will have to fill using different
  options within the Filled-Surface command.

- If the Feature Recognition dialog pops up, click **NO** to close it.

2. Enabling the Surfaces toolbar:

- Right click either the Features tab or the Sketch tab and select the Surfaces
  tool tab.

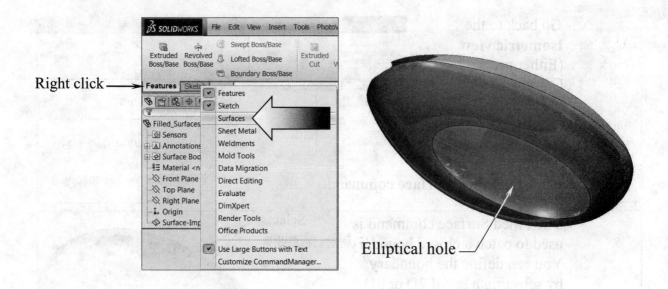

Right click

Elliptical hole

- Rotate the model and locate the elliptical-hole at the bottom of the model.

- This hole should forms a flat surface and we can use the Planar-Surface
  command to patch it

3. Creating a Planar surface 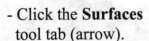:

- Click the **Surfaces** tool tab (arrow).

- Select the **Planar-Surface** command.

- Select the edge of of the elliptical hole.

- The preview of a new surface appears.

- Click **OK**.

- A planar surface can be created from a sketch, a set of closed edges, or a pair of planar entities such as curves or edges.

Select edge

4. Creating a Surface Fill with Tangent Control :

- Go back to the **Isometric view** (Either press Control + 7 or press the Spacebar and select the Isometric view).

- Click the **Filled Surface** command.

- The Filled Surface command is used to patch a closed boundary. You can define the boundary by selecting a set of 2D or 3D sketch entities, model edges or composite curves.

- Select the two edges of the elliptical hole as indicated.

Select 2 edges

- A preview mesh
  Is displayed to
  help you visualize
  the curvature of
  new surface.

- Change the
  Curvature Control*
  to **Tangent**.

- Enable the
  checkboxes as
  shown.

- Click **OK**.

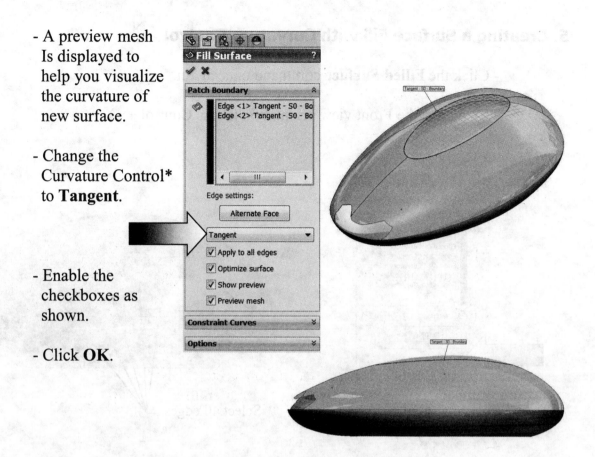

* The **Curvature Control** defines the type of control you want to exert on the patch you create. The types of **Curvature Control** include:

- **Contact**: Creates a surface within the selected boundary.

- **Tangent**: Creates a surface within the selected boundary, but maintains the tangency of the patch edges.

- **Curvature**: Creates a surface that matches the curvature of the selected surface across the boundary edge with the adjacent surface.

5. Creating a Surface Fill with Curvature Control :

- Click the **Filled Surface** command once again.

- Change to the Front view orientation (Press Control + 1).

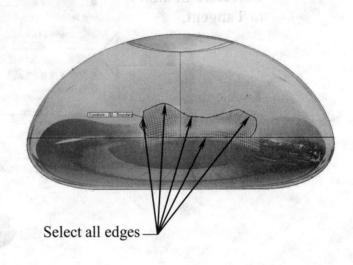

Select all edges ——

- Select <u>all edges</u> of the opening in the front as noted.

- The preview mesh appears indicating a closed boundary is found. (Enable the Preview Mesh checkbox if the preview is not visible).

- Under the Curvature Control change the Contact option to **Curvature** (arrow).

- Enable the other checkbox as shown in the dialog box.

- Click **OK**.

6. Knitting all surfaces :

- At this point all openings have been filled, we can now combine all surfaces into one by using the Knit option.

- Click the **Knit Surface** on the Surfaces tool tab.

Select 4 surfaces

- Select all for surfaces in the graphics area as indicated.

- Click the **Try To Form Solid** checkbox (arrow) to make the part solid.

- Click **OK**.

- To verify the interior of the part create a section view using the Right plane as the cutting plane. Click Cancel when done.

7. Saving your work:

- Save your work as **Using Filled Surface**.

Optional:

A closer look at the Edge Settings: Use the Edge Settings options to define the type of control you want to exert on the patch you create.

Contact Patch:

Creates a surface within the selected boundary.

Tangent Patch:

Creates a surface within the selected boundary, but maintains the tangency of the patch edges.

Curvature Patch:

Creates a surface that matches the curvature of the selected surface across the boundary edge with the adjacent surface.

Optional:

A closer look at the Zebra Stripes:

Use zebra stripes to visually determine which type of boundary to use between surfaces.

Zebra Stripes examples:

You can see small changes in a surface that may be hard to see with a standard display. Zebra stripes simulate the reflection of long strips of light on a very shiny surface.

With zebra stripes, you can easily see wrinkles or defects in a surface, and you can verify that two adjacent faces are in contact, are tangent, or have continuous curvature.

Questions for Review

Using Filled Surfaces

1. When opening a part document created from another CAD software, all of its features history will appear on the FeatureManager tree.
    - a. True
    - b. False

2. Tool tabs can be added as needed by right clicking on one of the one of the existing tool tab and select them from the list.
    - a. True
    - b. False

3. A planar surface can be created from a closed sketch or a set of closed edges.
    - a. True
    - b. False

4. An open sketch or a set of open edges can also be patched using the Planar surface command.
    - a. True
    - b. False

5. The Filled Surface command is used to patch a non-planar closed boundary.
    - a. True
    - b. False

6. The Filled Surface command will fail if the boundary is not closed.
    - a. True
    - b. False

7. The Preview Mesh can be toggled on/off during the creation of the filled surface.
    - a. True
    - b. False

8. The Knit Surface command can only Knit the surfaces, it cannot forms a solid from the surfaces.
    - a. True
    - b. False

7. TRUE	8. FALSE
5. TRUE	6. TRUE
3. TRUE	4. FALSE
1. FALSE	2. TRUE

CHAPTER 10 (cont.)

Boundary and Freeform Surfaces

Boundary Surface: Allows the user to create surfaces that can be tangent or curvature continuous in both directions (all sides of the surface). In most cases, this delivers a higher quality result than the loft tool.

Freeform feature: Modifies a face of a surface or a solid body. You can modify only one face at a time and the face can have any number of sides. Control curves and control points can be added to allow pushing and pulling the control points to modify the face. The triad is used to constrain the push or pull direction.

1. Opening a part file:

- Browse to the Training Files folder and open the part file named: **Freeform Surface**.

2. Creating the 1st Boundary Surface:

- Right click either the Features or the Sketch tab and enable the **Surfaces** option.

- Click the **Boundary Surface** button from the Surfaces toolbar or select: **Insert / Surface / Boundary Surface**.

Right click a tab and enable the Surfaces toolbar

- Zoom in on the left end of the image.

- For Direction 1: select the **1ˢᵗ Curve** approximately as shown.

- Curves are used to determine the boundary feature in Direction 1 and Direction 2.

- For each curve, select the point from which you want the path of the boundary feature to travel.

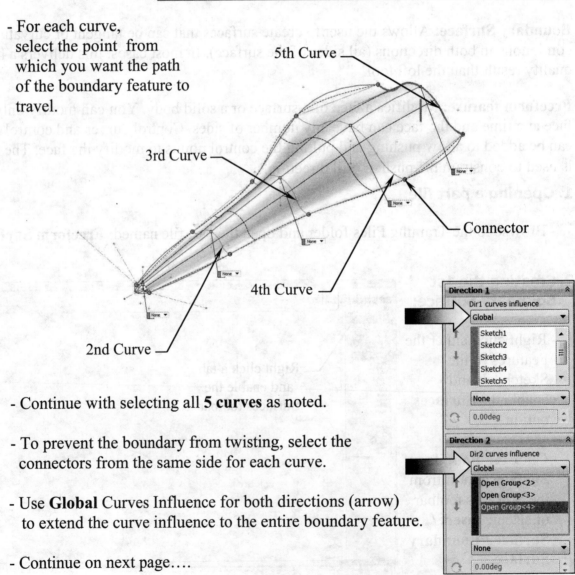

5th Curve

3rd Curve

Connector

4th Curve

2nd Curve

- Continue with selecting all **5 curves** as noted.

- To prevent the boundary from twisting, select the connectors from the same side for each curve.

- Use **Global** Curves Influence for both directions (arrow) to extend the curve influence to the entire boundary feature.

- Continue on next page....

- For Direction 2: select the **3 Curves** as indicated below.

- Since both Curve6 and Curve7 were created in the same sketch, the **Selection–Manager** pops up when one of them is selected, asking to confirm your selection. Click the OK button after selecting Curve6 and Curve7.

6th Curve

Click OK after the
6th and 7th Curves

7th Curve

8th Curve

- Enable the
**Merge Tangent
Faces** option.

- Click **OK**

3. Creating the 2nd Boundary Surface:

- Zoom in on the tip section of the surface.

- There are 5 other Curves on the Feature-
  Manager tree, 2 of them will be used as
  Direction 1 and the other 3, used as
  Direction2.

- Click the **Boundary Surface** button
  from the Surfaces toolbar or
  select: **Insert / Surface /
  Boundary Surface**.

- For Direction 1, select
  the **Curve1** and **Curve2**
  as noted.

Curve 1

Curve 2

- For Direction 2, select
  the **Curve3** as indicated.

- Click OK in the **Selection-
  Manager** dialog box after
  selecting the Curve3.

Curve 3

Click OK after the
3rd and 5th Curves

- Continue on next page…

- For Direction2, select the **Curve4** and **Curve5** as noted below.

- Enable the **Merge Tangent Faces** checkbox to force the boundary feature to be tangent to the corresponding segments.

- Click **OK** .

- The resulting Boundary Surface.

4. Creating the Freeform feature:

- From the **Insert** menus, select **Features / Freeform**.

- The **Freeform** Property-Manager appears when you create a freeform feature. Only one face can be modified at a time, but the face can have any number of sides.

- A set of Control Curves and Control Points are used to modify the face.

- **Select the face** as indicated to modify.

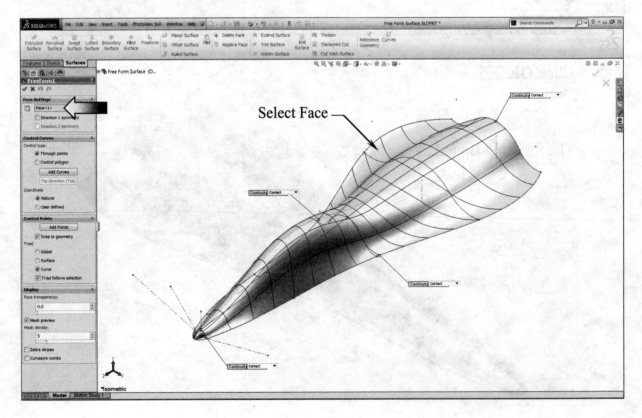

Select Face

- Go down to the **Control Curves** section and click the **Add Curves** button.

- Position the cursor approximately at the center of the face and click to **add a curve**.

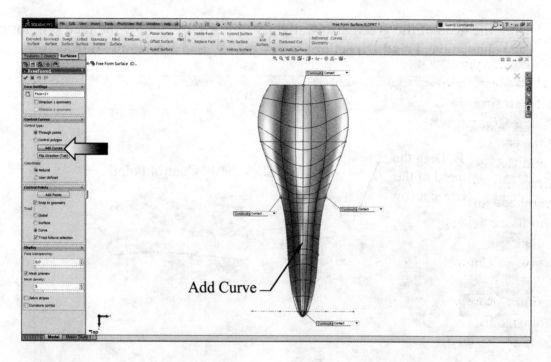

Add Curve

- Go down to the **Control Points** section and click the **Add Points** button.

- **Add 3 points** along the curve approximately as indicated.

Add 1st point

Add 2nd point

Add 3rd point

- Select the 1st Control Point to see the Triad. The arrows on the triad are used to push or pull the surface one direction at a time. Drag the center sphere in the middle of the 3 arrows to push or pull in all directions at the same time.

- Drag the head of the green arrow slightly upward to see how the face is deformed, then change the **Triad Directions** to **X= 0.375"** and **Y= 0.500"** (arrows).

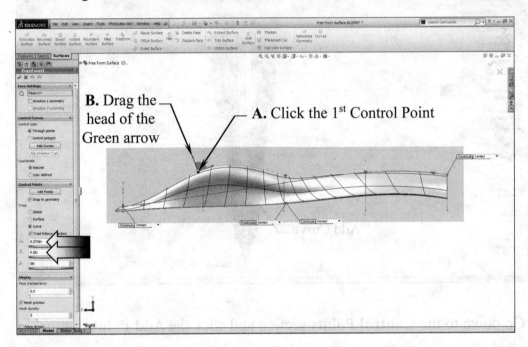

B. Drag the head of the Green arrow

A. Click the 1st Control Point

- Click the 2nd Control Point and set the **Triad Directions** to **X= -0.375"** and **Y= 0.050"**.

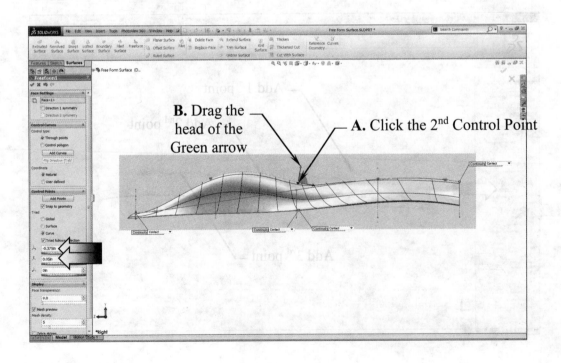

B. Drag the head of the Green arrow

A. Click the 2nd Control Point

- Click the 3rd Control Point, set the **Triad Directions** to **X= -0.700"** and **Y= 0.015"**.

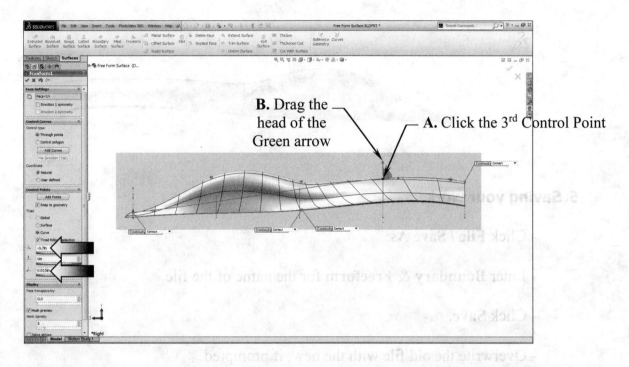

- Click the **Curvature combs** to see a visual enhancement of the surface' curvatures.

- Set the **Scale** to adjust the size of the curvature combs and set the **Density** to adjust the number of curvature combs.

- Click **OK** .

- The resulting Freeform Surface.

5. Saving your work:

- Click **File / Save As**.

- Enter **Boundary & Freeform** for the name of the file.

- Click **Save**.

- Overwrite the old file with the new, if prompted.

CHAPTER 10 (cont.)

Sweep with Solid Body

Sweep with Solid Body
Creating a Cam Feature

- Beside the traditional sweep using a sketch profile, we now have the option: Sweep using a solid body. It is only available for the Cut Sweep command.

- This feature is useful for end mill simulation, where a solid body is swept along a path to create cuts around cylindrical bodies, or some other cam features.

- Similar to the standard sweep using a profile and path, solid sweep requires the path to be tangent within itself and has no sharp corners.

- The path can either be an open or closed contour, and can be a set of 2D or 3D sketched lines, curves, or model edges.

Solid Body

Sweep Path

- The profile should be a revolved feature that consists of analytical geometry only, such as lines and arcs.

- A plane perpendicular to the path is be created, and the profile gets drawn on this plane and constrained to the sweep path.

Sweep with Solid Body
Creating a Cam Part

Dimensioning Standards: **ANSI**

Units: **INCHES** – 3 Decimals

Tools Needed:

 Insert Sketch   Circle   Convert Entities

 Helix/Spiral   Plane   Swept Cut

1. Creating the main body:

- Select the <u>Front</u> plane from the Feature tree and open a new sketch .

- Sketch 2 **circles** 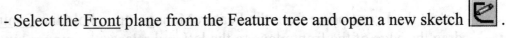 centered on the origin as shown.

- Add the OD and ID dimensions to fully define this sketch.

- From the Features toolbar click **Extruded Boss-Base** .

- Select the **Mid Plane** extrude option from the Direction 1 list.

- Enter **5.000**in for
  extrude depth.

- Click **OK** .

2. Creating an Offset-Distance plane :

- Select the **Front** plane from the FeatureManager tree, hold the <u>Control</u> key <u>drag</u> the edge of the front plane to the left and release the mouse button.

- This techniques makes a parallel copy of the selected plane.

- The plane options appear on the tree and the Offset-Distance button is selected automatically.

- Enter **2.000**in. for distance.

- Click **OK** .

3. Creating the sweep path:

- Select the <u>Plane1</u> and open a new sketch .

- Press **Control + 1** to change to the front orientation.

- Select the <u>outer</u> circular edge (as noted) and click:

   Convert Entities .

- The selected edge is converted into a circle.

- By converting the edge of the cylinder to a circle these 2 entities are now linked to one another.

- Click the Helix command from the **Features / Curves** toolbar.

Convert Entity

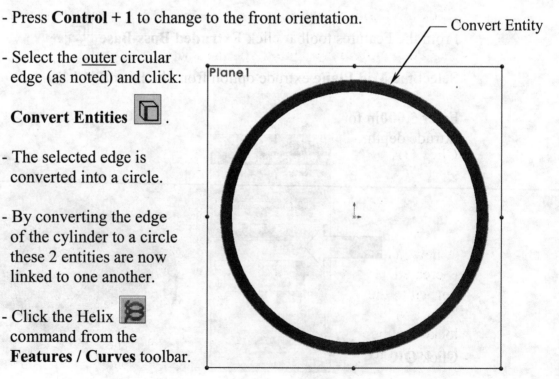

- Use the default Pitch and Revolution under Defined By section.

- Under Constant Pitch enter **7.750"** for Pitch.

- Click the **Reverse-Direction** checkbox.

- Enter **0.5** (1/2) for revolutions.

- For Start Angle, enter:**180deg**.

- Use the default **Clockwise** direction.

- Click **OK** .

4. Creating a plane Normal-To-Curve :

- Hold the <u>Control</u> key, select the Left endpoint of the helix <u>and</u> click the helix.

- Click the **Plane** command (or select **Insert / Reference Geometry / Plane**).

- The **Perpendicular** option should be selected already.

- Click **OK** .

- A new plane is created, normal to the helix and locked to the left end of it.

2. Click the helix...

1. Select the left endpoint

5. Creating the sweep body:

- Select the new <u>Plane2</u> and open a new sketch .

- Press <u>Control + 8</u> to change to the "Normal-To" orientation.

- Sketch a horizontal centerline from the origin to the left.

- Sketch a **rectangle** over the centerline.

- Add the dimensions shown to fully define the sketch.

- Notice the dimension Ø.500 is a virtual diameter dimension (dimension from the centerline to the bottom left vertex of the rectangle, and move the cursor upwards, pass the centerline to double it).

- Press **Revolve Boss-Base** from the Features toolbar.

- Use the default **Blind** and **360deg**. options.

- <u>Uncheck</u> the **Merge Result** check box (arrow) to make this feature a separate body from the first one.

- Click **OK** ✓ .

6. Creating the sweep cut with a solid body:

- Click **Swept Cut** 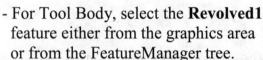 from the Features toolbar (or select: **Insert / Cut / Sweep**).

- Click the **Solid Sweep** option (arrow).

- For Tool Body, select the **Revolved1** feature either from the graphics area or from the FeatureManager tree.

- For Path, click the **Helix** from the graphics area.

- Expand the **Options** section and enable the **Preview** checkbox.

- Click **OK** ✓.

- Rotate the model to verify the result of the cut.

7. Saving your work:

- Click **File / Save As**.

- Enter **Sweep with Solid Body** for the name of the file.

- Click **Save**.

Questions for Review

Sweep with Solid Body

1. A Solid Sweep uses a solid body to move along the path to create the cut feature.
   a. True
   b. False

2. The Solid Sweep option is only available for sweep cuts only, not sweep bosses.
   a. True
   b. False

3. The Convert Entities command can be found on the Features toolbar.
   a. True
   b. False

4. The converted entities are <u>not</u> linked to the original geometry, where they were converted from.
   a. True
   b. False

5. The Path used in a Solid Sweep should be continuous; all of its entities should be tangent with one another, and have no sharp corners.
   a. True
   b. False

6. When the Solid Sweep option is selected, a sketch profile can be used in place of a solid body.
   a. True
   b. False

7. The Preview option is not available when using the Solid Sweep option.
   a. True
   b. False

8. The hot-keys Control+1 thru Control+8 are default keys for changing the view orientations.
   a. True
   b. False

1. TRUE   2. TRUE
3. FALSE   4. FALSE
5. TRUE   6. FALSE
7. FALSE   8. TRUE

CHAPTER 11

Surfaces vs. Solid Modeling

Surfaces vs. Solid Modeling

Surfaces are a type of geometry that can be used to create solid features. Surface tools are available on the Surfaces toolbar.

You can <u>create surfaces</u> using these methods:

- Insert a planar surface from a sketch or from a set of closed edges that lie on a plane
- Extrude, revolve, sweep, or loft, from sketches
- Offset from existing faces or surfaces
- Import a file
- Create mid-surfaces
- Radiate surfaces

You can <u>modify surfaces</u> in the following ways:

- Extend
- Trim existing surfaces
- Un-trim surfaces
- Fillet surfaces
- Repair surfaces using Filled Surface
- Move/Copy surfaces
- Delete and patch a face
- Knit surfaces

You can <u>use surfaces</u> in the following ways:

- Select surface edges and vertices to use as a sweep guide curve and path
- Create a solid or cut feature by thickening a surface
- Extrude a solid or cut feature with the end condition Up to Surface or Offset from Surface
- Create a solid feature by thickening surfaces that have been knit into a closed volume
- Replace a face with a surface

Safety Helmet
Surfaces vs. Solid Modeling

View Orientation Hot Keys:

Ctrl + 1 = Front View
Ctrl + 2 = Back View
Ctrl + 3 = Left View
Ctrl + 4 = Right View
Ctrl + 5 = Top View
Ctrl + 6 = Bottom View
Ctrl + 7 = Isometric View
Ctrl + 8 = Normal To
           Selection

Dimensioning Standards: **ANSI**

Units: **INCHES** – 3 Decimals

Tools Needed:

 Insert Sketch   Plane   Lofted Surface

 Swept Surface   Planar Surface   Knit Surface

 Revolve Cut   Sweep Cut   Surface Thicken

1. Opening the Existing file:

- From the Training Files folder open the part document named: **Helmet**.

- This part file has 3 sketch profiles and 3 guide curves previously created.

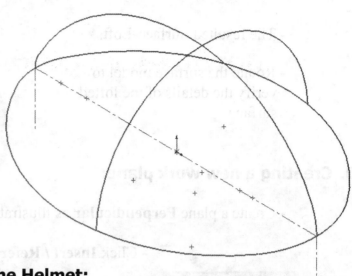

2. Constructing the Body of the Helmet:

- Click **Lofted Surface** OR – select **Insert / Surface / Loft**.

- Select the **3 Sketch Profiles**.

- Select the **3 Guide Curves** as noted.

- Click **OK** ✅.

Lofted Surface
Creates a lofted surface between two or more profiles.

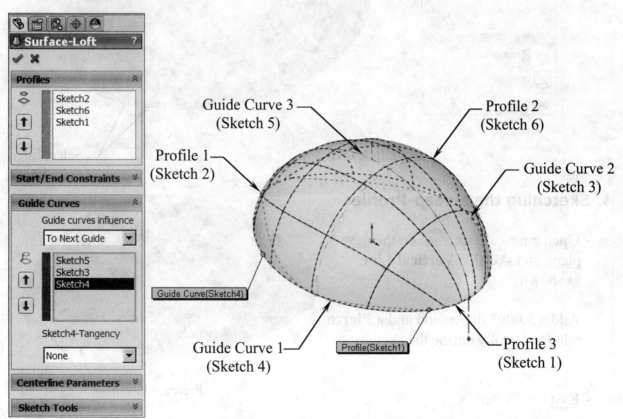

Guide Curve 3 (Sketch 5)

Profile 2 (Sketch 6)

Profile 1 (Sketch 2)

Guide Curve 2 (Sketch 3)

Guide Curve 1 (Sketch 4)

Guide Curve(Sketch4)

Profile(Sketch1)

Profile 3 (Sketch 1)

- The resulted Surface-Loft.

- Rotate the surface model to verify the details of the lofted surface.

3. Creating a new work plane:

- Create a plane **Perpendicular** as illustrated.

- Click **Insert / Reference Geometry / Plane** .

- Select the **circular edge** and its **endpoint** as noted.

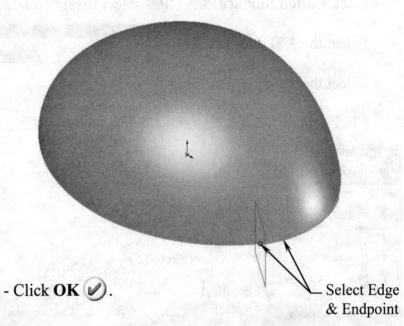

Select Edge & Endpoint

- Click **OK** ✅.

4. Sketching the Sweep-Profile:

- Open a new sketch 🖉 on the new-plane and sketch a **Vertical Line** as shown.

- Add a **3.000"** dimension and a **Pierce** relation to fully define the sketch.

- **Exit** the Sketch 🖉.

Pierce relation

3.000

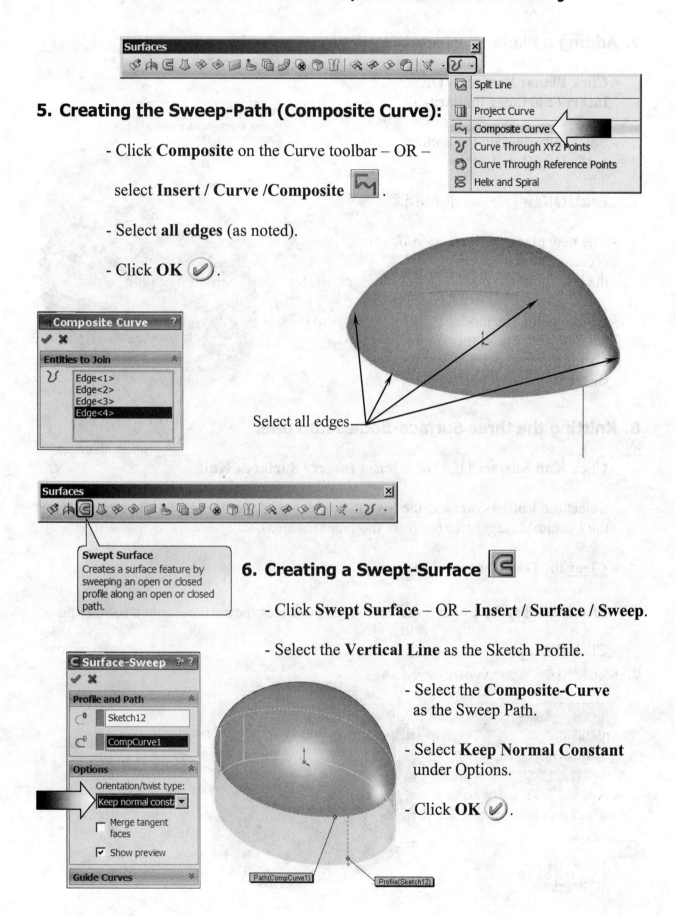

Surfaces

5. Creating the Sweep-Path (Composite Curve):

- Click **Composite** on the Curve toolbar – OR –

select **Insert / Curve /Composite** .

- Select **all edges** (as noted).

- Click **OK** .

| Split Line |
| Project Curve |
| Composite Curve |
| Curve Through XYZ Points |
| Curve Through Reference Points |
| Helix and Spiral |

Composite Curve ?

Entities to Join

Edge<1>
Edge<2>
Edge<3>
Edge<4>

Select all edges

Surfaces

Swept Surface
Creates a surface feature by
sweeping an open or closed
profile along an open or closed
path.

6. Creating a Swept-Surface

- Click **Swept Surface** – OR – **Insert / Surface / Sweep**.

- Select the **Vertical Line** as the Sketch Profile.

- Select the **Composite-Curve**
as the Sweep Path.

- Select **Keep Normal Constant**
under Options.

- Click **OK** .

Surface-Sweep ? ?

Profile and Path

Sketch12

CompCurve1

Options

Orientation/twist type:

Keep normal consta

☐ Merge tangent
faces

☑ Show preview

Guide Curves

Path(CompCurve1)

Profile(Sketch12)

7. Adding a Planar Surface:

- Click **Planar Surface** – OR – **Insert / Surface / Planar**.

- Select **all edges** on the bottom as the Bounding Entities.

- Click **OK** ✅.

- The new planar surface is created and it covers the bottom of the part.

- At this point, the model has 3 surfaces in it: the Lofted surface, the Swept surface, and the Planar surface.

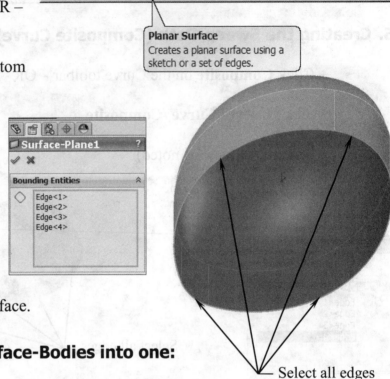

Select all edges

8. Knitting the three Surface-Bodies into one:

- Click **Knit Surface** 🔲 OR – select **Insert / Surface / Knit**.

- Select the **Lofted-Surface**, the **Swept-Surface**, and the **Planar-Surface** either from the FeatureManager tree (or from the graphics area).

- **Clear** the **Gap Control** checkbox.

- Enable the **Try To Form Solid** option, this changes the surfaces into a solid feature.

- Click **OK** ✅.

Select 3 surfaces to knit…

9. Creating a section view:

- Select the <u>Front</u> plane from the FeatureManager and click **Section View** (arrow). The model is a solid model. Click off the section view button when finished viewing.

10. Adding an Extruded Cut feature:

- Select the **Sketch8** from the FeatureManager Tree.

- This sketch will be used to remove the lower portion of the Helmet.

- Click **Extruded-Cut** OR – **Insert / Cut / Extrude**.

- Use **Through-All** end conditions for both **Direction 1** and **Direction 2**.

- Enable **Flip-Side-To-Cut** if needed to remove the lower portion of the part.

- Click **OK** ✅.

Arrow direction
indicates the
cutting side

*(The new option Through Both Directions
can also be used here).*

- <u>Hide</u> the Sketch8.

- Compare your model with
this illustration before moving
to the next step.

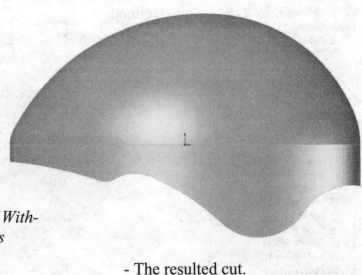

*- Change from Shaded to Shaded With-
Edges to be able to see the edges
more clearly.*

- The resulted cut.

11. Adding a Revolve-Cut feature:

- Select the **Sketch10** from the FeatureManager Tree.

- This sketch will be used to shape the <u>inside</u> of the Helmet.

- Click **Revolve-Cut** OR – select **Insert / Cut / Revolve**.

- Select the **vertical centerline** as Revolve-Direction.

- Revolve Angle: **360.00deg**.

- Click **OK** ✅.

- <u>Hide</u> the Sketch10.

Select this revolve line

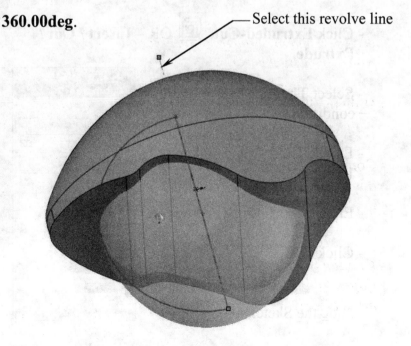

12. Adding the side cut features:

- Select the **Sketch9** from the FeatureManager Tree.

- This sketch will be used to cut from the <u>inside</u> with a **1.00deg.** draft angle.

Sketch9

- Click **Extruded-Cut** OR – **Insert / Cut / Extrude**.

- Select **Through-All** for end condition.

- Enable Draft Angle and enter: **1.00deg**.

- Enable **Draft Outward** option.

- Click **OK**.

- <u>Hide</u> the Sketch9.

13. Creating the cut-out slot:

- Select the **Sketch11** from the FeatureManager Tree.

- This sketch will be used to cut a slot from the <u>outside</u> with a **10.00deg**. draft angle.

- Click **Extruded-Cut** OR – select **Insert / Cut / Extrude**.

- For Direction 1, select **Up-To-Next** end condition.

- Enable Draft Angle and enter: **10.00deg**. (inward)

- For Direction 2, select **Through-All** end condition. (No draft)

- Click **OK**.

- <u>Hide</u> the Sketch11.

14. Mirroring the slot:

- Click **Mirror** – OR – select **Insert / Pattern-Mirror / Mirror** .

- Select the **Right** plane for Mirror Plane.

- Under Features to Mirror, select the cut feature (Cut Extrude3).

- Click **OK** ✅.

15. Mirroring the Cut Features:

- Click **Mirror** – OR – select **Insert / Pattern-Mirror / Mirror** 🔲.

- Select the **Front** plane as the Mirror Face/Plane.

- Select **both Slots** and the **Side-Holes** as Features to Mirror.

- Click **OK** ✅.

- Compare your model with the image below.

16. Creating the Sweep-Cut:

- Click **Insert / Cut / Sweep** .

- Select the sketch **Sweep-Profile** and the sketch **Sweep Path** from the FeatureManager tree.

- The preview graphics shows the proper transition of the sweep feature.

- Click **OK** .

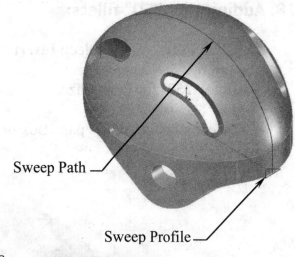

Sweep Path —

Sweep Profile —

17. Adding the .500" fillets:

- Click **Fillet** – OR – select **Insert / Features / Fillet-Round**

- Enter **.500"** for radius size.

- Select the **edges** of the Swept feature.

- Click **OK** .

18. Adding the .250" fillets:

- Click **Fillet** – OR – select: **Insert / Features / Fillet-Round**.

- Enter **.250**" for radius size.

- Select **all edges** of the part (Box or Lasso Select).

- Click **OK** ✅.

19. Saving your work:

- Click **File / Save As / Helmet / Save**. (Save on the Desktop)

Front Isometric   Back Isometric

Exercise: Advanced Loft – Turbine Blades

1. Open the existing document:

Turbine.sldprt from the Training Files folder.

- This part file has 6 sketch profiles and 4 guide curves previously created.

2. Create the 1st loft:
- Select the 3 Tall Blade sketches for Profiles.
- Select the 2 Tall Guide Curve sketches for Guide Curves.

The resulted Lofts.

3. Create the 2nd loft:
- Select the 3 Short Blade sketches for Profiles.
- Select the 2 Short Guide Curve sketches for Guide Curves.

5. Create a Revolve Cut:
- Use the Blade Trim Sketch and create a Revolve-Cut.

4. Circular pattern the Blades:
- Create a circular pattern for the Lofted Blades.
- Enter **10** for number of instances.

6. Save your work as:
- Turbine Blades.

Exercise: <u>Advanced Sweep – Candle Holder</u>

1. Opening the main sketch:

- From the Training Files folder open the part document named: **Candle Holder Sketch**.

- **<u>Edit</u>** this sketch and verify that the sketch is fully defined.

2. Revolving a surface:

- Click **Revolve Surface**.

- **Blind 360 deg**.

- Click **OK** ✅.

3. Creating a Helix:

- Select the <u>Top</u> plane and open a new sketch.

- Sketch a **10.00"** **circle** centered on the origin.

- Convert the Circle into a Helix using the settings as shown in the dialog box.

4. Creating a swept surface:

- Select the <u>Top</u> plane once again and open another sketch.

- Sketch a Line ◥ from the Origin and **Pierce** the other end of the line to the Helix.

- Click ▣ and sweep the Line along the Helix using the **Swept-Surface** option.

- Click **OK** ✅.

Pierce Relation

5. Create a new Axis: (to be used in step 9)

- Select **Insert / Reference Geometry / Axis** .

- Click the **Two-Planes** option.

- Select the **Front** and the **Right** planes from the FeatureManager tree.

- A preview of the new axis appears in the center of the part.

- Click **OK** .

6. Create the Intersection Curve:

- Hold the **Control** key and select the **Surface-Revolve1** and the **Surface Sweep1** from the FeatureManager tree.

- Click [ ] or select **Tools / Sketch Tools / Intersection Curve**.

- A 3D-Sketch is created from the intersection of the two surfaces.

- **Exit** the 3D Sketch.

Select 2 Surfaces

Intersection Curve

7. Hide the 2 Surface Bodies:

- From the FeatureManager tree, right click on each Surface and select **Hide**.

- Select the <u>Top</u> plane and open a new Sketch.

- Sketch a **Ø.260" circle** centered on the endpoint of the 3D Sketch.

- Click **OK** 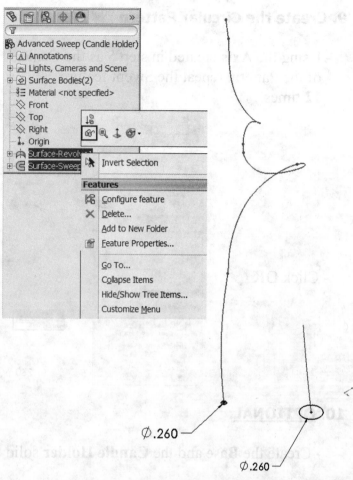.

8. Create a <u>solid</u> swept feature:

- Click or select **Insert / Boss-Base/ Sweep**.

- Select the **Circle** for Sweep Profile.

- Select the **3D-Sketch** for Sweep Path.

- Click **OK** .

9. Create the Circular Pattern

- Using the **Axis** created in step 5 as the Center of the Pattern, repeat the Swept feature **12** times.

- Click **OK** .

10. <u>OPTIONAL:</u>

- Create the **Base** and the **Candle Holder** solid features as shown below.

- Modify or design your own shapes if needed.

11. Save your work:

- Select **File / Save As**.

- Enter **Candle Holder** for file name.

- Click **Save**.

CHAPTER 11 (cont.)

Using PhotoView 360

1. Enabling PhotoView 360:

- Click: **Tools / Add Ins**.

- Enable the **Photo-View 360** check-box.

- Click **OK**.

- The **PhotoView 360** application appears in the drop-down menus.

2. Opening a file:

- Browse to the Training Files folder and open the document named: **Flying Hummer.sldprt**

Tools menu	
Measure...	
Mass Properties...	
Section Properties...	
Check...	
Geometry Analysis...	
Feature Statistics...	
Equations...	?
Import Diagnostics...	
Deviation Analysis...	
Thickness Analysis...	
Symmetry Check...	
DimXpert	▶
Macro	▶
Add-Ins...	
Customize...	
Options...	
Customize Menu	

Add-Ins dialog

Active Add-ins	Start Up
SolidWorks Premium Add-ins	
CircuitWorks	
FeatureWorks	
✓ PhotoView 360	
ScanTo3D	
SolidWorks Design Checker	
SolidWorks Motion	
SolidWorks Routing	
SolidWorks Simulation	
SolidWorks Toolbox	
SolidWorks Toolbox Browser	
SolidWorks Utilities	
SolidWorks Workgroup PDM 2011	
SolidWorks Workgroup PDM 2012	
TolAnalyst	
SolidWorks Add-ins	
Autotrace	
SolidWorks Flow Simulation 2012	
SolidWorks XPS Driver	
Other Add-ins	
3Dcontrol	
3DVIA SolidWorks Plug-in	
SolidProfessor LMS	

OK   Cancel

3. Setting the Appearance:

- Use Appearance to apply colors, material appearances, and transparency to parts and assembly components.

- Click **Edit-Appearance** from the PhotoView 360 pull down menu (arrow).

- From the Task Pane on the right side, Expand the **Metal** folder, the **Chrome** folder (arrows).

- Hold the **ATL** key, drag the sphere labeled: **Chromium Plate** and drop on the model (arrows).

- Click the Advanced tab and set the **Illumination** shown.

4. Setting the Scene:

- Use Scene to create a visual backdrop behind a model, including a realistic light source, illumination, and reflections. The objects and lights in a Scene can form reflections on the model and can cast shadows on the adjustable floor.

- Click **Edit Scene** from the Photo-View 360 pull down menu (arrow).

- Expand the **Scene** folder, the **Studio Scenes** folder (arrows) and double click the **Strip Lighting** to apply to the entire model.

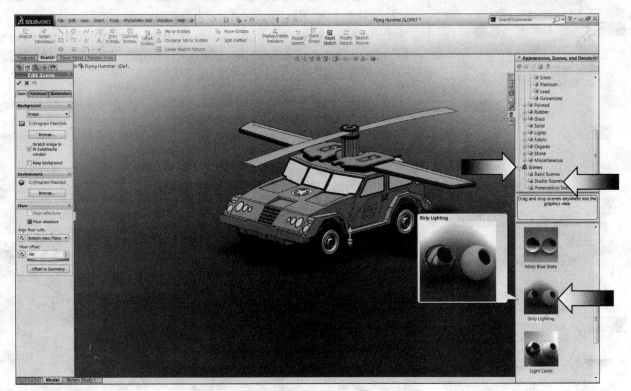

(more settings on the next page).

- The spacing between the model and the floor can be adjusted so that the shadow can look more realistic. From the **Basic tab**, set the following:

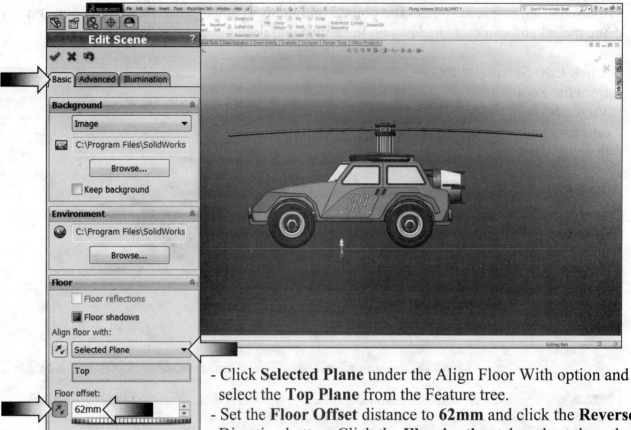

- Click **Selected Plane** under the Align Floor With option and select the **Top Plane** from the Feature tree.
- Set the **Floor Offset** distance to **62mm** and click the **Reverse** Direction button. Click the **Illumination** tab and set the values as shown below, then click **OK**.

5. Setting the final rendering quality:

- Click **Final Render** from the PhotoView 360 drop down menu.

- Using the drop down, set the **Output Image** to **1920x1080**.
- The **JPEG** file type should be selected by default.
- Under Render Quality, set the Preview Render to Good and **Final Render** to **Best** (arrow).
- Click **OK** to close.

6. Saving the rendered image:

- Click **Final Render**. After the rendering is completed, set the zoom to **Best Fit** and then click **Save Image** (arrow).

- Select the **JPEG** format from the Save-as-Type drop down list.

- Enter a file name and click **OK**.

- **Save** and **close** all documents.

NOTE:

- *Different file formats may reduce the quality of the image and at the same time, it may increase or decrease the size of the file.*

Level 3: Final Exam

- Create the part Bottle using the LOFT and SWEEP options where noted.

- All sketch profiles must be fully defined.

- The part must have no errors when finished.

1. Creating an Offset plane:

- Use the <u>Top</u> reference plane, create a new plane at **4.000 in**. offset distance.

2. Sketching the bottom profile:

- Select the <u>Top</u> plane and sketch the profile as shown.

- Use the Mirror option to create the **Symmetric** relations between entities.

- **<u>Exit</u>** the Sketch.

3. Creating the top profile:

- Use the <u>Plane1</u> sketch a **Circle** centered on the Origin.

- Add a diameter dimension to fully define the sketch.

- **Exit** the sketch.

4. Creating the 1st Guide Curve:

- Select the <u>Front</u> plane and sketch the profile as shown.

* <u>Note:</u> *The construction lines will be used later to create the Derived-Sketch and the Guide Curves.*

5. Creating the 2nd Guide Curve:

- Use the <u>Right</u> plane sketch a **3-Point-Arc** and add dimensions.

.700

Should the Pierce relation or the .700" dimension be used here?

R14.000

Right

1.000

- <u>**Exit**</u> the sketch.

Should the Pierce relation or the 1.000" dimension be used here?

6. Creating the 3rd Guide Curve:

- Use the <u>Right</u> plane sketch a **3-Point-Arc** and add dimensions.

.700

Should the Pierce relation or the .700" dimension be used here?

.700

Right

- The same arc from step 5 can be Derived to create this sketch.

- <u>**Exit**</u> the sketch.

7. Creating the 4th Guide Curve:

- Select the <u>Front</u> plane
  open a new sketch and
  convert the 3 entities
  as noted.

Convert
entities

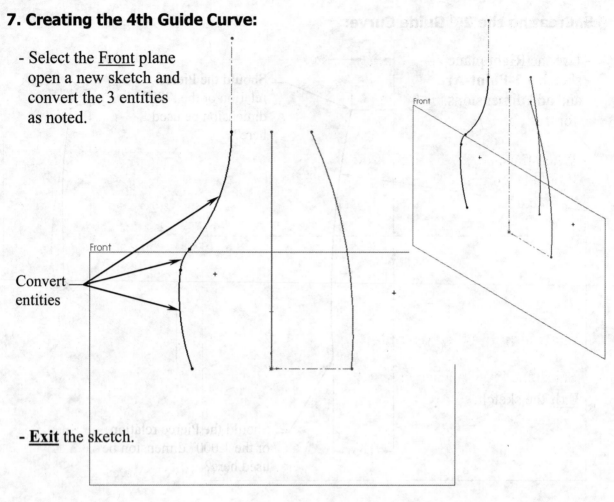

- **Exit** the sketch.

8. Creating the Lofted Surface:

- Use the Top and Bottom sketches as Loft Profiles.

- For Guide Curves, select the next 4 sketches.

9. Filling the bottom surface:

- Select **Insert / Surface / Planar**.

- Select **all edges** on the bottom for this operation.

- When finished, the bottom surface should be completely covered.

10. Sketching the Neck profile:

- Select the <u>Front</u> plane and sketch the profile below (2 lines).

- Revolve the sketch profile as a **<u>Surface</u>**.

- Revolve **One Direction**.

- Revolve a complete **360°**.

Pierce

.550

.500

Front

11. Knitting all surfaces into one:

- Select **Insert / Surface / Knit**.

- Select all **three surfaces**: the body, the Neck, and the Bottom surface.

- Clear the Gap Control option.

- When finished all 3 surfaces should now be combined as one continuous surface.

12. Adding fillet to the bottom edges:

- Add a **.250 in**. fillet to the bottom edges as shown.

Tips:

- *Right click on one of the edges and pick Select Tangency; this is the fastest way to select all edges at the same time.*

13. Adding fillet to the upper area:

- Add a **.093 in**. fillet to the upper edge as indicated.

Radius: 0.093in

Fillet 1 edge

14. Thickening the surface body:

- Select **Insert / Boss-Base / Thicken**.

- Enter a wall thickness of **.080 in**. to the **INSIDE** of the bottle.

15. Creating a new Offset plane:

- Select the Top face of the neck and create an Offset Distance plane at **.100 in**. Below it.

16. Creating the Sweep Path of the Thread (the Helix):

- Convert the upper **circular edge** and then click **Insert / Curves / Helix-Spiral**.

- Pitch = **.125 in**.

- Revolution = **2.5**.

- Starting Angle = **0 deg**.

- Click **OK** ✔.

Convert Entity

17. Creating the Sweep Profile of the Thread:

- Select the <u>Right</u> plane and sketch the thread profile as shown.

- Add Dimensions and Relations needed to fully define the sketch.

- Add the **R.015"** fillets after the sketch is fully defined.

Pierce relation

- **Exit** the sketch when finished.

18. Sweeping:

- Sweep the thread profile along the path to create the external threads.

19. Revolving:

- Convert the faces at the end of the thread and revolve them about the vertical centerlines to round off the ends.

20. Applying dimension changes:

- Change the dimension **R1.400** in the Sketch1 to **R1.500**.

- Change the Ø**1.400** in the Sketch2 to Ø**1.500**.

- Repair any errors caused by the changes.

21. Saving your work:

- Save your work as: **Level 3 – Final Exam**.

Designed by a CSWP student

Designed by a CSWP student

Designed by a CSWP student

Designed by a CSWP student

CHAPTER 12

SimulationXpress

SimulationXpress is a design analysis technology that allows SolidWorks users to perform first-pass stress analysis. SimulationXpress can help you reduce cost and time-to-market by testing your 3D designs within the SolidWorks program, instead of expensive and time-consuming field tests.

There are five basic steps to complete the analysis using SimulationXpress:

1. Apply restraints (Fixture)
Users can define restraints. Each restraint can contain multiple faces. The restrained faces are constrained in all directions due to rigid body motion; you must at least restrain one face of the part to avoid analysis failure.

2. Apply loads
User inputs force and pressure loads to the faces of the model.

3. Define material of the part
* EX (Modulus of elasticity).
* NUXY (Poisson's ratio). If users do not define NUXY, SimulationXpress assumes a value of 0.
* SIGYLD (Yield Strength). Used only to calculate the factors of safety (FOS).
* DENS (Mass density). Used only to include mass properties of the part in the report file.

4. Analyze the part
SimulationXpress prepares the model for analysis, then calculates displacements, strains, and stresses.

5. View the results
After completing the analysis, users can view results. A check mark on the Results tab indicates that results exist and are available to view for the current geometry, material, restraints, and loads. A report can also be created in MS-Word format.

SimulationXpress
Using the Analysis Wizard

von Mises (psi)

- 6.095e+004
- 5.587e+004
- 5.079e+004
- 4.572e+004
- 4.064e+004
- 3.556e+004
- 3.049e+004
- 2.541e+004
- 2.033e+004
- 1.525e+004
- 1.018e+004
- 5.101e+003
- 2.476e+001

View Orientation Hot Keys:

Ctrl + 1 = Front View
Ctrl + 2 = Back View
Ctrl + 3 = Left View
Ctrl + 4 = Right View
Ctrl + 5 = Top View
Ctrl + 6 = Bottom View
Ctrl + 7 = Isometric View
Ctrl + 8 = Normal To
           Selection

Dimensioning Standards: **ANSI**

Units: **INCHES** – 3 Decimals

Tools Needed:

SimulationXpress is part of
SolidWorks 2015 Basic,
SolidWorks Office Professional,
and SolidWorks Premium.

1. Starting SimulationXpress:

- SimulationXpress is an introductory version of fully featured simulation.

- SimulationXpress is a design analysis application that is fully integrated with SolidWorks. It is used by designers, analysts, engineers, students, and others worldwide to design safe, efficient, and economical products.

- To enable SimulationXpress, visit: www.my.solidworks.com/xpress, log in or create a user account and enter your SolidWorks Serial Number to generate the Xpress Product Codes. You can find your serial number from the Help menu > About SolidWorks.

- After entering the Xpress Product Code, click **OK** to launch the Simulation-Xpress application.

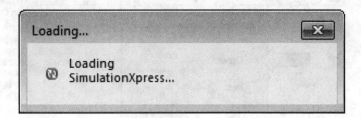

- The SimulationXpress program is launched and appeared on the right side of the screen

2. Opening a part document

- Open the part document that was created earlier: **Spanner** (or open a copy from the Training Files folder).

- **Suppress** the extruded text (the 5/8" and the Spanner text).

- From the **Tools** drop down menu, select **SimulationXpress** (Arrow).

3. Setting up the Units:

- Click **Options** (arrow), to set the system of units for the analysis.

SolidWorks SimulationXpress

Welcome to SolidWorks SimulationXpress.

SimulationXpress helps you predict how a part will perform under load and helps you detect potential problems early in the design cycle.

In SimulationXpress, you apply loads and fixtures to your part, specify its material, analyze the part, and view the results. All of this information is included in the Simulation study.

Note: Most analysis problems require a comprehensive analysis product for more accurate and complete real-world simulations before final sign-off on a design.

- Select **English (IPS)** for System Of Units (Inch, Pound, Second).

- Select the folder and the location to save the analysis results.

- Enable the option:

Show Annotation for Maximum and Minimum in the Result Plot.

- Creating a new folder for each study is recommended.

- Click **OK** .

- Click **Next** .

4. Adding a Fixture (restraint):

- The next step is to create the restraint area(s).

- Each restraint can contain one or multiple faces. The restrained faces are constrained in all directions. There must at least one fixed face of the part to avoid analysis failure due to rigid body motion.

- Click **Add a Fixture** .

Restraints

Restraint is used to anchor certain areas of the model so that they will not move or shift during the analysis.
At least one face should be restrained prior to running the analysis.

- Select the 3 faces as indicated to use as restraint faces.

- The Restraint faces are locked in all directions to avoid failure due to rigid body motion.

Restraint
face 1...

Restraint
face 2 & 3

- Click **OK** .

- When the restraint faces are selected, more faces
  can be added to create different restraint sets. They
  can also be edited or deleted at anytime.

- The information regarding the settings for this
  study is recorded on the lower half of the Feature-
  Manager tree (arrows).

- These settings can be modified at anytime.

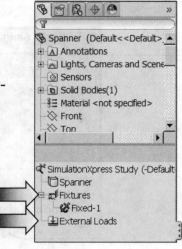

5. Applying a Force:

- Click **Add a Force** →.

- The **Forces** and **Pressures** options allow SolidWorks users to apply force or pressure loads to faces of the model. Multiple forces can be applied to a single face or to multiple faces.

- Select the 2 faces from the back side of the closed end as shown below.

Force & Load

* *Force infers a total force applied to a face in a specific direction.*

* *Load infers that the force is evenly distributed on the face.*

- Click the **Selected Direction** and select the **Front** plane from Feature Manager tree (arrow).

- Click the **Total** option (arrow). Enter **100** lbs. for Total Force value (arrow).

- Check the direction arrows and click Reverse Direction if necessary.

- Click **OK** ✓.

- At this point we will need to specify a material so that SimulationXpress can predict how it will respond to the loads.

6. Selecting the material:

- Click **Next** →.

- Select **Choose Material** →.

- Expand the **Steel** option (click the + symbol).

- Choose **Alloy Steel** from the list (arrow).

Material Editor

Material can be assigned to the part using the **Material Editor** PropertyManager. The material will then appear in SimulationXpress.

- The analysis results are dependent on the material selection. Simulation-Xpress needs to know the Visual and the Physical properties to run the analysis.

- Click **Apply** `Apply` and **Close** `Close`.
- The material **Alloy Steel** is now assigned to the part. SimulationXpress assumes that the material deforms in a linear fashion with increased load. Non-Linear materials (such as many plastics) require the use of Simulation Premium.

- The Modulus of Elasticity and the Yield Strength for the selected material are reported on the right.

- Click **Next** →.

- SimulationXpress is ready to analyze the model based on the information provided. Displacements, Strains, and Stresses will then be calculated.

7. Analyzing the model:

- Click **Run Simulation** →.

- SimulationXpress automatically tries to mesh the model using the default element size. The smaller the element size the more accurate the results, but more time is needed to analyze the model.

- To change mesh settings: First click **C**hange settings then click **Change mesh density**.

    * Drag the slider to the right for a finer mesh (more accurate, but takes longer).

    * Drag the slider to the left for a coarser mesh (quicker).

- Select **Yes, continue** .

8. Viewing the Results:

- Click **Show Von Mises Stress** →.

- SimulationXpress plots stresses on the deformed shape of the part.

- In most cases, the actual deformation is so small that the deformed shape almost coincides with the un-deformed shape, if plotted to scale.

- SimulationXpress exaggerates the deformation to demonstrate it more clearly.

- The Deformation Scale shown on the stress and deformed shape plots is the scale used to rescale the maximum deformation to **4.34794%** of the bounding box of the part.

- The **Stress Distribution Plot** is displayed below.

- To see the resultant displacement plot click **Show Displacement** ➡ .

- Click **Play Animation** ▶ or **Stop Animation** ◻ when finished viewing.

Displacement Plot

- To view regions of the model with a factor of safety less than a given value (1), click: **Show Where Factor Of Safety (FOS) Is Below: 1** (or enter any value).

- SimulationXpress displays regions of the model with factors of safety less than the specified value in red (unsafe regions) and regions with higher factors of safety in blue (safe regions).

- When finished viewing click: **Done Viewing Results**.

9. Creating the report:

- Click **Generate Report** .

- SimulationXpress cycles through the results, generates a report in Word format, and the MS Word program is launched to display the full report.

- The report includes:

1. Cover Page

2. Model Information

3. Load/Fixture Details

4. Solid Mesh Information

5. Stress Results

6. Displacement Results

7. Deformation Results

8. Factor of Safety Results

- In the Report Settings dialog box, enable the Description checkbox and enter the following:

* Spanner - SimXpress Study.

* Your Name.

* Your Company Name.

* Your Web Address (if applicable).

* Your Company Logo.

* Address and Telephone.

- Select the location to save the report.

- Click **Generate**.

The Report Cover Page

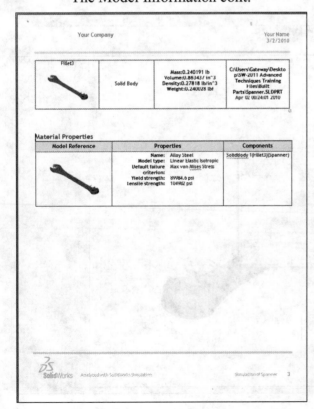

Your Company
www.yourwebaddress.com

Simulation of Spanner

Date: Tuesday, March 02, 2010
Designer: Your Name
Study name: SimulationXpress Study
Analysis type: Static

Description
Spanner - SimulationXpress Study

The Model Information

Your Company   Your Name
                            3/2/2010

Assumptions

Model Information

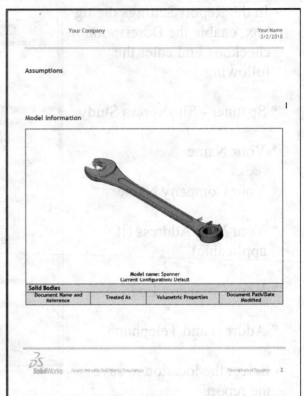

Model name: Spanner
Current Configuration: Default

Solid Bodies

Document Name and Reference	Treated As	Volumetric Properties	Document Path/Date Modified

The Model Information cont.

Your Company   Your Name
                            3/2/2010

Fillet3			
	Solid Body	Mass:0.240191 lb Volume:0.86343/ in^3 Density:0.27818 lb/in^3 Weight:0.240028 lbf	C:\Users\Gateway\Deskto p\SW-2011 Advanced Techniques Training Files\Built Parts\Spanner.SLDPRT Apr 02 06:24:01 2010

Material Properties

Model Reference	Properties	Components
	Name: Alloy Steel Model type: Linear Elastic Isotropic Default failure criterion: Max von Mises Stress Yield strength: 89984.6 psi Tensile strength: 104982 psi	SolidBody 1(Fillet3)(Spanner)

The Loads and Fixtures Details

Your Company   Your Name
                            3/2/2010

Loads and Fixtures

Fixture name	Fixture Image	Fixture Details
Fixed-1	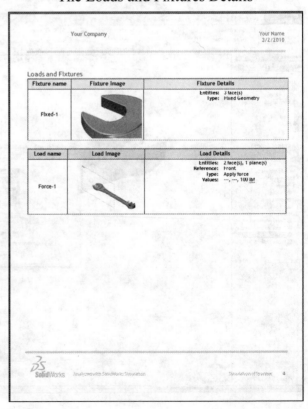	Entities: 3 face(s) Type: Fixed Geometry

Load name	Load Image	Load Details
Force-1		Entities: 2 face(s), 1 plane(s) Reference: Front Type: Apply force Values: ---, ---, 100 lbf

The Mesh Information

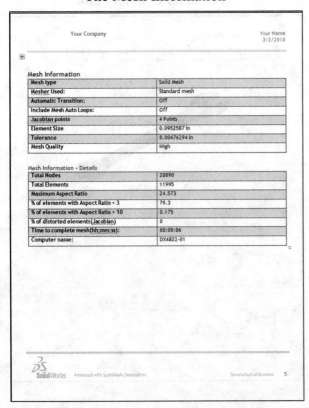

The Solid Mesh Plot

The Von Mises Stress Plot

The Displacement Plot

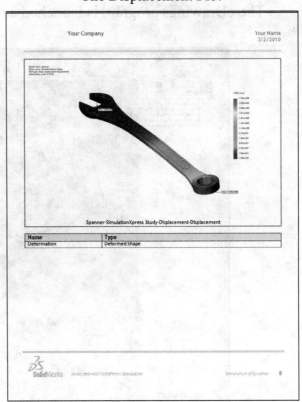

The Deformation Plot

The Factor of Safety Plot

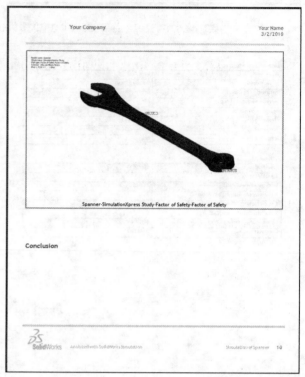

- When finished with viewing the Report, click: **Generate eDrawings File** ⟶.

- The eDrawings program is launched automatically.

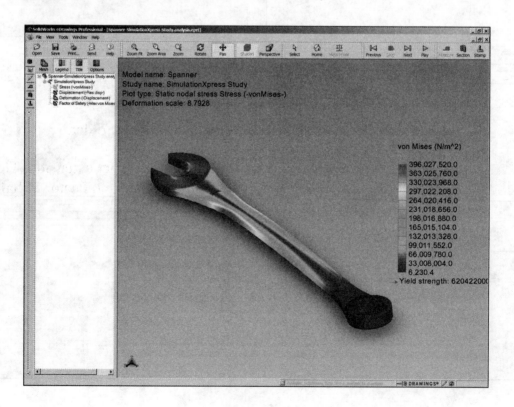

10. Generating the eDrawings file:

- An eDrawings file can be created for the SimulationXpress result plots.

- The eDrawings file allows you to view, animate and print your analysis results.

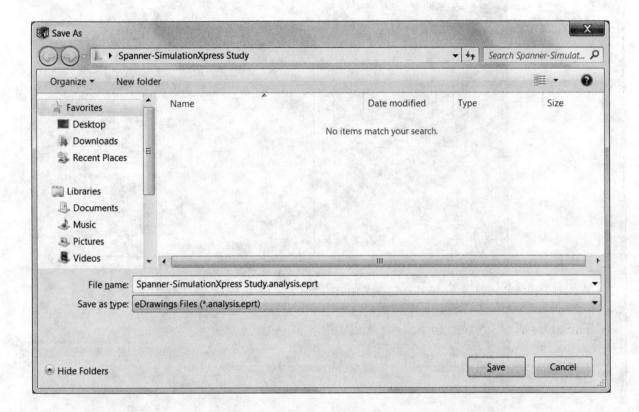

- When prompted, **Save** the analysis study in the default folder.

- SimulationXpress creates an eDrawing file with the **.eprt** extension. The file contains von Mises stress, displacement, deformation, and Factor of Safety plots. By default, the von Mises stress plot is displayed.

- Click the Play button 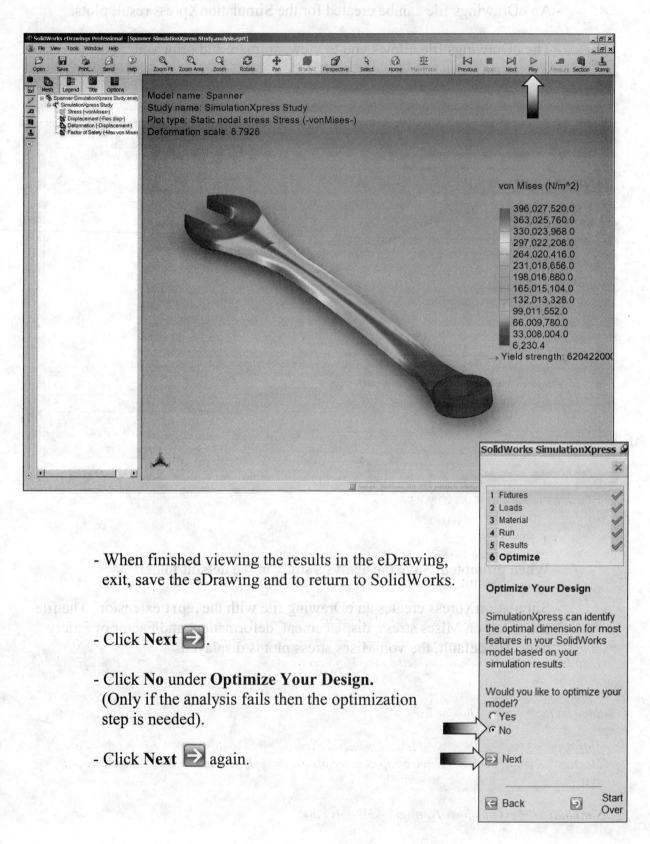 to see the animated results.

- When finished viewing the results in the eDrawing, exit, save the eDrawing and to return to SolidWorks.

- Click **Next** .

- Click **No** under **Optimize Your Design.**
(Only if the analysis fails then the optimization step is needed).

- Click **Next** again.

- At this point, you are prompted that the analysis has been completed. All 5 steps on the SimulationXpress property tree (right side) have the check marks in front of them.

11. Saving your work:

- Click **File / Save As**.

- Enter **Spanner Study** for file name and click **Save**.

Isotropic, Orthotropic & Anisotropic Materials:

Isotropic Material: If its mechanical properties are the same in all directions. The elastic properties of an Isotropic material are defined by the Modulus of Elasticity (EX) and Poisson's Ratio (NUXY).

Orthotropic Material: If its mechanical properties are unique and independent in the directions of three mutually perpendicular axes.

Anisotropic Material: If its mechanical properties are different in different directions. In general, the Mechanical properties of the anisotropic materials are not symmetrical with respect to any plane or axis.

SimulationXpress supports Isotropic materials only.

Questions for Review

SimulationXpress

1. SimulationXpress can be accessed from the Tools pull down menu.
   a. True
   b. False

2. System Of Units SI (Joules) is the only type that is supported in SimulationXpress.
   a. True
   b. False

3. The material of the part can be selected from the built-in library or input directly by the user.
   a. True
   b. False

4. SimulationXpress supports Isotropic, Orthotropic, and Anisotropic materials.
   a. True
   b. False

5. Restraints/Fixture are used to anchor certain areas of the part so that it will not move during the analysis.
   a. True
   b. False

6. Only one surface/face should be use for restraint in each study.
   a. True
   b. False

7. The elements size (mesh) can be adjusted to a smaller value for more accurate results.
   a. True
   b. False

8. The types of results reported are:
   a. Stress Distribution
   b. Deformed Shape
   c. Deformation
   d. Factor of Safety
   e. All of the above

7. TRUE	8. E
5. TRUE	6. FALSE
3. TRUE	4. FALSE
1. TRUE	2. FALSE

<u>Exercise 1:</u> SimulationXpress: Force

1. Open the existing part: **Extrude Boss & Extrude Cut.**

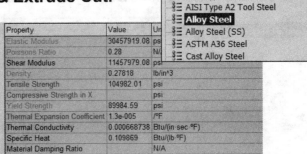

2. Set Unit to: **English (IPS)**.

5. Select Material: **Alloy Steel**.

3. Apply Restraint: **to 3 Holes.**

6. Run the Analysis.

7. Check the von Mises Stress results.

4. Apply Force of 50 Lbs, Normal to the FRONT Plane.

8. Save a copy as: **Simulation_Force**.

Exercise 2: SimulationXpress: Pressure

1. Open the existing part: **Bottle_SimulationXpress**.

2. Set Unit to: **English (IPS)**.

5. Select Material:
Nylon 6/10.

3. Apply Restraint:
to the **Top** face.

4. Apply Pressure
of **5 psi**. and
select all **Inside** faces.

6. Run the Analysis and show
the Von-Mises Stress.

7. Save a copy as:

Simulation_Pressure.

von Mises (psi)

6.095e+004
5.587e+004
5.079e+004
4.572e+004
4.064e+004
3.556e+004
3.049e+004
2.541e+004
2.033e+004
1.525e+004
1.018e+004
5.101e+003
2.476e+001

Free SolidWorks SimulationXpress Online Tutorial:
http://www.solidworks.com/sw/resources/videos/demo-library-solidworks-simulation.htm

CHAPTER 13

Sheet Metal Parts

Sheet Metal Parts

- This chapter discusses the introduction to designing sheet metal parts.

- Create a sheet metal part in the folded stage and add the sheet metal specific flange features such as:

  * Base Flange.
  * Edge Flanges.
  * Sketch Bends.
  * Cut with Link to Thickness.
  * Normal Cuts.

- There are at least 3 options for specifying the setback allowance, or the length difference between the fold and the flat patterns of a sheet metal part.

  * **Bend Table:** You can specify the bend allowance or bend deduction values for a sheet metal part in a bend table. The bend table also contains values for bend radius, bend angle, and part thickness.

  * **K-Factor:** Is a ratio that represents the location of the neutral sheet with respect to the thickness of the sheet metal part.
    Bend allowance using a K-Factor is calculated as follows:
    $$BA=\Pi(R + KT) \, A/180$$

  * **Use Bend Allowance:** Enter your own bend value base on your shop experience.

  * **Bend allowance Calculations:** The following equation is used to determine the total flat length when bend allowance values are used: $L_t = A + B + BA$

  * **Bend Deduction Calculations:** The following equation is used to determine the total flat length when bend deduction values are used: $L_t = A + B - BD$

Post Cap
Sheet Metal Parts

Dimensioning Standards: **ANSI**

Units: **INCHES** – 3 Decimals

Tools Needed:

Insert Sketch	Line	Circle
Dimension	Add Geometric Relations	Base Flange
Edge Flange	Sketch Bend	Extruded Cut
Flat Pattern		

1. Starting with the base profile:

- Select <u>Right</u> plane from FeatureManager tree and insert a new sketch .

- Sketch the profile below using the Line tool .

- Add dimensions and relations needed, fully define the sketch.

4.000

If Mid-Point relation is used, remove the dim 2.000

4.000

2.000

4.000

2. Extruding the Base Flange:

- Click or select **Insert / Sheet Metal / Base Flange**.

- Direction 1:   **Mid-Plane**.

- Extrude Depth: **4.00 in**.

- Use Gauge Table: **Sample Table - Steel**.

- Mat'l Thickness: **16 Gauge (.0598)** .

- Bend Radius: **.030 in**. (Override Radius) .

Set material thickness to **Outside**.

- Click **OK** ✓.

3. Creating an Edge Flange:

- Hold the Control key and select the **2 edges** as indicated.

- Click or select **Insert / Sheet Metal / Edge Flange**.

Select 2 edges

- Drag the cursor downwards and click anywhere to lock the preview of the 2 Edge Flanges.

- Select **Material Outside** under the Flange Position.

- Enter **90°** for Angle (default).

- Flange Length: **Blind**.

- Enter **5.000"** for depth.
- Relief Type: **Rectangle**.

- Relief Ratio: **.500**.

- Click **Edit Flange Profile** (arrow).

* The flange length will be modified in the next steps.

4. Editing the Edge Flange Profile:

- Move the Profile Sketch dialog to the upper corner.

- Drag the 2 outer lines inward as noted.

- Add the dimensions shown to fully define
the sketch.

Drag inwards

5.000

1.000

2.000

- After the 1st edge flange became fully define,
click the **Back** button (arrow) to switch back to
the previous screen.

- Select the **Edge 2** under the Flange Parameters section
and click the **Edit Flange Profile** once again (arrow).

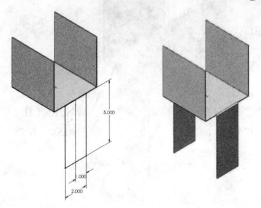

5.000

1.000

2.000

- Drag the 2 vertical lines inward similar to step
above, and add the same dimensions as the 1st
flange to ensure the 2 flanges are exactly the same
size (Collinear relations can also be used for the
width and height of the 2nd flange).

- Click finished [Finish] when the 2nd sketch
becomes fully defined.

- Zoom in on the upper end of the edge flange to see the relief details.

- Beside the Rectangular relief, there are two other types available: Obround and Tear.

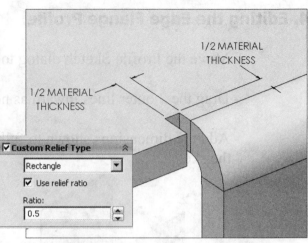

Custom Relief Type
Rectangle
☑ Use relief ratio
Ratio:
0.5

- Auto-Relief is added automatically after exiting the Sketch.
- Relief Width and Depth are defaulted to one-half (0.5) the Material Thickness.

5. Viewing the Flat Pattern:

- Click on the Sheet Metal toolbar:

- The flat pattern of the Part is displayed.

- Another way to view the flat pattern is to right click on the Flat-Pattern1 feature and select Suppress (arrow).

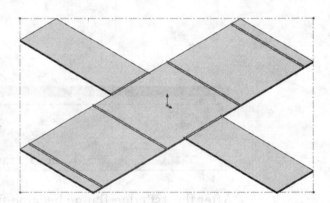

6. Changing the Fixed face:

- Edit the **Flat-Pattern** feature and select the <u>face</u> as indicated to use as the Fixed face.

Flat-Pattern

Parameters
Fixed face:
Face<2>
☑ Merge faces
☑ Simplify bends

Corner Options
☑ Corner treatment

Grain Direction

Faces To Exclude

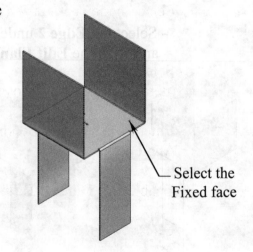

Select the Fixed face

7. Creating a Sketch Bend:

- Select the **side surface** and open a new Sketch .

- Sketch a **line** starting at one edge and Coincident with the other.

- Add dimensions to fully define the sketch.

Sketch Face

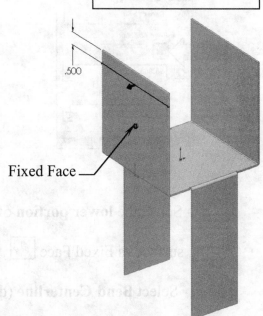

Fixed Face

- Click 🔽 or select **Insert / Sheet Metal / Sketch Bends**.

- Select the **lower portion** of the surface as Fixed Face.

- Select **Bend Centerline** (default) under Bend Position.

- Enter **90.00** deg for Bend Angle.

- Enable **Use Default Radius**.

- Click **OK** ⊘.

> ### Sketch Bends
>
> This command adds Bends or Tabs to the Sheet metal part with the sketch lines.
>
> Only sketch lines are allowed, but more than one line can be used in a same sketch to create multiple bends.

Sketched Bend1

Bend Parameters

Face<1>

Bend position:

90.00deg

☑ Use default radius

0.030in

☐ Custom Bend Allowance

8. Creating another Sketch Bend:

- Select the surface on the right and open a sketch or select **Insert / Sketch**.

- Sketch a line as shown and add dimensions to fully define.

- Click or select **Insert / Sheet Metal / Sketch Bend**.

Fixed Face

.500

- Select the **lower portion** of the

surface as Fixed Face.

- Select **Bend Centerline** (default) under Bend Position.

- Enter **90.00** deg for Bend Angle (default).

- Enable **Use Default Radius**.

- Click **OK**.

- The resulting bend.

- The upper portion of the surface is bent outward
90°, leaving the lower portion fixed.

9. Adding holes on the Edge Flange:

- Select the surface as shown and open a new sketch or select:
  Insert / Sketch.

Sketch Face

- Sketch two circles ⊕ on the face.

- Add dimensions ✏ as shown to
  position the circles.

- Add **Vertical** relations ⊥
  between the centers of the circles
  and the Origin, to fully define the
  sketch.

1.500

2.500

Vertical

Ø.225

- Click or select **Insert / Cut / Extrude**.

- End Condition: **Through All**.

- Enable **Normal Cut** (default).

- Click **OK** ⊘.

10. Adding holes on the Sketch Bend Flanges:

- Select the face as noted and open a new sketch 🖉 or select **Insert / Sketch**.

- Sketch 4 circles ⊕ and add dimensions ◈ as shown.

- Add the relations 🔟 as needed to fully define the sketch.

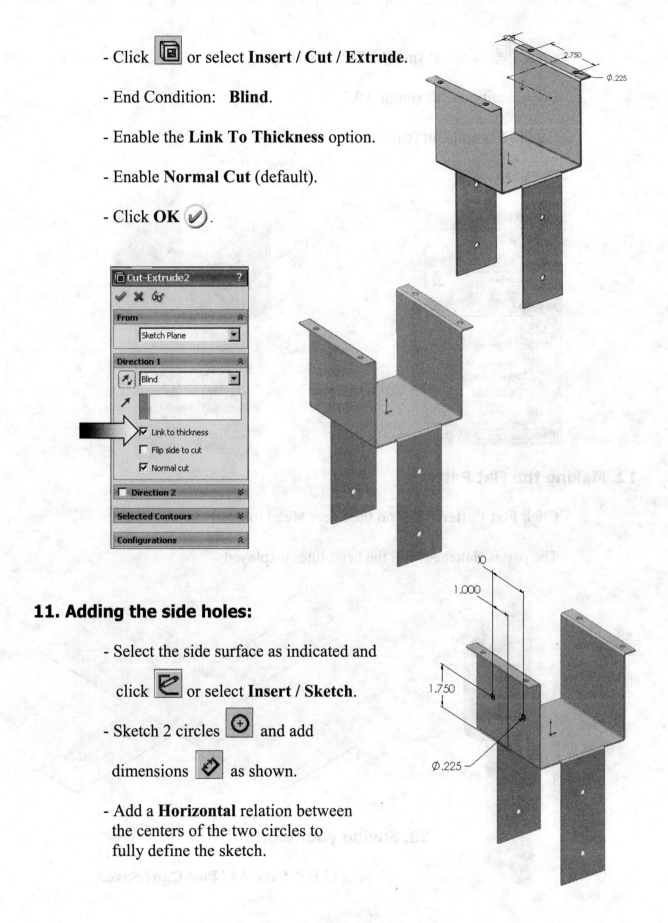

- Click [icon] or select **Insert / Cut / Extrude**.

- End Condition: **Blind**.

- Enable the **Link To Thickness** option.

- Enable **Normal Cut** (default).

- Click **OK** [icon].

Cut-Extrude2

From

Sketch Plane

Direction 1

Blind

☑ Link to thickness

☐ Flip side to cut

☑ Normal cut

☐ Direction 2

Selected Contours

Configurations

11. Adding the side holes:

- Select the side surface as indicated and

    click [icon] or select **Insert / Sketch**.

- Sketch 2 circles [icon] and add

    dimensions [icon] as shown.

- Add a **Horizontal** relation between
the centers of the two circles to
fully define the sketch.

- Click or select **Insert / Cut / Extrude**.

- End Condition: **Through All**.

- Enable **Normal Cut** (default).

- Click **OK** ✅.

12. Making the Flat Pattern:

- Click **Flat Pattern** on the Sheet Metal toolbar.

- The part is flattened with the bend lines displayed.

13. Saving your work:

- Select **File / Save As / Post Cap / Save**.

Using Sheet Metal Costing

Use SolidWorks sheet metal Costing tools to determine the cost of a sheet metal. Costing provides a comprehensive breakdown and comparison of manufacturing and material costs for sheet metal parts.

Costing Template Editor for Sheet Metal Parts

You can create and edit costing templates for sheet metal parts or bodies from the Costing Template Editor.

You can specify rates and costs for the procedures required to manufacture a sheet metal part or body in the sheet metal template. You can include customized information in the template, such as material cost and thicknesses, cost of manufacturing, and manufacturing setup costs.

You can determine how manufacturing operations affect the cost of your design. For example, you can set up templates for vendors that use different manufacturing operations.

You can specify the file location for Costing templates in Tools > Options > System Options > File Locations. In Show folders for, select Costing templates to add or delete a location. The default Costing template folder is *install_dir*\lang*language*\ Costing templates.

1. Opening an existing sheet metal part:

- Click **File / Open**.

- Browse to the Training Files folder, locate and open the **Sheet Metal Costing** document.

- The default template and all its values will be used in this exercise.

2. Inputting the information:

- Switch to the **Evaluate** tab and click **Costing** 🪙 .

- Click the **CostingManager** tab (arrow) on the left side tree to see how the Costing tool categorizes each operation required for manufacturing the part.

- Select the **Material** to **Steel AISI 304**) and **Thickness** to **1.90mm** (.075in). The sheet metal part is evaluated based on the selected material and processing costs as set in the default template.

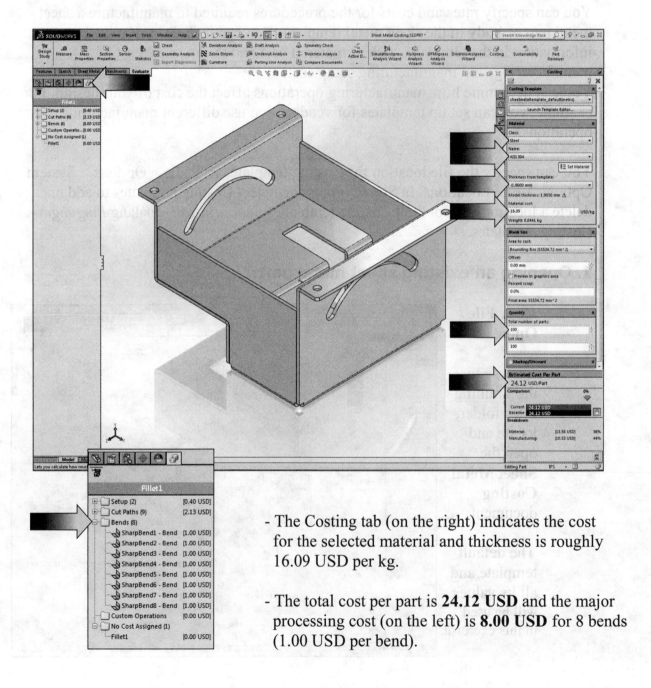

- The Costing tab (on the right) indicates the cost for the selected material and thickness is roughly 16.09 USD per kg.

- The total cost per part is **24.12 USD** and the major processing cost (on the left) is **8.00 USD** for 8 bends (1.00 USD per bend).

3. Setting the Baseline:

- The **Set Baseline** is used to set a baseline cost for comparison. If you change the design later on, the cost is compared to the baseline cost. When you set a baseline cost, any changes to the part are considered Current and the difference is displayed. While the baseline price is set, the part is rotated, flattened, and refolded because the software is capturing images for the Costing report.

- Click the **Set Baseline** button .

- The final cost is based on the values for manufacturing steps. The values that we are using here are only for samples only.

- Change the material to:
Aluminum Alloy 6061

- Use the same thickness (1.90mm or .075in)

- The SolidWorks Costing recalculates the cost based on the change in material.

- The recalculated cost is now almost half of what it was for Steel ($14.69 instead of $24.12)

4. Saving your work:

- Click **File / Save As**.

- Enter **Sheet Metal Costing** for the name of the document and click **Save.**

- **General**
  Use the General screen in the Costing Template Editor to set the units and currency options.

- **Material**
  Use the Material screen in the Costing Template Editor to set the materials you need to manufacture the sheet metal part.

- **Thickness**
  Use the Thickness screen in the Costing Template Editor to set the thickness and cost values for each class and material combination.

- **Cut**
  Use the Cut screen in the Costing Template Editor to define the cost of cutting methods based on length or stroke.

- **Bend**
  Use the Bend screen in the Costing Template Editor to define the cost of bending methods based on regular bends or hem bends.

- **Library Features**
  Use the Library Features screen in the Costing Template Editor to define the cost of library features, punch features, and forming tools in the part.

- **Custom**
  Use the Custom screen in the Costing Template Editor to define additional operations that contribute to a part's manufacturing cost, such as powder coating.

Questions for Review

Sheet Metal Parts

1. A sheet metal part can have multiple thicknesses.
    a. True
    b. False

2. An Edge Flange can be mirrored just like any other feature.
    a. True
    b. False

3. A sheet metal part can be created right from the beginning using the Base flange option.
    a. True
    b. False

4. Auto relief option is not available when extruding a Base Flange.
    a. True
    b. False

5. When the Sketched Bend option is used to create a bend, you'll have to specify at least two parameters:
    a. A fixed side and a sketched line.
    b. Fixed side and a bend angle value.
    c. A bend radius and a bend angle value.

6. The only time when the K-Factor option can be changed to Bend Table, is when extruding the Base Flange.
    a. True
    b. False

7. A sheet metal part can be designed from a flat sheet and other bends can be added later using Sketched Bend, Edge Flange, etc.
    a. True
    b. False

8. Link-to-Thickness option allows all sheet metal features in a part to have the same wall thickness and they can all be changed at the same time.
    a. True
    b. False

7. TRUE   8. TRUE
5. A   6. FALSE
3. TRUE   4. FALSE
1. FALSE   2. TRUE

CHAPTER 13 (cont.)

Sheet Metal Parts

Sheet Metal Parts

Sheet metal parts can be created using one of the following methods:

- Create the part as a solid and then insert the sheet metal parameters such as rips, bend radius, material thickness, bend allowance, and cut relief so that the part can be flattened.

- Create the part as a sheet metal part from the beginning by using the Base Flange command to extrude the first feature.

- Sheet metal parameters can be applied onto the sheet metal part during the extrusion or after the fact.

This chapter will guide you through the use of the sheet metal and forming tool commands to create a sheet metal part and a louver form tools:

- Creating the parent feature with the Base Flange command.
- Using the Miter-flange command.
- Create a sheet metal part in the flat or folded stage.
- Create Revolved features.
- Accessing the Design Library.
- Using the forming tool to form the louvers.
- Create a Linear pattern of features.
- Create a Circular pattern of features.
- Create a pattern of patterned features.

Vents
Sheet Metal Parts

Dimensioning Standards: **ANSI**

Units: **INCHES** – 3 Decimals

Tools Needed:

Insert Sketch	Line	Dimension
Rectangle	Add Geometric Relations	Linear Pattern
Base Flange	Miter Flange	Circular Pattern
Flat Pattern	Extruded Cut	Design Library

1. Sketching the first profile:

- Select <u>Front</u> plane from the FeatureManager tree.

- Click from Sketch toolbar OR select **Insert / Sketch**.

- Click and sketch a horizontal line **below the Origin**.

- Click and dimension the length of the line to **18.00 in**.

Origin

2. Adding a Midpoint relation:

- Click from the Sketch toolbar OR select **Tools / Relations /Add**.

- Click on the Origin point and select the line as shown.

- Select **Midpoint** option from the Add Geometric Relation dialog box.

- Click **OK**.

Mid-Point relation

3. Extruding the Base-Flange:

- Click (Base Flange) from the Sheet Metal toolbar OR select:
Insert /Sheet Metal / Base Flange.

- Enter / select the following:

Direction 1:	**Mid-plane**.
Extrude Depth:	**18.00 in**.
Use Gauge table:	**Sample Table – Steel**.
Thickness:	**16 Gauge (.0598")**.
Bend Radius:	**.030 in**. (Override radius).
Bend Allowance:	**K-Factor / Ratio: 0.5**.
Auto Relief:	**Rectangular**
Relief Ratio:	**0.5**.

- Click **OK** ✅.

4. Creating the Miter-Flanges:

- Hold the control key, select the <u>Edge</u> and the vertex as indicated below, and click 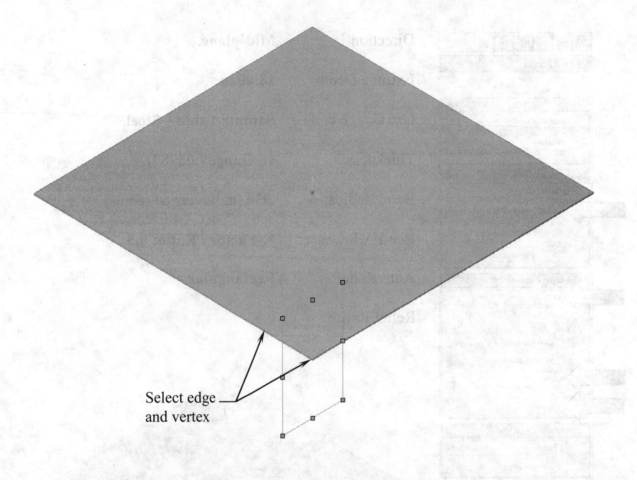 OR select: **Insert / Sketch**.

- SolidWorks automatically creates a new plane <u>normal</u> to the selected edge.

Select edge
and vertex

- Click **Zoom-to-Area** from the View toolbar and zoom in on the corner as shown below.

- Sketch a vertical line staring at the upper corner.

- Click (Dimension) and make the length of the line **.375 in**.

- Click (**Miter-Flange**) from the Sheet Metal toolbar OR select:
  Insert / Sheet Metal / Miter Flange.

- Select the **4** upper edges as indicated.

- Choose **Material Outside** under Flange Position .

- Set Gap Distance to **.010 in** .

- Click **OK** .

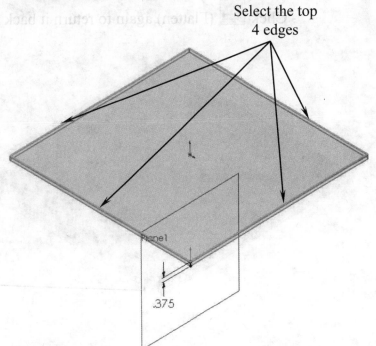

Select the top
4 edges

5. Flattening the part:

- The Flat Pattern can be toggled at anytime during or after the part is created.

- Click (Flatten) from the Sheet Metal toolbar to flatten the part.

6. Switching back to the folded-model:

- Click (Flatten) again to return it back to the folded stage.

7. Saving your work: Select **File / Save As / Sheet Metal Vent / Save**.

---

8. Creating a new Forming Tool – The Louver:

- Start a new Part file: click **File / New / Part / OK**.

- Set Units to Inches – 3 Decimal (Tools/Options/Document Properties/ Units).

9. Sketching on the TOP reference plane:

- Select the <u>Top</u> plane and click 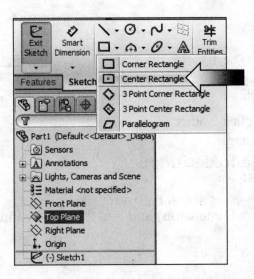**Insert / Sketch** from the Sketch toolbar.

- Select the 🔲 (Center Rectangle) from the Sketch-Tools toolbar.

- Sketch a rectangle that centered on the Origin, as shown below.

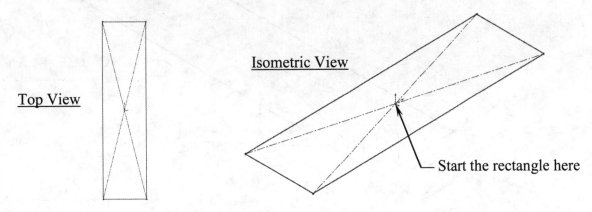

10. Other Rectangle options:

 Corner Rectangle

P1

P2

Click 2 diagonal points.

 3-Point Corner Rectangle

P1

P3

Click 3 points to
define the angle.

P2

 3-PointCenter Rectangle

P1

P3

P2

Start at Center point and click 2 other
points to define the angle.

Parallelogram

P3

P1

P2

Click 3 points to define the parallelogram.

11. Adding dimensions:

- Click (Smart Dimension) and add the dimensions shown below.

8.000

2.000

12. Extruding the Base:

- Click (**Extruded Boss/Base**) and fill in the following parameters:

- End Condition: **Blind**.

- Depth: **.125 in**.

- Click **OK** ✅.

> ### 💡 Forming Tools
>
> Forming tools are solid parts that used to bend, stretch, and form sheet metal.

13. Building the louver body:

- Select the <u>upper face</u> of the part and open a new sketch ✏️ .

- Change to the Top View Orientation 🔲 (Ctrl+5).

- Sketch the profile of the Louver-Forming tool and add Dimensions ◇
  as illustrated below:

- Select the horizontal Centerline and click (**Revolve Boss/Base**).

- Use **Blind** for Revolve Type.

- For revolve Angle, enter **90°**.

- Toggle (Reverse) and make sure the preview looks like the one below.

- Click **OK** ✅.

- The resulting of a 90° revolved.

14. Adding a fillet at the base:

- Click **Fillet** and enter **.125 in**. for Radius size.

- Select the **edge** as indicated.

- Select **Tangent Propagation** checkbox (default), the system applies the same fillet to all connected tangent edges.

- Click **OK** ✓.

- Rotate the model to see the resulting fillet from the backside.

- The new fillet should runs around the back but not on the front.

15. Removing the base:

- The Rectangular block was created
  so that a fillet can be added between
  the two features. We no longer
  need it at this point.

- Select the <u>side surface</u> of the part and
  open a new sketch.

Sketch face

- While the side surface is still highlighting
  press the **Convert Entities** command.
  The selected face is converted to a
  rectangle.

- Switch to the **Features** tool tab
  and click the **Extruded Cut** command.

- Change the End Condition to **Through All**.

- Click **OK** ✓.

- The base is removed and
  only the form portion
  is kept.

16. Creating the Positioning Sketch:

- The Positioning Sketch displays the preview of the Form tool while it is being dragged from the Design Library. Its sketched entities can be dimensioned to position the Formed feature.

- Select the **bottom face** of the part and open a new sketch 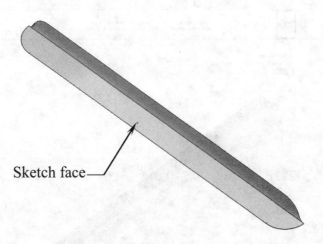.

Sketch face

- Select the bottom face of the part and click **Convert Entities** .

- Add a Centerline as shown to help position the tool when it is placed on a sheet metal part.

Convert the edges
of the Louver

Add Centerline

- **Exit** the sketch or click .

- Re-name the sketch to **Position Sketch** from the FeatureManager tree.

17. Establishing the Stop and Remove faces:

- In order for the forming tools to work properly, a set of Stopping Face and Removing Faces will have to be established prior to saving as a forming tool.

- Change to the Sheet metal tool tab and click the **Forming Tool** command.

Face to Remove

Stopping Face

- For **Stopping Face**, select the **bottom face** of the part.

- For **Faces to Remove**, select the **face on the right side** of the part.

- Click **OK**.

18. Saving the Forming Tool:

- Click: **File / Save As.**

- Enter **Long Louver** for the name of the file.

- Select **Form Tool** (*.sldftp) in the Save As Type.

- The following directories should be selected automatically:
Program Files\ SolidWorks\ SolidWorks 2015\ Design Library\ Forming Tools\ Louvers.

- Select the Louver folder and click **Save**.

<u>**NOTE:**</u> *The Design Library is a Hidden Folder (Explorer / Organize / Folder and Search Options / View / Show Hidden Files, Folders and Drives).*

- After the forming tool is saved, it can be accessed through the Task pane, by dragging and dropping it from the Design Library folder.

19. Opening the previous part:

- Open the Sheet Metal Vent that was saved earlier. (**Alt+Tab**)

- Click the push pin to lock the Task Pane in place (arrow).

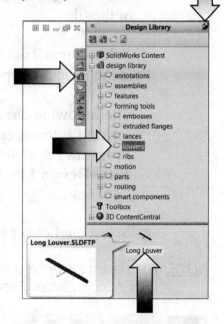

- Expand the **Design Library** folder .

- Expand the **Forming Tool** folder and double click on the **Louvers** folder to see its content.

- Hover the mouse cursor over the name Long Louver to see the preview of the Forming tool.

20. Applying the form tool:

- **Drag** the Long Louver form tool from the Design Library and **drop** it approximately as indicated.

> ### 💡 Forming Tools
>
> Forming tools should be inserted from the Design Library window and applied onto parts with sheet metal parameters such as material thickness, bend allowance, fixed face, cut relief, etc…

- Change the Angle to **180°** and click **Flip Tool**.

Place the Louver here

21. Positioning the form tool:

- Click the **Position** tab (arrow).

Position

Message

Please use sketch points to locate sub-instances of the tool.

Use dimensions and other sketch tools to position the points used for tool centers.

💡 **Push / Pull**

While dragging the Forming Tool from the Design Library, (still holding the mouse button) press the TAB key to reverse the direction from push to pull.

- Add the locating dimensions 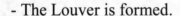 as shown to fully define this sketch.

- Use the <u>outer edges</u> of the sheet metal part when adding the dimensions.

- Click **OK** ⊘.

- The Louver is formed.

22. Adding a mounting hole:

- Select the <u>upper face</u> of the part as indicated.

- Click to open a new sketch or select **Insert / Sketch**.

Sketch Face

- Sketch a circle ⊕ on the left side of the louver.

- Add dimensions ◇ to define the circle.

Ø.325

1.000

1.000

23. Extruding a cut:

- Click or select **Insert / Cut / Extrude**.

- End Condition: **Blind**.

- Link to Thickness: **Enabled**.

- Normal Cut: **Enabled**.

- Click **OK** ✅.

24. Creating a Linear Pattern:

- Click 🔲 or select **Insert / Pattern Mirror / Linear Pattern**.

- Select the **bottom edge** as Pattern Direction.

- Enter **.703 in**. as Spacing.

- Enter **10** as Number of Instances.

- Select the **Long Louver** as Features to Pattern.

- Click **OK** ✅.

- The completed Linear Pattern.

25. Creating an Axis:

- An axis can be created at anytime so features can be arrayed around it. In this case, an axis in the center of the part will be made and used as the center of the next Circular Pattern.

- Click [ ] or select **Insert / Reference Geometry / Axis**.

- Click the **Two Planes** option [ ].

- Select **Front** and **Right** planes from FeatureManager tree.

New Axis

- Click **OK** ⊘.

26. Creating a Circular Pattern:

- Click or select **Insert / Pattern Mirror / Circular Pattern**.

- Select the new **Axis** for Pattern Axis.

- Enter **360 deg**. for Pattern Angle.

- Enter **4** for Number of Instances.

- For Feature to Pattern select the **Cut-Extrude1, LPattern1** and the **Long Louver** from the FeatureManager tree.

- Click **OK** ✅.

27. Saving your work:

- Save the model with the same file name and override the previous file.

Finished Part (Folded)

Flat Pattern*

* After the formed features are created they will retain their formed shapes even when toggled back and forth between Folded or Flattened.

Questions for Review

Sheet Metal Parts

1. The mid-point relation can be used to center a line onto the Origin.
   a. True
   b. False

2. The base flange command can also be selected from Insert / Sheet Metal / Base Flange.
   a. True
   b. False

3. When a linear model edge is selected and the sketch pencil is clicked, the system creates a plane Normal To Curve automatically.
   a. True
   b. False

4. The Miter Flange feature can create more than one flange in the same operation.
   a. True
   b. False

5. The Flat and the Folded patterns cannot be toggled until the part is completed and saved.
   a. True
   b. False

6. An existing forming tool cannot be edited or changed; forming tools are fixed by default.
   a. True
   b. False

7. When applying a form tool onto a sheet metal part, the push or pull direction can be toggled when pressing:
   a. Up arrow
   b. Tab
   c. Control

8. The Modify Sketch command can be used to rotate or translate the entire sketch.
   a. True
   b. False

9. A formed feature(s) cannot be copied or patterned.
   a. True
   b. False

	9. FALSE
8. TRUE	7. B
6. FALSE	5. FALSE
4. TRUE	3. TRUE
2. TRUE	1. TRUE

CHAPTER 14

Sheet Metal Forming Tools

Sheet Metal Forming Tools

- Forming tools act as dies that bend, stretch, or otherwise form sheet metal.

- SolidWorks includes some sample forming tools to get you started. They are stored in: *Installation_Directory\Data\Design Library\Forming Tools\folder_name*.

- Some types of form features, such as louvers and lances, create openings on sheet metal parts. To indicate which faces of the form tool will create the openings, the system changes the color of these faces to **red,** the stopping faces to **blue** and the rest to **yellow**.

- The user can only insert (drag & drop) forming tools from the **Design Library** window and apply them only to sheet metal parts. The Design Library window gives you quick access to the parts, assemblies, library features, and form tools that are used most often.

- Users can create their own forming tools and apply them to sheet metal parts to create form features such as louvers, lances, flanges, and ribs.

- The Design Library window has several default folders. Each folder contains a group of palette items, displayed as Thumbnail Graphics.

- Design Library can include:
  - Parts (.sldprt)
  - Assemblies (.sldasm)
  - Sheet Metal Forming Tools (.sldftp)
  - Library Features (.sldlfp)

- In this 1st half of the chapter we will learn how to create and save a forming tool.

Button with Slots
Sheet Metal Forming Tools

Dimensioning Standards: **ANSI**

Units: **INCHES** – 3 Decimals

Tools Needed:

Insert Sketch	Boss/Base Revolve	Convert Entities
Dimension	Add Geometric Relations	Extrude Cut
Split Line	Fillet/Round	Forming Tool

1. Creating the base block:

- Select the <u>Right</u> plane and Insert a new Sketch .

- Sketch a **Center-Rectangle** [image] that centered on the origin.

- Add the width and height dimensions [image] as shown.

(The sketch should be fully defined at this point).

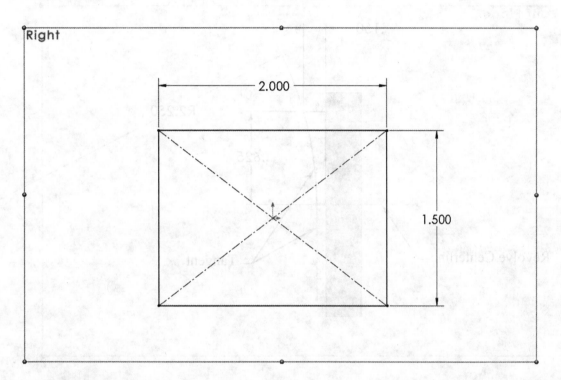

2. Extruding the base:

- Click **Extruded Boss/Base** [image] .

- Enter the following:

- Direction 1: **Blind**.

- **Reverse** Direction.

- Depth: **.250in**.

- Click **OK** ✅ .

3. Creating the forming tool body:

- Select the <u>Front</u> plane and open a new sketch .

- Sketch the profile as shown.

- Add dimensions and relations to fully define the sketch.

Front Plane

.150

R2.250

.625

Revolve Centerline —

Tangent

4. Revolving the body:

- Click **Revolved Boss/Base** .

- Revolve **Blind** with a full **360 deg**.

- Click **OK** .

.150

.625   R2.250

Revolve

Axis of Revolution

Line1

Direction1

Blind

360.00deg

☑ Merge result

5. Adding a fillet:

- Click **Fillet** and enter **.080 in**. for Radius .

- Select the edge as indicated.

- Click **OK** .

Select edge to fillet

Fillet1

Items To Fillet

Edge<1>

☑ Tangent propagation
◉ Full preview
○ Partial preview
○ No preview

Fillet Parameters

0.080in

☐ Multiple radius fillet
Profile:

Circular

Radius: 0.08in

6. Sketching the 1st slot profile:

- We will take a look at two different methods to create the slots. For the 1st Arc Slot, let us try out the **Offset Entities** option.

- Select the **face** as indicated and open a new sketch. Draw a Center-Point-Arc approximately as shown.

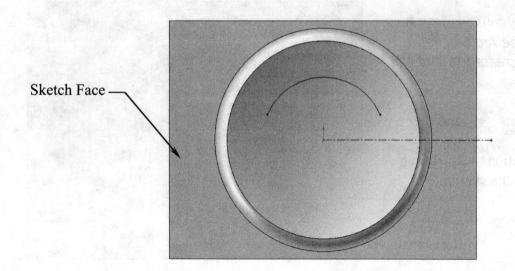

Sketch Face

- While the arc is still highlighting, click the **Offset Entities** command.

- Enter **.0625 in**. for Offset Distance.

- Enable the following:

  * Select Chain   *** Bi-Directional**

  * Make Base Construction   *** Cap End / Arcs**.

- Click **OK** ✅.

Note:

- *We will use the Arc-Slot command to create the 2nd slot.*

- Add dimensions ⬦ and the

  horizontal relations ⊥ shown to fully define the sketch.

135.00°

.063

.063

R.388

Horizontal

7. Creating the 1st Split Line:

- Click **Split Line** from the **CURVES** toolbar or select: **Insert / Curve / Split Line.**

- Select the <u>face</u> as indicated to split .

- Click **OK** ✅.

135.00°

.063

.063

R.388

Face to Split

- The selected face is split into a new, separate surface.

- This new surface can now be used as Faces-to-Remove, when the form tool is inserted into a sheet metal part.

- The Faces to Remove option specifies what features/area will get a through cut.

8. Creating the 2nd slot profile:

- This time we will try another method to create the 2nd curved slot. (The Copy & Paste option also works well).

- Select the **Face** as noted and open a new sketch.

- Select the **Center Arc Slot** under the Straight-Slot button.

- Enable the **Add Dimensions** checkbox.

- Start at the Origin and click **point 1**, move outward and click **point 2**, swing the cursor to the other side and click **point 3**, then drag down or upward to **point 4**.

- The arc-slot is completed with the Radius, Width, and Angular dimensions.

Add a horizontal centerline

Sketch face

- Change the values of the dimensions to:

 * Width: **.125"**
 * Radius: **R.325"**
 * Angle: **135 deg.**

- Create the **2nd split line** as shown in step 8.

9. Adding more fillets:

- Click **Fillet** and enter **.062 in**. for Radius.

- Select the edge as indicated.

- Click **OK**.

10. Inserting the Forming Tool feature:

- Select **Insert / Sheet Metal / Forming tool** from the pull down menu

- Select the **Stopping-Face** and the **Faces-to-Remove** as indicated.

Stopping Faces

Faces to Remove:
creates the openings
when the form tool
is applied onto the
sheet metal parts.

- Click **OK**.

- The completed form tool.

11. Saving the Forming tool:

- Click **File / Save As / Button w-Slots**, change the Save as Type to **Form Tool** and save the part in the following directories:

C:\Program Files\SolidWorks\Data\Design Library\Forming Tools\File Name

Note:

The Design Library is a Hidden Folder, to enable it, go to: *Windows Explorer / Organize / Folder and Search Options.*

Click the *View* tab and enable the option: *Show Hidden Files, Folders and Drives.*

Note:

- *The Sheet metal forming tools can also be saved by dragging and dropping from the FeatureManager tree to a folder (i.e. Forming Tools) inside the Design Library.*

- *The file name, file type, and path can be selected to save the forming tool at this time.*

12. Applying the new forming tool: (Optional)

- Create a sheet metal part using the drawing below and test out your new forming tool.

Questions for Review

Sheet Metal Forming Tools

1. Forming tools can bend or stretch sheet metal parts.
    a. True
    b. False

2. Forming tools can be stored in the Design Library window using the file extension:
    a. slddrw
    b. sldftp
    c. dwg

3. Forming tools can be dragged and dropped from the Design Library window.
    a. True
    b. False

4. Forming tools can be used to formed surfaces and solid parts as well.
    a. True
    b. False

5. The Red color on the face(s) of the forming tool creates openings on the sheet metal parts.
    a. True
    b. False

6. The Split Line command divides a selected face into multiple separate faces.
    a. True
    b. False

7. Only one single closed sketch can be used with the Split Line command.
    a. True
    b. False

8. The _____ key is used to reverse the direction of the forming tool (push/pull):
    a. Shift
    b. Tab
    c. Alt

1. TRUE
2. B
3. TRUE
4. FALSE
5. TRUE
6. TRUE
7. TRUE
8. b

CHAPTER 14 (cont.)

Designing Sheet Metal Parts

Designing Sheet Metal Parts

- Sheet metal components are normally used as housings or enclosures for parts or to strengthen and support other parts.

- A Sheet Metal part can be created as a single part or it can also be designed in the context of an assembly that has enclosed components.

- Forming tools are dies that can bend, stretch, or form sheet metal.

- In SolidWorks, forming tools are applied using the "Positive Half" (the raised side) to form features.

- When inserting a forming tool, its direction can be reversed using the TAB key (Push or Pull).

- The Sheet Metal part can be flattened either by using the Unfold 🔼 or Flattened 🔲 button, and drawings can be made to show views of the bent or flattened part. Bend lines are also visible in the drawing views.

- By default, only the Bend-Lines are visible at all time, but not the Bend-Regions. To show the Bend Regions, right click on the Flat Pattern1 icon at the bottom of the FeatureManager tree, then select Edit Feature and clear the Merge Faces check box.

- In this 2nd half of the chapter, besides learning how to create a sheet metal part, we will also learn how to apply the form tool that was created earlier in the 1st half of the lesson.

Mounting Tray
Designing Sheet Metal Parts

| Dimensioning Standards: **ANSI** |
| Units: **INCHES** – 3 Decimals |

Tools Needed:

Insert Sketch		Base Flange		Edge Flange	
Unfold		Fold		Extruded Cut	
Linear Pattern		Flattened		Break Corner	

1. Creating the base block:

- Select the <u>Front</u> plane from FeatureManager Tree.

- Click or select **Insert / Sketch**.

- Sketch the profile below and add dimensions to fully define the sketch.

Front Plane

2.000

1.000

> 💡 **Base Flange**
>
> A Base Flange is the first extruded feature in a sheet metal part.
> Sheet metal parameters are added automatically

2. Extruding the Base Flange:

- Click on the Sheet Metal toolbar, or select:

   Insert / Sheet Metal / Base Flange.

- End Condition: **Blind**.

- Extrude Depth: **5.000**.

- Thickness: **18 Gauge**.

- Override Radius: **Enabled**.

- Bend Radius: **.010**.

- Click **OK**.

Base Flange

Direction 1
Blind
5.00000000in

Direction 2

Sheet Metal Gauges
☑ Use gauge table
SAMPLE TABLE - STEEL -
Steel Air Bending
Browse...

Sheet Metal Parameters
18 Gauge
0.04780000in
☐ Override thickness
☐ Reverse direction
0.01000000in
☑ Override radius

3. Creating an Edge Flange:

- Select the **outer edge** as shown and click on the Sheet Metal toolbar or select: **Insert / Sheet Metal / Edge Flange**.

Select the outer edge

> ☀ **Edge Flange**
>
> The Edge Flange command adds a flange to the selected linear edge and shares the same material thickness as the sheet metal part.

- Position the flange towards the left side and set the following:

- Use Default Radius: **Enabled**.

- Flange Direction: **Blind**.

- Bend Angle: **90deg**.

- Flange Depth: **.985**.

- Use **Inner Virtual Sharp** .

- Flange Position: **Material Outside** .

- Click **OK** .

4. Adding cut features:

- Select the <u>face</u> as shown and insert a new sketch .

- Sketch the profile and add dimensions .

- The horizontal dimensions are measured from the Centerline.

Sketch face

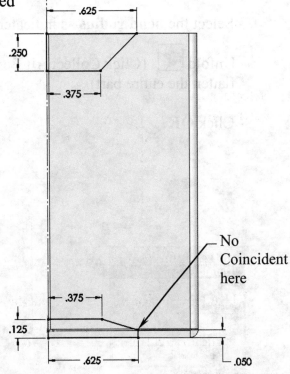

No Coincident here

5. Extruding a cut:

- Click or select **Insert / Cut / Extrude**.

- End Condition: **Blind**.

- Extrude Depth: **.165 in.**

- Click **OK** .

6. Using the Unfold command:

- Click 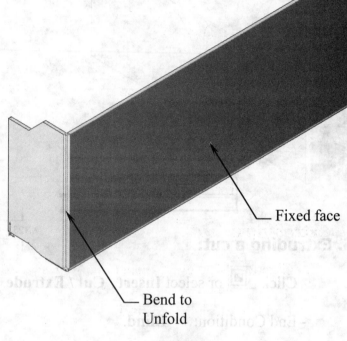 on the Sheet metal toolbar or select:
  Insert / Sheet Metal / Unfold.

- Select the **right face** as Fixed face .

- Select the **bend radius** as indicated for Bends to

  Unfold . (Click Collect All Bends if you want to
  flatten the entire part).

- Click **OK** .

Unfold

When adding cuts across a bend, the Unfold command flattens one or more bend(s) in a sheet metal part.

Fixed face

Bend to
Unfold

Unfold

7. Creating a Rectangular Window:

- Select the <u>face</u> as indicated and insert a new sketch .

- Sketch a **Corner rectangle** as shown below.

- Add dimensions and Sketch Fillets .

Symmetric

R.032

Sketch face

.875

.625

.500

8. Extruding a Cut:

- Click or select **Insert / Cut / Extrude**.

- End Condition: **Blind**.

- Link to Thickness: **Enabled** (default) .

- Normal Cut: **Enabled**.

- Click **OK** .

Link To Thickness

- The Link-to-Thickness option is only available in sheet metal parts.

- When this option is enabled, the extruded depth is automatically linked to the part thickness.

R.032

.875

.625

.500

9. Using the Fold command:

- Click on the Sheet metal toolbar or select:

   Insert / Sheet Metal / Fold.

- Select the **right face** as Fixed face .

- Select the **bend radius** as indicated for Bends to Fold . (If Collect All Bends was selected last time, click it again this time).

- Click **OK** .

> ✨ **Fold**
>
> The Fold command returns the bends to their folded state.

Fixed face

UnFold

Bend to Fold

Hide the Sketches

Folded

10. Unfolding multiple bends:

- Click or select **Insert / Sheet Metal / Unfold**.

- Select the <u>bottom face</u> as Fixed face .

- Select the **faces** of the 2 bends as shown for Bends To Unfold .

- Click **OK** .

Bends to Unfold

Fixed face

11. Adding more Cuts:

- Select the **upper face** as noted and insert a new sketch .

- Sketch **2 Circles** and add dimensions for size and position.

- Add an **Equal** and a **Vertical** relation between the circles.

Sketch face

ϕ.500

1.000

1.125

2.500

- Click or select **Insert / Cut / Extrude**.

- End Condition: **Blind**.

- Link To Thickness: **Enabled**.

- Click **OK** ✅.

12. Folding multiple bends:

- Click 🔳 on the Sheet Metal toolbar or select: **Insert / Sheet Metal / Fold**.

- The Fixed face 🔳 is still selected by default.

- Under Bends to Fold 🔳, click **Collect All Bends** [Collect All Bends].

- Click **OK** ✅.

Unfold

Folded

13. Inserting a Sheet Metal Forming Tool:

- Click the **Design Library** icon and click the push pin to lock it.

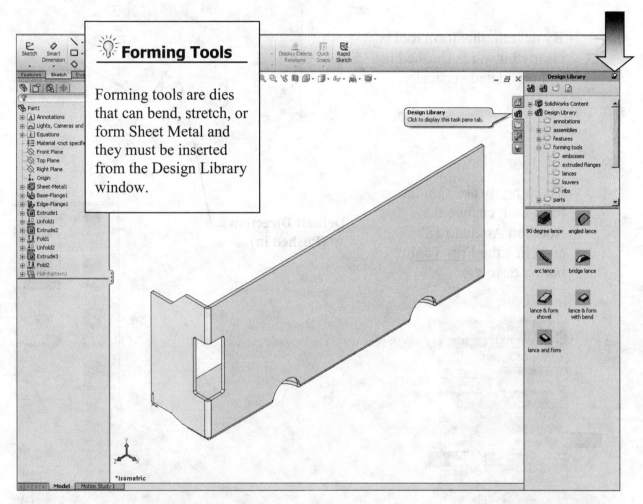

Forming Tools

Forming tools are dies that can bend, stretch, or form Sheet Metal and they must be inserted from the Design Library window.

- Expand the **Design Library** folder .

- Click on the **Forming Tools** folder forming tools .

- Click on the **Lances** folder lances .

- Locate the **Bridge Lance** form tool.

- Hover the mouse cursor over the Bridge Lance icon to see its preview graphics.

- SolidWorks includes some sample forming tools to help get you started. These form tools can be customized and used in different sheet metal parts.
- Drag the Bridge Lance* from the Task Pane and drop it on the sheet metal part approximately as shown.

- By default, this form tool is inserted inwards (pushed in) and orientated vertically.

- To correctly position the form tool, change the Rotation Angle to **180°** and click the **Flip Tool** button (arrows).

Default Direction (Pushed in)

Drag & Drop

If the Bridge Lance fails to form, double click on its icon to open the actual part, and re-save it in the same location, but using the new Forming Tool extension (.sldftp)

14. Locating the Bridge Lance:

- Click the **Position** tab (arrow).

- Add the dimensions shown below to correctly position the formed feature.

- Dimensions <u>from the centerlines</u> to the outer-most edges of the part.

- Click Finish .

- Un-pin the Design Library tree to put it away temporarily.

15. Creating the Linear Pattern of the Bridge Lance:

- Click or select **Insert / Pattern Mirror / Linear Pattern**.

- Select the top **horizontal edge** of the part as Pattern Direction.

- Enter **1.500** in. for Instance Spacing.

- Enter **3** for Number of Instances.

- Select the **Bridge-Lance** as Features to pattern.

- Click **OK**.

Direction arrow

Direction 1
Spacing: 1.500in.
Instances: 3

.787   R.157236
       R.118
       50.00°

1.000

1.125

LPattern1

Direction 1
Edge<1>
1.50000000in
3

Direction 2

Features to Pattern
bridge lance1

Faces to Pattern

Instances to Skip

Options
☐ Vary sketch
☐ Geometry pattern
☑ Propagate visual properties
○ Full preview
● Partial preview

16. Mirroring the body:

- Rotate the part and select the face as indicated (for mirror face).

Mirror face

- Select **Insert / Pattern Mirror / Mirror**.

- Expand the **Bodies to Mirror** section and select the body as shown.

- Click **OK** ✅.

Body to mirror

17. Adding the rear Edge Flange:

- Select the <u>edge</u> as indicated.

- Click or select **Insert / Sheet Metal / Edge Flange**.

Select edge

- Position the flange downwards and enter the following:

- Use Default Radius: **Enabled**.

- Flange Length: **Blind**.

- Bend Angle: **90deg**.

- Flange Position: **Material Inside**.

- Use **Inner Virtual Sharp**.

Note:
The Flange depth will be
edited in the next step.

18. Resizing the Edge Flange:

- Click the **Edit Flange Profile** button (arrow).

- The 2D sketch of the flange is activated so that its shape and size can be altered.

- **Drag** the 2 outer-most vertical lines inward (pictured).

Drag inwards

- Sketch **2 Circles** and add the Dimensions as shown.

- Click [icon] to **exit** the sketch

or click **Rebuilt** [icon] .

.750

.375

.375

.188

Ø.125
(2 Plcs)

.625

1.250

19. Adding Chamfers:

- Click or select **Insert / Sheet Metal / Break-Corner**.

- Break Type: **Chamfer** .

- Enter **.060** for chamfer depth.

- Select the **4 Edges** as shown.

- Click **OK** ✓.

Select 4 Edges

Front Isometric

Back Isometric
See note below

Rotate Option 1: Shift + Up or Down Arrow twice to rotate 90° each time.
Rotate Option 2: Set the View rotation to 15 degrees – Press the **Right** arrow 12 times and the **Down** arrow 4 times).
OR: use the new option **View Selector** (Space Bar) and click one of the faces (or projected faces) on the cube to rotate the model to that orientation.

20. Switching to the Flat Pattern:

- Click or select **Insert / Sheet Metal / Flattened***.

- Verify that the part is flattened properly and there are no rebuild errors.

Fixed face

* *To change the Fixed face of the part, edit the **Flat-Pattern1** feature and select the face as noted and press OK.*

21. Saving your work:

- Select **File / Save As / Mounting Tray / Save**.

Questions for Review

Designing Sheet Metal Parts

1. A Sheet Metal part can be created as a single part or in context of an assembly with enclosed components.
   a. True
   b. False

2. A Base Flange is the first extruded feature in a sheet metal part. Sheet metal parameters are added automatically.
   a. True
   b. False

3. A sheet metal part designed in SolidWorks can have multiple wall thickness.
   a. True
   b. False

4. The Edge Flange command adds a flange to the selected linear edge and shares the same material thickness of the sheet metal part.
   a. True
   b. False

5. Only one bend can be flattened at a time using the Unfold command.
   a. True
   b. False

6. Forming tools have to be inserted from the Feature Palette window.
   a. True
   b. False

7. To reverse the direction of the forming tool while being dragged from the Feature Palette window, press:
   a. Tab
   b. Control
   c. Shift

8. After the features are created by the forming tools, their sketches can only be moved or re-positioned, and their dimension values cannot be changed.
   a. True
   b. False

1. TRUE   2. TRUE
3. FALSE 4. TRUE
5. FALSE 6. TRUE
7. A   8. TRUE

CHAPTER 15

Sheet Metal Conversions

Sheet Metal Conversions
From IGES to SolidWorks

- Parts created from other CAD systems (using IGES or **I**nitial **G**raphics **E**xchange **S**pecification) can be imported and converted into SolidWorks Sheet Metal.

- When importing other CAD formats into SolidWorks, read them in as follows:

  • If there are blank surfaces, they are imported and added to the Feature Manager design Tree as surface features.
  • If the attempt to knit the surfaces into a solid succeeds, the solid appears as the base feature (named **Imported1**) in a new part file.
  • If the surfaces represent multiple closed volumes, then one part is generated for each closed volume.
  • If the attempt to knit the surfaces fail, the surfaces are grouped into one or more surface features (named **Surface-Imported1...**) in a new part file.
  • If you import a **.dxf** or **.dwg** file, the **DXF/DWG import wizard** appears to guide you through the import process.

- The imported parts must be of uniform thickness to fold and unfold properly.

- After the part is opened in SolidWorks, sheet metal parameters such as Rip ⬚ , Fixed face or edge ⬚ , Bend radius ⬚ , etc., should be added before the Flat Pattern can be created.

- The converted part appears on the Feature Manager Design tree, it contains the features Sheet Metal1 ⬚ , Flatten Bend1 ⬚ , and Process Bend1 ⬚ .

- The sheet metal part can now be Flattened and Folded by toggling the Suppression state ⬚ of the Process Bends.

Sheet Metal Conversions
From IGES to SolidWorks Flat Pattern

Dimensioning Standards: **ANSI**
Units: **INCHES** – 3 Decimals

Tools Needed:

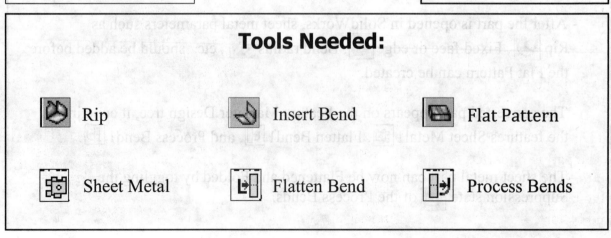

Rip

Insert Bend

Flat Pattern

Sheet Metal

Flatten Bend

Process Bends

1. Opening an IGES document:

- Go to **File / Open**. Change Files of Type to **IGES**.

- Browse to the Training Files folder and open: **Sheet Metal Conversion**.

- Click **No** to skip the Import-Diagnosis option.

- Click **No** to skip the Feature-Recognition option.

- The part is imported into **Solid**Works as the base feature with no history.

2. Creating the Rips:

- Click **Rip** on the sheet metal toolbar or select **Insert / Sheet Metal / Rip**.

- Select the **inner edge** as shown.

- The 2 arrows indicate that the Rip command is going to cut both walls.

Select the 1ˢᵗ edge.

RIP

The RIP command creates a tear between the 2 walls. A Gap is entered and the rip direction can be toggled to achieve the Butt, Over-lapped, or Under-lapped results.

Rip1

Rip Parameters

Edge<1>

Change Direction

0.01000in

- Click on the arrow as noted, to keep the correct sides from being ripped.

- Use the **Default Gap** (.010).

Either click on Change Direction -OR- click on the arrow itself.

Default

Direction 1
(Over lapped)

Direction 2
(Under lapped)

- Select a total of **4 edges** (2 on each side) as indicated.

- Click **OK** .

Arrows indicate
the trimmed side

Select
4 edges

3. Inserting the Sheet Metal Parameters:

- Click **Insert Bends** command or select **Insert / Sheet Metal / Bends**.

- Select the inside **face** to use as the Fixed Face.

- Enter **.015 in.** for inside Bend Radius.

- Click **OK** .

- The system reports some Auto Relief Cuts were made for some bends.

- Click OK .

Fixed Face

Sheet Metal

Bends

Bend Parameters

Face<1>

0.01500in

0.00000in

☑ **Bend Allowance**

K-Factor

K 0.5

☑ **Auto Relief**

Rectangular

0.5

Rip Parameters

SolidWorks

Auto relief cuts were made for one or more bends.

OK

4. Adding Fillets:

- Click **Fillet** command or select **Insert / Features / Fillet/Round** (or use the Break Corner option on the Sheet Metal toolbar).

Edges to
fillet (2X)

- Enter **.100 in**. for Radius.

- Select the **2 edges** as noted.

- Click **OK**.

- Rotate the model to
verify the resulted fillets.

5. Switching to the Flat pattern:

- To examine the part in the flattened view; click the

Flatten command on the Sheet Metal toolbar.

6. Saving your work:

- Click **File / Save As**.

- Enter **Sheet Metal Conversion** for file name.

- Click **Save**.

Questions for Review

Sheet Metal Conversions

1. An IGES file can be imported into SolidWorks and converted into a sheet metal part.
   a. True
   b. False

2. DXF and DWG are imported into SolidWorks as 2D Sketches, using the DXF/DWG Import- Wizard.
   a. True
   b. False

3. After being imported into SolidWorks, the IGES file can be flattened instantly.
   a. True
   b. False

4. The imported parts must be of uniform thickness to fold and unfold properly.
   a. True
   b. False

5. The Rip feature removes 1 material thickness based on the side of the direction arrow that you select.
   a. True
   b. False

6. When applying the sheet metal parameters you do not have to specify a fixed face.
   a. True
   b. False

7. The width and depth of the relief cuts are fixed and cannot be changed.
   a. True
   b. False

8. The Folded and the Flat pattern can be toggled by moving the Rollback Line up or down.
   a. True
   b. False

7. FALSE	8. TRUE
5. TRUE	6. FALSE
3. FALSE	4. TRUE
1. TRUE	2. TRUE

Sheet Metal Gussets

Sheet Metal gussets can now be created in SolidWorks 2015 with specific indents that go across bends. This exercise with guide us through the creation of a gusset in a sheet metal part.

1. Opening a sheet metal part document:

- Click **File / Open**.

- Browse to the Training files folder and open a part document named: **Sheet-Metal Gusset**.

2. Creating a gusset:

- Click the **Sheet Metal Gusset** command from the Sheet Metal tool tab (arrow).

- Under the **Position** section, select the **2 Faces** as indicated in the balloon number 1 for Supporting Faces.

- Select the **horizontal edge** in the middle of the 2 supporting faces as noted in the balloon number-2 to be used as a reference to align the gusset.

- Select the **Vertex** as noted in the balloon number 3 to be used for dimensioning.

Reference edge ②

Reference point ③

2 supporting faces ①

- Move down to the **Profile** section and click the **Profile Dimensions** option (arrow).

- Enter **.500 in**. for Profile Length.

- Enter **.500 in**. for Profile-Height.

- Click the **Rounded Gusset** button to create a gusset with a rounded edge.

- Move down to the Dimensions section and enter the following:

    * Indent Width Dimension: **.1875 in**.

    * Indent Thickness Dimension: **.060 in**.

    * Inner Corner Fillet: **.030 in**.

    * Outer Corner Fillet: **.090 in**.

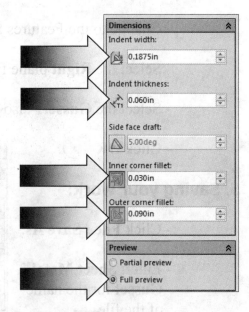

- Enable the **Full Preview** option in the Preview section.

- Click **OK** ✓ to complete the gusset.

3. Viewing the resulted gusset:

- Zoom in on the new gusset to see its details. Also rotate the view to see the indent from the back side.

- Click on the feature itself to see its dimensions

- The gusset has a built in sketch that can be edited to change to a custom profile if needed.

4. Mirroring the gusset:

- Change to the Features tool tab and click the **Mirror** command.

- Select the **Right** plane from the Feature tree for Mirror-Plane.

- Select the **Gusset1** also from the Feature tree for Features-to-Mirror.

- Click **OK** ✓.

5. Saving your work:

- Click **File / Save As**.

- Enter: **Sheet Metal Gusset** for the name of the file.

- Click **Save**.
  Click Yes to replace the old file with the new when prompted.

CHAPTER 15 (cont.)

Flat Pattern Stent

Flat Pattern Stent
A Different Approach

- Using the built-in Sheet Metal features in SolidWorks you can flatten or roll solid models such as wire mesh screens, grill meshes, or stent patterns.

- When designing a sheet metal part, the material setback is something we must keep in mind: The Bend allowance and bend deduction calculations are methods you can choose to determine the flat length of sheet stock to give the desired dimension of the bent part. This lesson uses the default settings of the K-Factor to calculate the bend allowance (BA=P(R + KT) A/180).

- K-Factor is a ratio that represents the location of the neutral sheet with respect to the thickness of the sheet metal part. When you select K-Factor as the bend allowance, you can specify a K-Factor bend table. The SolidWorks application also comes with a K-Factor bend table in Microsoft Excel format.

- There are several known methods for creating this types of patterns, this lesson will walk you through the use of rolling and unrolling a cylinder and its pattern, using the Sheet Metal functions in Solidworks.

Flat Pattern Stent
Flat Pattern Approach

Dimensioning Standards: **ANSI**

Units: **INCHES** – 3 Decimals

Tools Needed:

 Revolve Boss-Base   Flatten   Unfold

 Fold   Extruded Cut   Fillet / Round

Sheet Metal **STEP Files** and **Smart Fasteners**

1. Opening an Assembly Step File:

- Go to **File / Open**. Browse to the Training Files folder, change the Files of Type to **STEP** and open the STEP document named: **SM-Assembly.step**.

- The part files from the STEP document will appear as SolidWorks documents on the FeatureManager tree without any model history.

- Click **OK** if the message Improve Free Curves appears.

- There are 4 components in this assembly and they have not yet been constrained.

- The Housing will be used as the Fixed Component and the 3 Card Guides will be left un-constrained for the purpose of this exercise.

- Change the Shading option to: **Shaded with Edges** (arrow).

Shaded with Edges

2. Mating the components:

- In order to mate the Housing Component to the assembly's Origin, we'll need to align the 3 Front, Top & Right planes.

Coincident 2 Front Planes

- Click the **Mate** command from the Assembly toolbar.

- Select the **Front** plane of the Housing and the **Front** plane of the Assembly.

- Select **Coincident** from the list.

- Click **OK**.

- Add the same Coincident mate to the **Top** plane of the Housing and the **Top** plane of the Assembly.

Coincident 2 Top Planes

- Repeat the Coincident mate for the **Right** plane of the Housing and the **Right** plane of the Assembly.

Coincident 2 Right Planes

- The Housing component should be **Fixed** (f) at this time.

3. Adding other Mates:

- Other mates can be added to constrain the other components, but later on they'll need to be suppressed so that the final sheet metal components can be flattened properly.

- In this exercise we will leave the components un-constrained to help focus on other areas.

4. Examining the components:

- The imported components have **Sharp corners** all around, which is not suitable for the Sheet Metal processes.

- Sheet Metal parameters* must be added to fully convert the imported part into a SolidWorks Sheet Metal part.

Sharp Corner(s)

5. Adding the Sheet Metal tool tab:

- In an assembly, if the Sheet Metal tool tab is not visible on the CommandManager, do the following to add it:

Right Click

Select Customize CommandManager

- Right click on the Assembly tool tab and select the **Customized CommandManager** option (arrow).

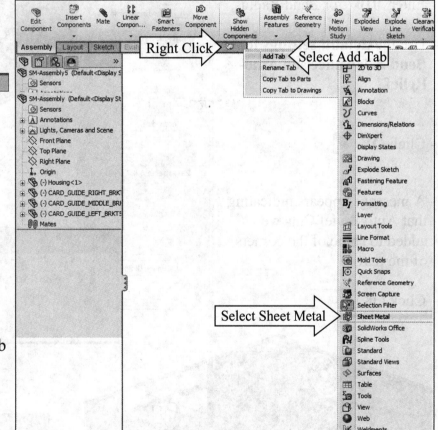

Right Click — Select Add Tab

Select Sheet Metal

- Right click the tab and pick **Add Tab** (arrow).

- Select the **Sheet Metal** toolbar from the list (arrow).

- The Sheet Metal tool tab is now added to the CommandManager.

- Switch to the Sheet Metal tool tab (arrow).

Sheet Metal Tab

6. Inserting Sheet Metal parameters*:

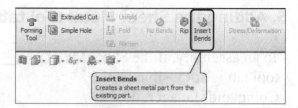

- Select the component **Housing** and click the

Edit Component command .

- From the Sheet Metal tool tab

click the **Insert Bends** command.

- Select the **Fixed face** as noted.

- Enter **.010"** for Bend Radius.

- Use the **default settings** for **Bend Allowance** and **Auto-Relief**.

- Click **OK** .

- A message appears indicating that Auto Relief Cuts were added to some of the corners of the part.

- Click OK .

Select Fixed face

Relief Corner(s)

- Zoom in to see the relief corners.

7. Viewing the Flat Pattern:

- From the Sheet Metal tool tab, click the

  Flatten command .

- The Housing is flattened. The orientation of the flattened view is based on the Fixed face that was specified in step number 6.

- Click **Flatten** again to fold it back.

- Click-off the **Edit Component** command.

8. Converting the 2nd component:

- Select the **Card Guide Left** as shown and click the

  Edit Component command.

- From the Sheet Metal tool tab, select **Insert Bends** command.

- Select the **Fixed face** as noted.

- Enter **.010"** for Radius.

- Click **OK** .

Select Fixed face

- Click off the **Edit Component** command.

9. Converting the 3rd component:

- Select the **Card Guide Middle** as shown and click the **Edit-Component** command.

- From the Sheet Metal tool tab select **Insert Bends** .

- Select the **Fixed face** as noted.

- Enter **.010"** for Bend Radius and use the **default settings** for the Bend Allowance and K-Factor.

- Click **OK** ✓ .

- Click-off the **Edit Component** command.

10. Converting the 4th component:

- Select the **Card Guide Right** as shown and click the **Edit Component** command.

- From the Sheet Metal tool tab, click:
Insert Bends .

- Select the **Fixed face** as noted.

- Enter **.010"** for Bend Radius.

- Click **OK** ✓ .

Select Fixed face——

- Click-off the **Edit Component** command.

11. Using the Hole Series:

- The hole series is an Assembly Feature, used to create a series of holes through the individual parts of an assembly.

- Unlike other assembly features, the holes are contained in the individual parts as externally referenced features. If you edit a hole series within an assembly, the individual parts are modified.

- From the Assembly tool tab, select **Assembly Features / Hole Series** .

- From the FeatureManager, click: **Create New Hole** (arrow).

- The mouse cursor changes into the **Sketch Point** command .

- Create **3 points** approximately as shown.

- Each point will become the center of a hole.

- Add an **ALONG Z** relation (Vertical) between the 3 points.

- Add the dimensions as indicated to fully define the positions of the points.

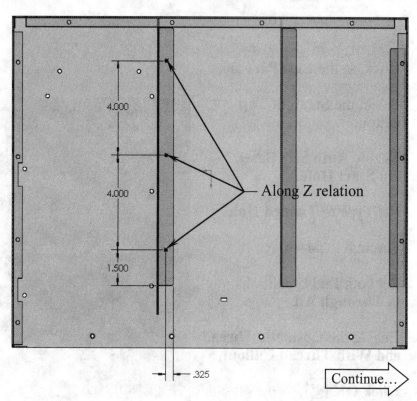

Continue…

- Click the **First Part** tab.

- Click the **Countersink** option.

- Select the following:

Standard: **Ansi Inch**

Type: **Flat Head Screw**

Size: **#4**

Fit: **Normal**

- Use the default settings for Custom Sizing.

- Click the **Middle Part** tab.

- Select the Hole button.

- Enable the check box:

  Auto Size based on Start Hole.

- Click on the **Last Part** tab.

- Select the **Straight Tap** button.

- Enable **Auto Size Based On Start Hole**.

- Set Type to **Tapped Hole**.

- Set Size to **#4-40**.

- Set both End Conditions to **Through All**.

- Enable the **Cosmetic Thread** and **With Thread Callout**.

- Click **OK** ✓ .

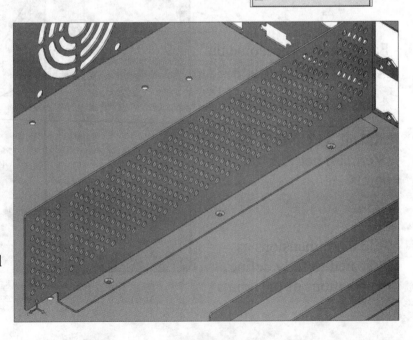

12. Using the Hole Wizard:

- Hole wizard is an Assembly Feature, which creates these types of holes:

- Counterbore
- Countersink
- Hole
- Straight Tap
- Tapered Tap
- Legacy

Feature Scope

○ All components

◉ Selected components

Enable → ☑ Propagate feature to parts

☑ Auto-select

- From the Assembly tool tab, click **Assembly Features / Hole Wizard**.

Hole Wizard

- Select the **Countersink** option under the **Type** tab.

- Set the options **to match** the last 3 holes in step number 11.

- Switch to the **Positions** tab.

- Click approximately as shown to create **3 points**.

- Each point represents the center for that hole.

- Add relation and dimensions as indicated.

- Click **OK** ☑.

Type tab

Positions tab

4.000

4.000

1.500

Along **Z** relation

.325

13. Verifying the two hole types:

- Even though the 6 holes were created with 2 different hole options, they are exactly identical.

- Open the Card Guide Middle to verify that the holes are actually there on the part.

- The new feature in step 12 (propagate feature to parts) allows these Assembly Features to appear in the part mode as well.

14. Adding holes on the Card Guide Right:

- Repeat either step number 11 (Hole Series) or step number 12 (Hole Wizard) and create 3 more holes for the last Card Guide.

Add 3 more C'Sinks

- Use the same dimensions from the previous step to position the holes.

15. Adding the Smart Fasteners:

- Click **Smart Fasteners** 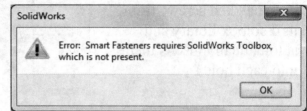 from the Assembly tool tab.

- An error message appears asking for SolidWorks Toolbox to be activated** (Required SolidWorks Office Professional or SolidWorks Premium).

** To activate Toolbox, go to:

> - **Tools / Add Ins**.

Enable Toolbox & Browser

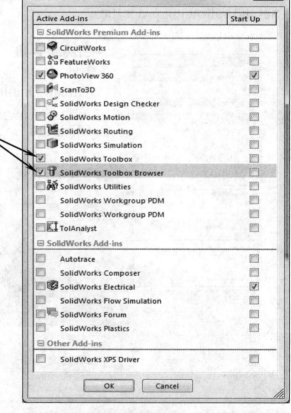

> - Enable **SolidWorks Toolbox** <u>and</u> **SolidWorks Toolbox Browser**.
>
> - Click **OK** 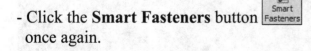.

- Click the **Smart Fasteners** button 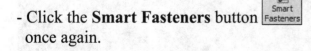 once again.

- Another message pops up indicating that the Smart Fasteners calculation may take extra time, click **OK** [OK].

- Select one of the C'sink
  holes from the graphics area.

- Click **Populate All** (arrow).

- The system searches for the
  best matched screws from
  its Toolbox library and
  automatically inserts them
  into each hole.

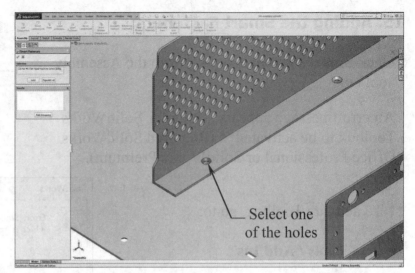

Select one
of the holes

- Set the following properties:

- Size: **#4-40**   Length: **.125"**   Drive Type: **Cross**

- Thread Display: **Simplified**

Flat Head
screw

- Click **OK** .

Optional: A washer and a hex nut
can be added if required.

16. Creating an Exploded View:

Option 1

- Create an exploded view with all 4 parts show in folded stage as shown.

- When an exploded view is created, SolidWorks also creates an animated configuration, which can be played back and saved as an AVI file format.

Option 2

- Create a 2nd exploded view with all 4 parts as shown in the Flatten view below.

NOTES:

- *Edit each component in order to switch from the Folded to flatten stage.*

- *Configurations can also be used to capture the flat pattern of each component.*

17. Saving your work:

- Click **File / Save As**.

- For the name of the file enter:
  SM_Assembly_Smart Fasteners.

- Click **Save**.

- Close all documents.

Adding Parts to the Toolbox Library

Customized parts or fasteners can be added to existing Toolbox folders.

For parts that are stored in the shared library, administrators can control who can add or change parts by creating a Toolbox password and setting permissions for Toolbox functions for each user (see Toolbox Permission in the SolidWorks Help section).

1. Starting the Toolbox Settings Utility:

    - From the Windows desktop select the following:
    Start / Programs / SolidWorks 2015 /
    SolidWorks Tools / Toolbox Settings.

    - Select the option number 2:
    Customize your hardware.

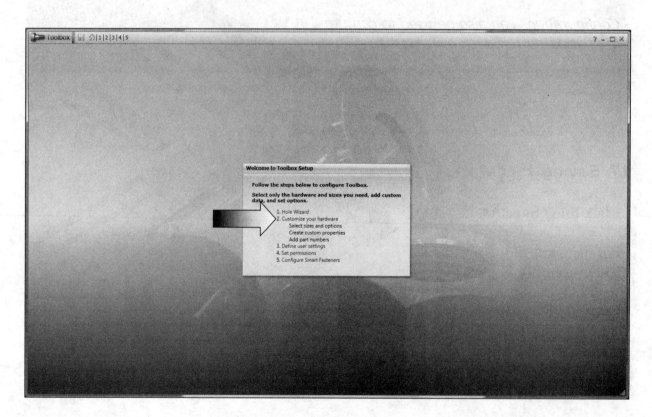

2. Adding a part to a folder:

- From the upper left side of the tree, select the following:

ANSI Inch.
Bolts and Screws
Countersunk Head

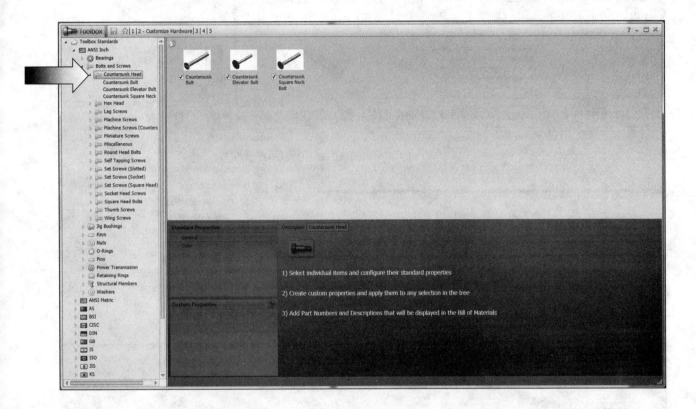

- In this folder there are 3 existing screw / bolt types: Countersunk Bolt, Countersunk Elevator Bolt, and Countersunk Square Neck Bolt.

- Right click the Countersunk Head folder and select **Add File** (arrow).

- Browse to the Training Files folder and select the document named:
C-Sink .250-20x1x0.75-Bolt.sldprt and open it.

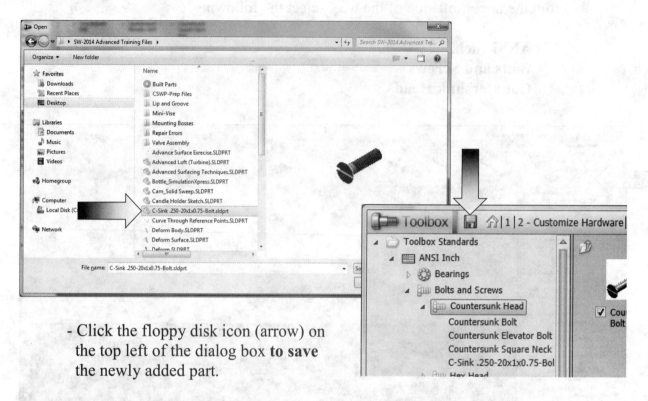

- Click the floppy disk icon (arrow) on
the top left of the dialog box **to save**
the newly added part.

- The new part and its name appear in the display window (arrow).

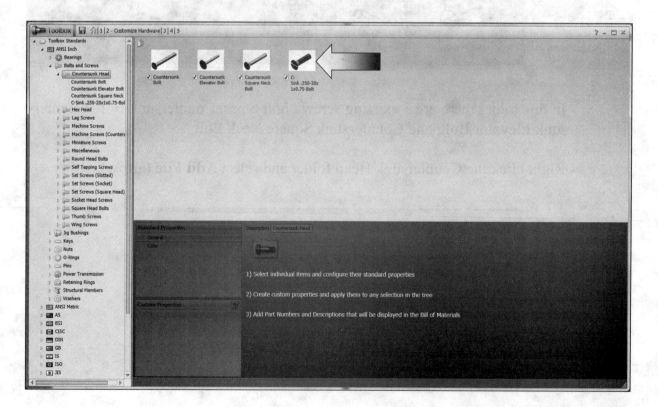

3. Activating Toolbox:

- Launch the Solidworks application.

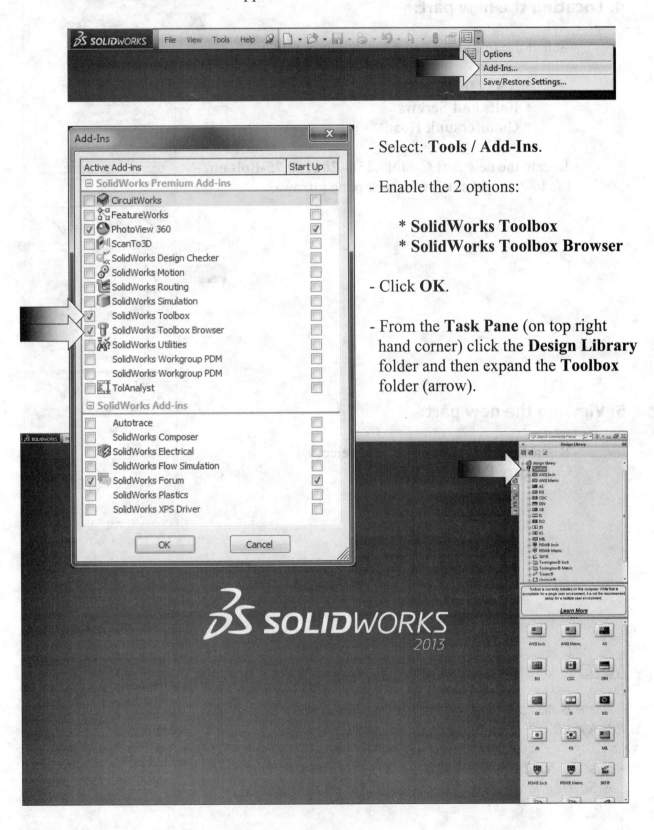

- Select: **Tools / Add-Ins**.

- Enable the 2 options:

    * SolidWorks Toolbox
    * SolidWorks Toolbox Browser

- Click **OK**.

- From the **Task Pane** (on top right hand corner) click the **Design Library** folder and then expand the **Toolbox** folder (arrow).

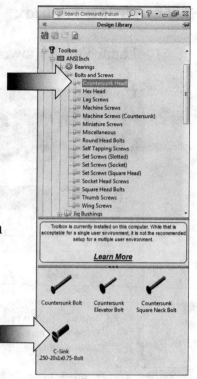

4. Locating the new part:

- Select the following under the Toolbox folder:

    * **ANSI Inch**
    * **Bolts and Screws**
    * **Countersunk Head**

- Locate the new part **C-Sink .250-.20x1x0.75-Bolt** on the lower right side of the task pane (arrow).

5. Viewing the new part:

- Right click on the new part and select: **Configure Part**.

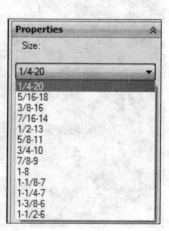

NOTE:

- _There is no configuration created for this custom screw, its length will have to be modified manually._

- _Existing Toolbox parts will have several configurations such as Size, Length, Thread Display, etc., to choose from._

- The new Toolbox part appears in its own window.

6. Adding a Part Number and Description:

- Click the Edit button (arrow).

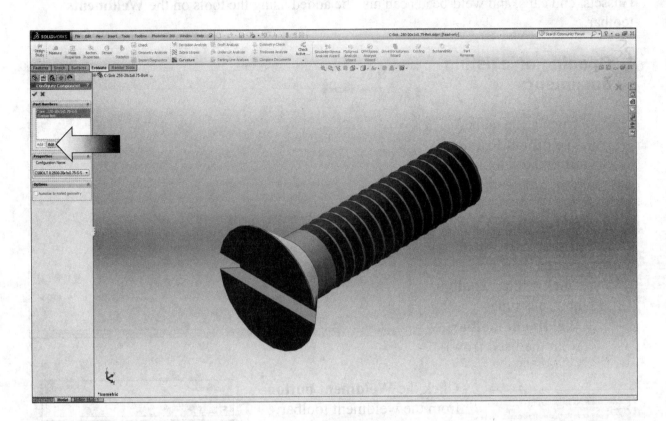

- Enter a new **Part Number** (if applicable).

- Enter **Custom Bolt** as Description.

- **Save** and close your documents.

Weldments – Structural Members

The options in Weldments allows you to develop a weldment structure as a single multibody-part. The basic framework is defined using a 2D or a 3D sketch, then structural members like square or round Tubes are added by sweeping the tube profile along the framework. Gussets, end caps, and weld-beads can also be added using the tools on the **Weldments** toolbar.

1. Opening an existing document:

- Open a file named **Weldment Frame** from the Training CD.

2. Enabling the Weldment toolbar:

- Click **View / Toolbar** and select the **Weldment toolbar** from the list (arrow).

- Click the **Weldment button** from the weldment toolbar.

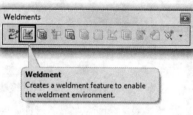

Weldment
Creates a weldment feature to enable the weldment environment.

- A Weldment Feature appears on the feature tree along with a Weldment Cut List (arrows), which indicates the items from the model to include in this cut list.

- A single 3D Sketch is created for the purpose of this exercise. In reality, multiple sketches (2D & 3D) can be used to work with weldments.

3. Adding Structural Members:

- Click the **Structural Member** button from the Weldment toolbar.

Weldments

Structural Member
Creates a structural member feature by sweeping pre-defined profiles along user defined paths.

- Select the following:

- **Ansi Inch.**
- **Square Tube**
- **4 X 4 X 0.25**

- Click the **4 lines** on the top of the frame.

- Select the **MITER** under Apply Corner-Treatment.

- Click **OK**.

Structural Member

Message
Select sketch segments for defining path. You can rotate the profile by a specified angle.

Selections
Standard:
ansi inch

Type :
Tube (square)

Size:
TS4x4x0.25

Groups:
Group1

New Group

Settings
Path segments:
Line3@3DSketch1
Line4@3DSketch1
Line1@3DSketch1
Line2@3DSketch1

☑ Apply corner treatment

☐ Merge miter trimmed bodies

G1 0.000in

G2 0.000in

☐ Mirror profile

Select the 4 upper lines

1st Group

- By default, the profile of the tube is automatically centered on the end of each line.

- Try out all 3 options for corner treatments: End Miter, End Butt1, and End Butt2.

- Switch back to the End Miter option when finished.

End Miter

End Butt1
(Overlapped)

End Butt2
(Under-lapped)

4. Adding Structural Members to Contiguous Groups*:

- Repeat the previous Step and add another 4 square tubes to the 2nd group as shown.

- Use these same settings:

- **Ansi Inch.**
- **Square Tube**
- **4 X 4 X 0.25**

2nd Group —

Contiguous Group

* A group is a collection of related segments in a structural member. There are 2 types of groups, one is called Contiguous, where a continuous contour of segments is joined end-to-end. The other is called Parallel, which includes a discontinuous collection of parallel segments. Segments in the group cannot touch each other.

3rd Group —

Contiguous Group

- Repeat the same step for the 3rd group

- Follow the same procedure and add the same size tubing to the vertical members as note for the 4th group.

Note: Select the exact same members on both sides (total of 12).

4th Group —
(both sides)

Parallel Group

5. Adding Structural Members to the Parallel Groups:

- Repeat the previous step and add the same structural members to the 5th group as indicated.

Note

You can define a group in a single plane or in multiple planes. A 3D sketch is best suited for weldment designs since all entities can be drawn and controlled in the same sketch.

5th Group
(both sides)

Parallel Group

- Create the same type of structural Members for the 6th and 7th group, which has only 2 lines in each group...

6th Group
Rotate 30 deg.

- Rotate the profile to **30 deg.** for the 6th group and **60 deg.** for the 7th group.

- There are several over-lapped areas that need trimming, we will look into that in the next steps.

Parallel Group

7th Group
Rotate 60 deg.

6. Hiding the 3D sketch:

- Right click on one of the lines
  in the 3D sketch and select **Hide** .

- Notice the overlapping areas in the enlarged view below?
  For practice purposes, we will learn to use different trim
  options to cut the tubes to their exact lengths and angles.

Overlapped

Overlapped

7. Trimming the Structural Members:

- Click **Trim/Extend** on the Weldment toolbar.

- Under **Corner Type**, use the default **End Trim**.

Select 4 **Bodies To Be Trimmed**

- Under **Bodies To Be Trimmed**, select the 4 vertical tubes as shown.

- Under **Trimming Boundary**, select the **Body** option (arrow).

- Select the 6 horizontal tubes as indicated, for use as trimming bodies.

Select 6 **Trimming Bodies**

> ### Trim with Bodies
>
> *This option allows either to Trim or Extend 2 segments so they butt up correctly.*
>
> *Selecting **Face/Plane** as the **Trimming Boundary** is normally more efficient and offers better performance.*

- Click **OK**.

8. Trimming the Parallel Groups:

- Select the **Trim/Extend** command once again from the weldment toolbar.

- Click in the **Bodies To Be Trimmed**

Select 4 **Bodies To Be Trimmed**

dialog to activate it and select the next 4 vertical tubes as noted.

- For **Trimming Boundary**, select the **Body** option again (Arrow).

- Select the 6 horizontal tubes as shown, for use as trimming bodies.

Select 6 **Trimming Bodies**

- Click **OK**.

9. Trimming the next sets of Parallel Groups:

- Select the **Trim/Extend** command from the weldment toolbar.

- Click in the **Bodies To Be Trimmed** dialog to activate, and select the 4 structural members as noted.

Select 4 **Bodies To Be Trimmed**

- For **Trimming Boundary**, click the **Body** option (Arrow).

- Select the 4 horizontal tubes as shown, for use as **Trimming Bodies**.

Select 4 **Trimming Bodies**

- Click **OK** .

10. More Trimming:

- Select the **Trim/Extend** command from the weldment toolbar.

Select 6 **Bodies To Be Trimmed**

- For **Bodies To Be Trimmed** select the 6 structural members as indicated.

- For **Trimming Boundary**, click the **Body** option (Arrow).

- Select the 8 horizontal structural members as shown, for **Trimming Bodies**.

Select 8 **Trimming Bodies**

- Click **OK** ✓.

11. Trimming with Face/Plane:

- Select the **Trim/Extend** command from the weldment toolbar.

Select 2
**Bodies To
Be Trimmed**

- For **Bodies To Be Trimmed** select the 2 structural members as indicated.

- For **Trimming Boundary**, click the **Face / Plane** option (Arrow).

- Select the planar surface as noted, for **Trimming Bodies**.

Select **Face**
for **Trimming
Boundary**

💡 Trim with Face/Plane

This option allows a planar face(s) as a trimming boundary to trim one or more solid bodies.

*Selecting **Face/Plane** as the **Trimming Boundary** is normally more efficient and offers better performance.*

- Click **OK** .

12. More Trimming with Face/Plane:

- Select the **Trim/Extend** 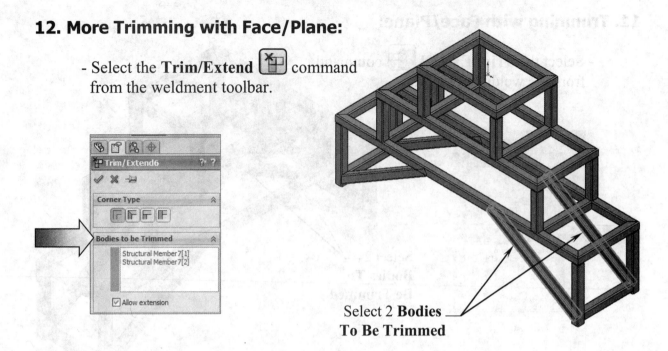 command from the weldment toolbar.

Select 2 **Bodies**
To Be Trimmed

- For **Bodies To Be Trimmed** select the 2 structural members as indicated.

- For **Trimming Boundary**, click the **Face / Plane** option (Arrow).

- Select the planar surface on the back of the vertical tube as noted, for **Trimming Bodies**.

Select **Face**
(rotate around)
for **Trimming
Boundary**

- Click **OK**.

13. Trimming the last 4 structural members:

- Select the **Trim/Extend** 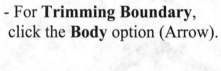 command from the weldment toolbar.

Select 4 **Bodies**
To Be Trimmed

- For **Bodies To Be Trimmed** select the 4 structural members as shown.

- For **Trimming Boundary**, click the **Body** option (Arrow).

- Select the 2 horizontal tubes as noted, for **Trimming Bodies**.

Select 2
Trimming
Bodies

(Front View)

- Click **OK** ✓.

14. Adding the foot pads:

- Insert a new sketch on the bottom surface of one of the 4 legs.

- Sketch the profile as shown.

- The 4 circles are concentric with the corner radius.

- Add the dimensions and relations needed to fully define the sketch.

- Mirror the sketch to make a total of 4 foot pads.

Note:
Add a couple of centerlines as shown prior to making the mirror.

Add centerlines to mirror

- Since the 4 foot pads have the same thickness, we can extrude them at the same time.

- Click **Extruded Boss/ Base**.

- Enter the following:

  * Type: **Blind**

  * Depth: **1.000**

- Click **OK** .

15. Adding the Gussets:

- Rotate and zoom to an orientation that looks similar to the view below.

- Click the **Gusset** Command.

- For **Supporting Faces**, Select the **2 faces** as indicated.

- Enter the following:

  * Distance1: **5.00 in.**

  * Distance2: **5.00 in.**

  * Distance3: **.500 in.**

  * Thickness: **.500"**
    (Both Sides)

  * Location: **Midpoint**

- Click **OK** .

Supporting Faces

16. Adding more Gussets:

- Repeat the step 15 and add a gusset to each corner of the frame.

- Next, we're going to add the weld beads around the gussets. Weld beads can be added as full length, intermittent, or staggered fillet weld beads between any intersecting weldment

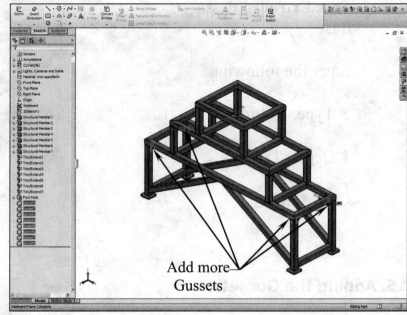

Add more Gussets

entities such as structural members, plate weldments, or gussets.

17. Adding the Fillet-Beat icon to the Weldments toolbar:

- The **Fillet Beat** icon may need to be added to the Weldments toolbar.

- Do the following to add the missing icon:

- Select **Tools / Customize**.

- Click the **Commands** tab (circled).

- Select the **Weldments** option under **Categories** (arrow).

- Drag the Fillet Bead icon and drop it to the left of the Weld Bead icon as illustrated.

- Click **OK** to close the Customize dialog box.

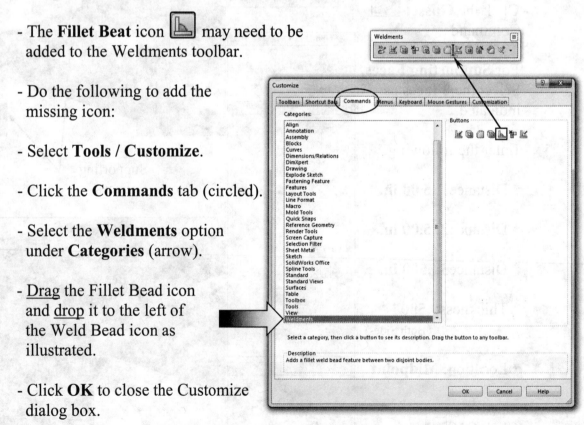

18. Adding the Fillet Beads:

- Click Fillet Bead on the Weldment toolbar.

- From the Weld Bead properties tree, enter the following:

* Bead Type: **Full Length**

* Fillet Size: **.250 in.**

* Tangent Prop: **Enabled**

* Face Set1: **Select the 2 faces** as noted.

Select **2 Faces** (front & back)
for Face Set1

- For **Face Set2**, select the next 2 faces as indicated.

(Intersecting Edges.
Highlights edges where
Face Set1 *and* ***Face Set2***
intersect. You can right-
click an edge and select
Delete *to remove from*
the weld bead).

Select **2 Faces**
for Face Set2

- Enable the **Other Side** checkbox and apply the same settings to the back end of the gusset.

- Different bead type or fillet size can be added to the other side, but we are going to use the same settings as the first side.

- Click **OK** .

- A bead call out is added automatically (see example below).

Example: 0.25 = *Length of the leg of the fillet bead.*
0.375 = *Length of each bead segment.*
0.7   = *Distance between the start of each bead.*

Intermittent or Staggered

19. Adding more Fillet Beads:

- Repeat step 17 and add a set of fillet beads to each gusset that was created earlier.

- When adding the fillet beads, try using the different types of beads: Full Length, Intermittent, and Staggered to see the different results and callouts.

Add more Fillet Beads

20. Viewing the Weldment Cut List:

- Locate the **Cut List** on the FeatureManager tree and click the Plus (+) sign to expand.

- The Cut List needs to be updated every time something is added to the model.

- An icon in front of the cut list indicates that it needs updating and the icon indicates the list is up to date.

- The current list displays all items in the order that they were created. We will update the list in the next step.

21. Updating the Cut List:

- Right click on the cut list and select **Update** (arrow).

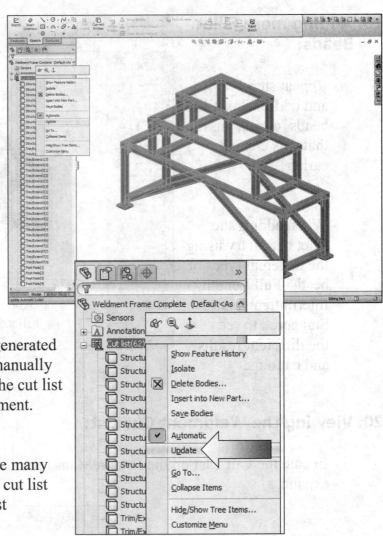

- Notice the option **Automatic** is on by default? This option organizes all of the weldment entities in the cut list for the new weldment parts.

- Although the cut list is generated automatically, you can manually specify when to update the cut list in a weldment part document.

- This enables you to make many changes, then update the cut list once; however the cut list updates automatically when you open a drawing that references the list.

- At this time, the icon in front of the cut list is changed to ⊞ which indicates the cut list is now up to date.

- The cut list <u>Table</u> can now be viewed by accessing the Properties of one of the item folders.

22. Creating a drawing (OPTIONAL):

- A drawing that includes the cut list can be generated. (Refer to the Part 1 Basic Tools textbook for more information on how to create a detail drawing in SolidWorks 2015).

ITEM NO.	QTY.	DESCRIPTION	LENGTH
1	2	TUBE SQUARE .ADD X .ADD X .25	46
2	6	TUBE SQUARE .ADD X .ADD X .25	40
3	2	TUBE SQUARE .ADD X .ADD X .25	94
4	2	TUBE SQUARE .ADD X .ADD X .25	142
5	8	TUBE SQUARE .ADD X .ADD X .25	20
6	4	TUBE SQUARE .ADD X .ADD X .25	72
7	4	TUBE SQUARE .ADD X .ADD X .25	38
8	4	TUBE SQUARE .ADD X .ADD X .25	76.58
9	4	FOOT PADS	
10	1	CHASSIS	
11	7	HUB PADS	

COMPANY NAME

XXXXX

C XXXXX XX

23. Saving your work:

- Click **File / Save As**.

- Enter **Weldments Frame** for the name of the file.

- Click **Save**.

- Replace the existing file when prompted.

<u>Optional:</u>
Use either the Move/Copy command
(Insert / Features) or the Exploded
View command (Insert /Exploded
View) to create the view similar to
the one shown here.

CHAPTER 17

Core & Cavity - Linear Parting Lines

Creating a Core and Cavity
Linear parting Lines

- A mold is normally designed in SolidWorks using a sequence of intergraded tools that control the mold creation process.
Using the finished model, these mold tools can be used to analyze and correct deficiencies in the part.

- The process usually follows these steps: Draft analysis, Undercut Detection, Parting Lines, Shut-Off Surfaces, Parting Surfaces, Interlock Surfaces (Ruled Surfaces), and Tooling Split.

- The Parting Lines ⬡ lie along the edge of the molded part, between the core and the cavity surfaces. They are used to create the Parting Surfaces and to separate the surfaces.

- The Shut-Off Surfaces ⬖ are created after the Parting Lines. A shut-off surface closes up a through hole by creating a surface patch along the Edges that form a continuous loop -OR- a parting line you previously created, to define a loop.

- After the Parting Lines and the Shut-Off Surfaces are determined, the Parting Surfaces 🗈 are created. The Parting Surfaces extrude from the parting lines and are used to separate the mold cavity from the core.

- After a parting surface is defined, the Tooling Split tool 🗈 is used to create the core and cavity blocks for the model. To create a tooling split, at least three surface bodies are needed in the Surface Bodies folder 🗈 Surface Bodies.

- With most mold parts, the interlock surfaces 🗈 need to be created. The interlock surfaces help prevent the core and cavity blocks from shifting, and are located along the perimeter of the parting surfaces. Usually they have a 5-degree taper.

Creating a Core and Cavity
Linear Parting Lines

| Dimensioning Standards: **ANSI** |
| Units: **INCHES** – 3 Decimals |

Tools Needed:

 Parting Lines Parting Surfaces Shut-Off Surfaces

 Tooling Split Planes 2D Sketch

1. Opening an existing Parasolid document:

- Select **File / Open**.

- Browse to the Training Files folder, change the Files of Type to **Parasolid**.

- Select **Remote Control.x_b** and click **Open**.

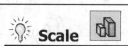

☀️ **Scale** 🏢

The Parasolid part has already been scaled to 1.05%, about its Centroid.

2. Creating the Parting Lines:

- Click or select:

Insert / Molds / Parting Line.

Parting Lines
Establishes parting lines to separate core and cavity surfaces.

- From the Feature tree, select the **Top** plane for Direction of Pull.

- Enter **1deg** for Draft Angle.

- Click **Draft Analysis**.

Straddle Faces
Negative Drafts
No Drafts
Positive Drafts

- The system automatically selects the lower edges of the part and places them in the Parting Lines section.

Straddle Faces

* Displays any faces that contain both positive and negative types of draft.
* Typically, these are the faces that require creating a split line.

- Click **OK** ✅.

3. Creating the Shut-Off Surfaces:

- Click or select **Insert / Molds / Shut-Off Surfaces**.

Shut-Off Surface1

Message

The mold is separable into core and cavity.

Edges

Edge<1>
Edge<2>
Edge<3>
Edge<4>
Edge<5>
Edge<6>
Edge<7>
Edge<8>
Edge<9>
Edge<10>
Edge<11>
Edge<12>
Edge<13>

Undo   Redo

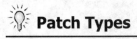 ☑ Knit
☑ Show preview
☑ Show callouts

Reset All Patch Types

- The system automatically selects the edges of all through openings and labels them as Loop/Contacts.

Reset All Patch Types

Resets all through hole surface patches to one of the 3 settings.

— All No-Fill —
— All Contact —
— All Tangent —

Patch Types

Only one Shut-Off Surface feature is allowed in a model. Therefore, within the one feature, you must assign a fill type of **Contact**, **Tangent**, or **No Fill** to every hole.

- Click **OK** ✅.

4. Creating the Parting Surfaces:

- Click or select **Insert / Molds / Parting Surfaces**.

Parting Surfaces
Creates parting surfaces between core and cavity surfaces.

- In the Mold Parameters, select **Perpendicular to Pull**.

- In the Parting Line selection, select the **Parting Line1** from the FeatureManager Tree.

- In the Parting Surface selection, enter **1.500 in**.

- Select **Sharp Edges** under Smoothing section.

Smooth Edges

Sharp Edges
(A higher value creates a smoother transition between adjacent edges)

- Click **OK**.

5. Sketching the profile of the mold-blocks:

- Select the <u>Top</u> plane and open a new sketch .

- Sketch a Center Rectangle approximately as shown.

- Add the width and the height dimensions .

- The sketch should be fully defined at this point.

- **Exit** the Sketch .

(The next step is to create the upper and lower blocks using the Tooling Split command. This is only available when the Sketch is off)

6. Creating the Tooling Split:

- Click or select:
  Insert / Molds / Tooling Split.

- In the Block Size selection, enter:

  1.500 in for upper block.
  1.50 in for lower block.

— Upper block thickness

— Lower block thickness

- The Cavity and the parting surfaces options should already be filled.

- Click **OK** ✓.

* *The Interlock Surface surrounds the perimeter of the parting lines in a slight tapered direction, it helps seal the mold to prevent resins from leaking, prevents shifts, and maintains alignment between the tooling entities.*

8. Patching with Filled Surface:

- The Filled Surface command creates a surface patch with any number of sides, within a boundary defined by existing model edges, sketches, or curves, including composite curves.

- Zoom in on the upper portion of the opening. We will patch it up with the Filled Surface command.

- Click the **Filled Surface** command from the Surfaces toolbar.

- Keep the Curvature Control at the default: **Contact**.

- Select all of the remaining edges on the upper portion of the same opening.

Select all edges

- A preview of a filled surface appears filling the upper portion of the opening.

- Click **OK**.

Filled surface

9. Patching all openings:

- Repeat the steps 7 and 8 and patch / fill the rest of the openings in the model.

Lofted surface
(left side)

Filled surface
(left side)

Lofted surface
(right side)

Lofted surface
(right side)

- The Filled Surface command requires the boundary to be closed in order to fill or patch that area. The Curve Through Reference Points command can be used to create the missing entities in those openings.

Missing entity

- From the **Surfaces** toolbar, select **Curves / Curve Through Reference Points**.

- Select the **2 vertices** as indicated and the preview of a curve appears.

- Click **OK**.

Curve Through 2 Reference Points

Filled surface

- Continue with creating the patches to fill the rest of the openings.

Lofted surface

Filled surface

- After all openings are patched, expand the Surface Bodies folder and <u>show all surfaces</u>.

10. Knitting the surfaces:

- To help selecting multiple surfaces more easily, we will need to knit all the ruled surfaces and the patched surfaces together as one surface.

- Click the **Knit Surface** command (arrow).

- Expand the <u>Surface Bodies</u> folder and select all surfaces inside of the <u>Parting Surface</u> folder.

- Click **OK**.

11. Creating a new plane:

- The bottom of the interlock surface is not flat. We will create a plane and a planar surface and use it to trim the bottom.

- Click **Reference Geometry / Plane**, from the **Surfaces** tool tab.

- Select the **Front** plane for **First Reference**.

- Click the **Offset Distance** button and enter **.750in** for **Distance**.

- Place the new plane <u>below</u> the Front plane and click **OK**.

New plane

Interlock surface

12. Creating a new sketch:

- Select the new **plane1** and open a new sketch.

- Sketch a Rectangle around the model and add the dimensions shown to
  to fully position it.

Sketch rectangle

Dimension
to vertex

- While the sketch is still active
  click **Planar Surface** from the
  Surfaces tool tab.

- The rectangular sketch is
  converted into a planar surface.

- Click **OK**.

13. Trimming the bottom of the ruled surface:

- Select the **Trim Surface** command from the Surfaces tool tab.

- Click the **Mutual** trim option (arrow). Select the **Planar Surface** and <u>all</u> of the surfaces along the perimeter of the Interlock Surface.

- Click the **Remove Selections** options and select the <u>inside</u> of the Interlock Surface plus all of its surfaces along the perimeter as indicated.

- Click **OK**.

Remove

Trim tools

Flat bottom

- The resulting Trimmed Surface. Change to the side view to verify the trim. The bottom of the interlock surface should be flat at this point.

14. Knitting the surfaces:

- Select the **Knit Surface** command from the Surfaces tool tab.

- Expand the FeatureManager tree and the Surfaces Bodies folders.
  Select the Parting Surface and all of the surfaces that
  belong to the Ruled Surface.

- Click **OK**.

Knit the Parting
Surface with the
Ruled Surfaces

15. Creating the tooling split sketch:

- Select the **Planar Surface** and open a new sketch.

Offset from Sketch1

- Locate the
  Sketch1
  under the
  Planar
  Surface and
  Show it.

- Create an
  offset of
  .125in
  (smaller)
  from the
  Sketch1.

.125

- <u>Exit</u> the sketch and click **Tooling Split**. The Tooling Split properties appears.

- For Block Size, enter the following:

      Upper block: 2.500in
      Lower block: 1.500in

- Click **OK**.

- There are 3 solid bodies
  on the FeatureManager
  tree. The Original part,
  the Upper Mold Block,
  and the Lower Mold
  Block.

- We will separate them
  in the next step.

16. Separating the solid bodies:

- Select **Insert / Features / Move-Copy**.

- Click the **Translate / Rotate** button at the bottom of the tree.

- Select the <u>bottom half</u> of the mold (the core) for Bodies To Move/Copy.

- Enter **-6.500in** for Delta Z distance. The bottom half is moved downward.

- Click **OK**.

- Repeat step number 16 and move the upper half of the mold (the cavity).

- Move the cavity block about the **Delta Z** direction, use a distance of **8.00in**.

17. Making the body transparent:

- From the
Feature tree,
Expand the
Solid Bodies
folder. Right-
click on the
Cavity body
and select:
**Change-
Transparency**
(arrow).

18. Hiding the surface bodies:

- The Core, Cavity, and other surfaces are still visible in the graphics making it difficult to see the molded part. We will need to hide them.

- From the FeatureManager tree, right click the Surface Bodies folder and select: **Hide**.

Hide all surfaces

19. Saving your work:

- Select **File / Save As**.

- Enter **Mold Manual Creation** for the file name.

- Click **Save**.

CHAPTER 18

Top-Down Assembly

Top-Down Assembly

- This chapter will guide us through some techniques
  of creating new parts in the context of an assembly or Top Down mode.

- By using the existing geometry of other parts such as their locations,
  features, and sizes to construct new components is referred to as In Context
  Assembly. This option greatly helps capture your design intent and reduces
  the time it takes to do a design change, having the parts update within
  themselves based on the way they were created.

- While working in the top down assembly mode, every time a face or a
  plane is selected as a sketch plane to create a feature of the new part, the
  system automatically creates an INPLACE mate to reference the new part.

- The Inplace mates can be suppressed so that components can be moved or
  repositioned and the Inplace mates can also be deleted as well, new mates
  can be added to establish new relationships with other components.

- When a part is being edited in the Top Down Assembly mode, the Edit-
  Component icon is selected and the part's color changes to Blue (or
  Magenta depending on the color settings in the system options).

- Upon the successful completion of this lesson, you will have a better
  understanding of the 2 assembly methods in SolidWorks: the traditional
  Bottom Up assembly (where parts are created separately, then inserted
  into an assembly document and mated together) and the dynamic Top-
  Down assembly (where parts can be created together, in the context
  of an assembly).

Miniature Vise
Top-Down Assembly

View Orientation Hot Keys:

Ctrl + 1 = Front View
Ctrl + 2 = Back View
Ctrl + 3 = Left View
Ctrl + 4 = Right View
Ctrl + 5 = Top View
Ctrl + 6 = Bottom View
Ctrl + 7 = Isometric View
Ctrl + 8 = Normal To
        Selection

Dimensioning Standards: **ANSI**

Units: **INCHES** – 3 Decimals

Tools Needed:

Insert Sketch	Rectangle	Circle
Dimension	Add Geometric Relations	Sketch Mirror
Offset Entities	Planes	Fillet/Round
Base/Boss Extrude	Loft	Edit Component

1. Starting a new assembly template:

- Select **File / New / Assembly**.

- Click **Cancel** to exit the **Begin Assembly** mode.

- **Save** the new assembly document as **Mini Vise.sldasm**.

2. Creating the Base part:

- Select **Insert / Component / New Part**.

- Select the <u>Front</u> plane from the FeatureManager tree to reference the new part (Inplace1).

- A new component is created using a default name **[Part1^Assembly]<1>**.

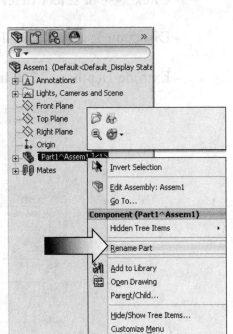

- To rename the part, right click on the default name and select **Rename Part**.

- Enter: **Base** as the new name for the 1st part.

- The new part has the default Blue color.

- To change the part's color, go to: **Tools/ Options / System Options / Colors / Assembly Edit Part.**

- A new sketch is created automatically when a new component is inserted.

- Sketch the profile shown below; keep the Origin at the lower right corner.

- Add the Dimensions ⬦ or Relations ⏄ needed to fully define the sketch.

3. Extruding the Base:

- Click ⬛ or select **Insert / Boss-Base / Extrude**.

- Direction 1:   **Mid-Plane**.

- Extrude Depth: **.750 in.**

- Click **OK** ✓.

4. Adding the side flanges:

- Select the <u>bottom face</u> of the base and open a new sketch 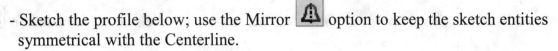 .

- Sketch the profile below; use the Mirror ⚠ option to keep the sketch entities symmetrical with the Centerline.

- Add dimensions ◇ as shown. (Hold the **Shift** key when adding the .625 dim.)

Sketch Face

1.500
R.313
Ø.175
.625

5. Extruding the Flanges:

- Click ⬜ or select **Insert / Boss-Base / Extrude**.

- Direction 1:   **Blind** (Reverse).

- Extrude Depth: **.200 in.**

1.500
R.313
Ø.175
.625

- Click **OK** ✓ .

6. Adding the side cuts:

- Select the <u>face</u> as indicated and click or select **Insert / Sketch**.

- Sketch a Centerline starting at the Origin and click **Dynamic Mirror** .

- Sketch a rectangle and add the dimensions shown below.

Sketch Face

Coincident with corner

.100

.140

7. Extruding the side cuts:

- Click or select **Insert / Cut / Extrude**.

- Direction 1: **Up-To-Surface**.

- Select the <u>face</u> as indicated.

Select Face

Cut-Extrude 1

From
Sketch Plane

Direction 1
Up To Surface

Face<1>@Base -1

Flip side to cut

Draft outward

.100

- Click **OK** .

8. Creating an offset distance plane:

- Select the <u>face</u> as shown and click or select **Insert / Reference Geometry / Plane**.

- Click **Offset Distance** option.

- Enter **.150 in**. (the new plane is placed **away** from the face)

- Click **OK**.

9. Creating the Fixed Jaw, sketch 1 of 4:

- Select the <u>new plane</u> and click or select **Insert / Sketch**.

- Sketch a rectangle approx. 2 inches above the origin.

<u>NOTE:</u> *The dimension .450 can be replaced with a centerline and a symmetric relation.*

More...

- Add dimensions to fully position the sketch.

.900

.275

2.000

.450

- **Exit** the sketch or select **Insert / Sketch**.

10. Creating the 2ⁿᵈ profile, sketch 2 of 4:

- Select the <u>face</u> as indicated and click or select **Insert / Sketch**.

Sketch Face

- Hold the CONTROL key and select the 4 edges as shown (or simply select the rectangular face and click the Convert Entities command).

- Click **Convert Entities** on the Sketch-Tools toolbar.

Convert these 4 Edges

- The 4 selected edges are converted into a new 2D rectangle.

- **Exit** the sketch or select **Insert / Sketch**.

11. Creating the 3D Guide Curves:

- Select **3D Sketch** from the Sketch tool tab or select **Insert / 3D Sketch**.

- Sketch a 3-Point-Arc approximately as shown and add the **Coincident** relation between the ends of the arc and the corners of the rectangles.

Tangent

A = 94.39 R = 0.679

- Add a **Perpendicular** relation between the <u>endpoint</u> of the arc and the <u>upper face</u> of the part as noted.

- Repeat the last step and create the other 3 arcs the same way.

Perpendicular
or Tangent

- **Exit** the 3D Sketch or select **Insert / 3D Sketch** (Control + Q).

12. Creating the Fixed Jaw loft:

- Click or select **Insert / Boss-Base / Loft**.

- Select the 2 sketch profiles as labeled (Profile 1 and Profile 2) .
  (Click near the ends of the rectangles will work just fine. SolidWorks will select the nearest endpoints automatically).

Loft Profile 1

Loft Profile 2

- Expand the **Guide Curve** section and select one of the guide curves in the 3D Sketch.

- Because this sketch has multiple entities that are not connected with one another, you will have to click the OK button (the check mark) on the <u>SelectionManager</u> after selecting <u>each</u> arc.

- Click **OK** .

- The resulted loft with four guide curves.

13. Creating the Fixed Jaw Clamp:

- Select the <u>Front</u> plane from the FeatureManager tree and click or select **Insert / Sketch**.

- Sketch a Rectangle and add Dimensions and Relations as indicated. *(Add a horizontal centerline and a midpoint relation between the right endpoint and the model edge).*

14. Extruding the Fixed Jaw Clamp:

- Click or select **Insert / Boss-Base / Extrude**.

- Direction 1:   **Mid-Plane**.

- Extrude Depth: **1.250 in**.

- Click **OK** ✓.

15. Creating the Lead Screw Hole:

- Select the <u>face</u> as indicated

  and open a new sketch.

- Sketch a Circle ⊕ and add the dimensions ◇ and relations ⊥ as shown.

16. Extruding the Hole:

- Click 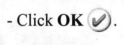 or select **Insert / Cut / Extrude**.

- Direction 1: **Through All**.

- Click **OK** ✓.

17. Adding Fillets:

- Click Fillet 🔘 or select **Insert / Features /Fillets-Rounds**.

- Enter **.032 in**. for Radius 🗘 .

- Select the edges as shown for Edges to Fillet 🔲 .

- Click **OK** ✓.

Edges to Fillet

No fillet

Edges to Fillet

- The Base part is shown in Front and Back Isometric views.

18. Saving your work:

- Select **File / Save As / Base / Save**.

- Click to <u>exit</u> the Edit Component mode.

19. Creating a new component: The Slide Jaw

- Select **Insert / Component / New Part**.

- Rotate the model to the right, the planar surface on the left side will be used next.

- Select the <u>face</u> indicated as sketch plane for the new component (Inplace2). A new part and a new sketch are created in the FeatureManager tree.

- **Rename** the component to **Slide Jaw**.

Select face ———

- A new part is created in the FeatureManager tree and the sketch pencil is activated.

- An INPLACE mate is also created for the new component to reference its location.

20. Using the Offset Entities command:

- Select the **4 edges** of the model (as shown) and click **Offset Entities** ⟲ .

- Enter **.010 in**. for offset value. This offset distance between 4 the lines and the model edges will remain locked and get updated at the same time when the value is changed.

Edges to Offset*

.125

.010

.010

45.00°

.010

(.010)

(.010)

.275

💡 Offset Entities

* The geometry of a model such as edges, faces, and other sketch entities can be offset or converted to use in the new part.
* The offset entities can be set to one direction or bidirectional.
* An On-Edge relation is created for each converted sketch entity.

- Sketch the rest of the profile
  and add the dimensions or
  relations needed to fully
  define the sketch.

Note:

The mirror option *can be used
to help speed up the sketching
process and keep the profile
symmetrical at the same
time.*

Horizontal
4 places

Collinear
2 places

21. Extruding the Slide Jaw:

- Click ⬚ on the Features toolbar or select:
  Insert / Base / Extrude.

- Direction 1: **Blind** and reverse direction 📐 .

- Extrude Depth: **1.000 in**.

- Click **OK** ✓.

> 💡 **Transparency**
>
> * The transparent images are
> sometimes toggled on/off for
> clarity purposes.

22. Adding the support wall:

- Select the <u>face</u> indicated and open a new sketch or select **Insert / Sketch.**

Select Face

- Sketch the profile and add the dimensions and relation as shown below to fully define the sketch.

Ø.210

Vertical

Ø.210

.585   .225

.585

.225

NOTE: *Remove the dimension .585 if the Concentric relation is used.*

23. Extruding the Support Wall:

- Click on the Features toolbar or select **Insert / Base / Extrude.**

- Direction 1: **Blind** and reverse direction ⬈ .

- Extrude Depth: **.375 in.**

- Click **OK** ✅.

- The Support wall is built with a guide hole.

24. Creating a new work plane:

- Select the face as indicated and click or select: **Insert / Reference Geometry / Plane.**

- Enter **.150 in**. in the Offset Distance box and place the new plane on the **outside**.

25. Creating the Slide Jaw, 1st sketch:

- Open a new sketch on the **new plane** or select **Insert / Sketch.**

- Sketch a rectangle and add the dimensions as shown to fully define the sketch.

- **Exit** the sketch or select: **Insert / Sketch.**

26. Creating the Slide Jaw, 2ⁿᵈ sketch:

- Select the <u>face</u> indicated and open a new sketch or select: **Insert / Sketch.**

- Sketch a rectangle as shown.

Sketch Face

Mid-Point relation between endpoint and edge

.750

.500

.750

.500

- Add dimensions to fully define the sketch.

- <u>**Exit**</u> the Sketch or select **Insert / Sketch.**

27. Creating the Guide Curve to connect the two sketches:

- Select the <u>Right</u> plane of the part from the FeatureManager tree.

- Click to open a new sketch or select: **Insert / Sketch.**

💡 Guide Curves

* Guide curves are used to control the profile from twisting as the sketch is swept along the path.
* Guide curves are also used in Sweep to shape the 3D Features.
* Each profile is Pierced or coincident with the guide curve.

- Sketch either a **Centerpoint Arc** or a **3-Point Arc** that connects the two sketches.

- Add the Relations as shown below to fully define the sketch.

Pierce Relation

3 Point Arc or
Centerpoint Arc

Pierce Relation

Add centerline
and make it
tangent w/arc.

- **Exit** the sketch or Select **Insert / Sketch**

28. Creating the Slide Jaw Loft:

- Click on the Features toolbar or select **Insert / Boss / Loft.**

- Select the upper corners of the 2 rectangular sketches to use as Loft Profiles.

- Expand the **Start/End Constraints** section and set the following:

Select line
for
Direction Vector.

* Start Constraint: **Normal to Profile**

* End Constraint: **Direction Vector** and select the centerline as noted

- Expand the Guide Curves dialog box and select the Arc (sketch4) to use as a Guide Curve.

(see next page for details).

Start/End Constraints

* The Start constraint and End constraint option applies a constraint to control tangency to the start and end profiles.

* The Direction Vector option applies a tangency constraint based on a selected entity used as a direction vector.

OPTIONAL:
4 Guide Curves
(in one 3D Sketch)

Tangent

- Click **OK** ✓.

29. Creating the Clamp block:

- Select the part's <u>Right</u> plane from the FeatureManager tree.

- Click to open a new sketch or select: **Insert / Sketch.**

- Sketch a Rectangle and add Dimensions as shown.

- Add a Centerline in the middle of the rectangle and position it on the Mid-Point of the vertical edge.

Mid-Point with vertical edge

30. Extruding the Clamp block:

- Click or select **Insert / Boss-Base Extrude.**

- Direction 1:   **Mid-Plane**.

- Extrude Depth: **1.250 in**.

- Merge Result: **Enabled**.

- Click **OK** .

31. Which option is better?

- Instead of using the Mid-Plane extrude, the **Up-To-Surface** option can be used to link the length dimensions of the 2 Clamp Blocks together.

- Right click on the last Extruded feature and select **Edit Feature**.

- Change **Direction 1** from Mid-Plane to **Up-To-Surface** and select the face on the left side.

- Change **Direction 2** to **Up-To-Surface** and select the face on the right side as indicated.

- Click **OK** .

> **Up-To-Surface**
>
> * Extends the feature from the sketch plane to the selected surface.
> * When the driving surface is changed in length, the referenced extruded feature will also be reflected.

Direction 2:
Up-To-Surface
(Right side)

Direction 1:
Up-To-Surface
(Left side)

32. Adding fillets:

- Click or select **Insert / Features / Fillet-Round.**

- Enter **.032** for Radius value .

- Select the edges as shown .

- Click **OK** .

- The fillets are shown in the Front and Back Isometric views for clarity.

33. Creating the internal threads:

- Starting with the sweep path.

- Select the <u>face</u> indicated and open a new sketch or select: **Insert / Sketch.**

Sketch face —

- Sketch a Circle ⊕ that is Concentric with the hole. (Converting the ID of the hole is another good way to link the diameter of the circle to the hole's diameter)

- Add a **Ø.210** dimension ⬦ to fully define.

Ø.210 —

> ### 💡 Wake up Center Points
>
> * Center-points of existing geometry can be "woke-up" for use as snap points in a sketch.
>
> * With a Circle tool selected, position the mouse cursor over the circumference of the hole; the 4 quadrant points appear, and the center-point of the circle is visible for snapping.

- Select **Insert / Curve / Helix-Spiral.**

- Enter the following parameters:

Defined by: **Pitch and Revolution**.

Pitch: **.080 in**.

Revolution: **5.000**.

Starting Angle: **90.00 deg**.

Reverse Direction: **Enabled**.

Clockwise: **Selected**.

- Click **OK** ✅.

Click **View / Curves** if
the helix is not visible.

- Sketching the Sweep Profile:

- Select the part' <u>Right</u> plane from the Feature tree and open a new sketch or select: **Insert / Sketch.**

- Sketch the profile as shown below.
  (Use Mirror to keep the entities symmetrical)

- Add Dimensions and Relations to fully define the sketch. Pierce the endpoint of the centerline to the 1st revolution of the helix.

- Use the Front view with Hidden Lines Visible option.

- **Exit** the sketch or Select **Insert / Sketch.**

34. Sweeping the thread Profile along the Helix:

- Click or select **Insert / Cut / Sweep.**

- Select the thread profile to use as Sweep Profile .

- Select the Helix to use as Sweep Path .

- Click **OK** .

35. Creating a Section View:

- Click the **Section View** command or select **View / Display / Section View**.

- Use the **Right** plane for cutting.

- Verify the details of the threads.

- Click the **Section View** icon again to turn it off.

36. Saving your work.

- Save your work once again using the same file name: **Mini-Vise.sldasm**

- Overwrite the old file when prompted.

37. Assembly Exploded view (Optional):

- Create the additional components: Lead Screw, Crank Handle, and Crank Knob using the Top Down Assembly method.

- Create an assembly exploded view as shown (details on next page).

* To define the Helix, use the
Height and Pitch option.
Height = 2.116
Pitch   = .080

LEAD SCREW

CRANK HANDLE

CRANK KNOB

Questions for Review

Top-Down Assembly

1. New parts can be created in context of an assembly.
    a. True
    b. False

2. Geometry of other components such as model edges, hole diameters, and locations etc., can be used to construct a new part.
    a. True
    b. False

3. Part documents can be inserted into an assembly using:
    a. Insert menu
    b. Windows Explorer
    c. Drag and drop from an open window
    d. All of the above

4. The suffix (f) next to the first part's name in the FeatureManager tree stands for:
    a. Fail
    b. Fixed
    c. Float

5. When inserting new components into an assembly, the Inplace mates are created by the user.
    a. True
    b. False

6. Either in the part or assembly mode, the guide curves are used to help control the profiles from twisting, as they are swept along the path.
    a. True
    b. False

7. Centerpoint Arcs are drawn from its center, then radius, and angle.
    a. True
    b. False

8. The Link Values option allows a user to link only two dimensions at a time.
    a. True
    b. False

7. TRUE   8. FALSE
5. FALSE   6. TRUE
3. D   4. B
1. TRUE   2. TRUE

CHAPTER 19

Top Down Assembly

Top Down Assembly
Water Control Valve

- When a component is built in the context of an assembly external references are created to reference how it was constructed, and which plane or surface was used to create it with. Starting from the very <u>Top</u> level assembly, information regarding the new component are added and flow <u>Down</u> to the component level, and gets repeated every time a new component is added.

- For example: The mounting holes in the second part can be converted from the first, so that the hole diameters and the location dimensions are the same for both parts. When the holes in the 1st part are changed, the holes in the 2nd part would also changed. Thus the sketch of the holes in the 2nd part is defined in the assembly, not by sketching and dimensioning them as in the part mode.

- Using the Top Down assembly design, one of the better approaches is to use the geometry of the existing parts to create the new. This way several parts can be controlled and changed at the same time.

- There are many advantages for creating parts in Top Down mode, and just to mention a few: not only this method is much quicker than the others due to the ability to use existing geometry to reference the new parts, but because all the parts are always visible in the assembly to help developing the <u>Form</u> of the new part, how it supposed to <u>Fit</u> with other parts , and therefore, it is more predictable how it is going to <u>Function</u>. Interference, friction and or clearance fits can be created and controlled within the very same screen.

- However, there are a few things to consider when designing in Top Down mode:
    * External references are created to the geometry that the new part is referenced, and that means:
    * When changes occurred, the assembly updates all of its internal parts, and if drawings were made from these parts earlier, they will get updated as well.

Top Down Assembly
Water Control Valve

Dimensioning Standards: **ANSI**

Units: **INCHES** – 3 Decimals

Tools Needed:

🖊	Insert Sketch	✏	Line	⊕	Circle
⊥	Add Geometric Relations	⌐	Sketch Fillet	✳	Trim
◇	Dimension	⫶	Centerline	◔	Fillet/Round
⊕	Base/Boss Revolve	⬚	Extruded Boss/Base	▧	Assembly

1. Starting with a new Assembly Template:

- Click **File / New**.

- Select an **Assembly** template either from the Template or the Tutorial tab.

- Click the **Advance** button at the lower left corner of this dialog box if you do not see the similar templates.

- The **Begin Assembly** dialog appears on the left side, click **Cancel**. We're going to use a different approach to create the new components.

- At the bottom right of the screen, set the Units to **IPS (Inch, Pound, Second).**

- From the **Assembly tab**, click the **drop arrow** below the Insert Components command and select: **New Part**.

- Creating components in context of an assembly will requires a few additional steps:

    a/. A new part is inserted into an Assembly and the Part's name is entered.

    b/. A plane is selected at this time to reference the new part.

    c/. The Edit Component command is activated and the Sketch mode is enabled for the plane selected in step b.

    d/. The active part will change to the blue color by default.

2. Creating the 1st component:

- When the symbol √ appears next to your mouse cursor, click the <u>Front</u> plane from the Feature tree. An Inplace mate is created to reference the new part.

- Press **Control + 1** to switch to the Front orientation.

<u>**NOTE:**</u> *To automatically rotate normal to the sketch plane, go to System **Options / Sketch**, and enable the checkbox: **Auto Rotate View Normal to...***

3. Creating the Base Profile:

- Sketch the profile <u>above</u> the origin.

- Add the dimensions shown. Notice the diameter dimensions are created as Virtual Diameters.

- Click **Revolve** .

- The centerline should be selected automatically.

- Use the default Blind option and revolve the sketch one complete revolution.

- Click **OK**.

4. Adding the Inlet Flange:

- Select the <u>face</u> indicated and open a new sketch.

- Sketch the profile shown below. Use the Dynamic Mirror option to help speed up the sketching process.

Sketch face

- Add the dimensions and relations needed to fully define the sketch.

- The number of places are added to help clarify the sketch, you do not have to add them.

- Click **Extruded Boss-Base**.

- Use the **Blind** extrude option.

- Enter **.650"** for thickness.

- Enable the Merge Result checkbox.

- Click **OK**.

5. Adding the mounting holes:

- Select the <u>face</u> indicated and open a new sketch.

- Sketch a couple of center-lines to help locate the center and directions for this sketch.

- Add a circle and either mirror it or circular pattern it 4 times around.

- Add the dimensions and relations needed to fully define the sketch.

- Press **Extruded Cut**.

- Select the **Up-To-Next** extrude option.

- Click **OK**.

6. Adding other mounting holes:

- Select the <u>face</u> as noted and open a new sketch.

- Sketch a circle and **convert** it to **construction** (click the For-Construction checkbox on the Feature tree).

- Add a couple of **centerlines** as shown.

- Sketch a **smaller circle** that's coincident with the construction circle and the endpoint of the centerline.

- Use the **Circular-Sketch-Pattern** option to array the small circle 4 times around.

- Add the dimensions and relations needed to fully define this sketch.

NOTE: *An additional Vertical or Horizontal relation between the centers of the small circles is needed when using the 2D sketch pattern.*

- Click **Extruded Cut**.

- Use the **Up-To-Next** extrude option to ensure that the cut only goes through the thickness of the flange.

- Click **OK**.

- Rotate the view to verify the cut result.

The center of the circle is coincident with the construction circle and the endpoint of the angled centerline.

Sketch face

45.00°

Ø4.750

Ø.525

Coincident

Horizontal

7. Adding the .032" chamfers:

- Click **Chamfer** (below the Fillet command).

- Enter **.032"** for Depth and use the default **45°** angle.

- Select the edges of the 8 holes and the 2 edges of the round flange.

- To un-select an edge simply click it once again.

- Click **OK**.

Fillet edges

8. Adding the .060" fillets:

- Click the **Fillet** command.

- Enter **.060"** for radius size.

- Select the **3 edges** of the transition body.

- Enable the Full Preview checkbox.

- Change to the Top orientation (Control + 5) to verify the selection.

- Click **OK**.

Fillet edges

9. Adding the .125" chamfers:

- Click **Chamfer** once again.

- Enter **.125"** for Depth and use the default **45°** angle.

- Select the **2 edges** of the center hole.

- Selecting the face of the hole would be the same as selecting its 2 edges.

- Click **OK**.

Fillet edges

Chamfer2

Chamfer Parameters

Edge<1>@Outlet Housing-1
Edge<2>@Outlet Housing-1

○ Angle distance
○ Distance distance
○ Vertex
☐ Flip direction

0.125in

45.00deg

☑ Select through faces
☐ Keep features
☑ Tangent propagation
◉ Full preview
○ Partial preview
○ No preview

Distance: 0.125in
Angle: 45.00deg

10. Exiting the Edit Component mode:

- Click off the **Edit Component** button to return to the Edit Assembly mode.

- When the Edit Component command is <u>not active,</u> the part's color goes back to its default color (grey).

- In the Edit Assembly mode, new components can be created or existing parts can be inserted and mated to others.

11. Renaming the component:

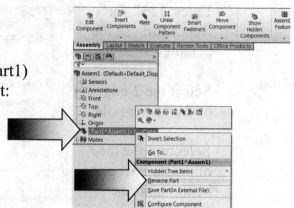

- Right click the name of the part (Part1) from the FeatureManager and select: **Rename Part** (arrow).

- Enter **Outlet Housing** and press enter.

12. Saving as Virtual Component:

- Virtual component are quite useful in the Top-Down Assembly mode. These components are saved internally, or embedded in the assembly document, instead of as separate part or sub-assembly documents.

- Click **File /Save As**.

- Enter **Water Control Valve** for the file name and press **Save**.

- The Save As Virtual Component dialog appears, click the **Save Internally** (Inside the Assembly) option and click **OK**.

- When the parent assembly is opened, all virtual components are also loaded into RAM. The virtual components can then be opened so that the detail drawings can be generated from them, or they can simply be saved as external part documents to share with others.

13. Creating the 2nd component:

- Click the **New Part** command from below the Insert-Components button (arrow).

- When the symbol √ appears next to your mouse cursor, click the <u>Face</u> of the flange as indicated.

- At this point, another Inplace mate is create for the new part.

- A new (blank) component is inserted on the Feature tree.

- The Outlet Housing turns to transparent (inactive).

- The **Edit Component** command is activated.

Select face

- The Sketch pencil is also enabled automatically.

   a/. Right click on one of the outer edges and pick **Select Tangency**.

   b/. Press **Convert Entities**. The selected edges are converted to new sketch entities.

- Convert also the **circular edges** of the 4 holes.

b/. Convert Entities

a/. Select Tangency

- Click **Extruded Boss-Base**.

- Use the default **Blind** extrude option.

- Enter **.650"** for thickness.

- Click **OK**.

- The new flange is created using the geometry of the 1st component.

- If the 1st component is changed the 2nd component will also gets updated. We will take a look at some of the changes toward the end of this chapter.

14. Creating the transition body:

- Select the part's <u>Right</u> plane and open a new sketch.

- Sketch the profile shown below and add the dimensions and any relations needed to fully define this sketch. (Add the R2.00 fillet after fully defined).

- Click **Revolve Boss-Base**.

- The revolve centerline is selected by default.

- Use the default settings:
  * **Blind**
  * **360deg**

- Click **OK**.

15. Adding another mounting flange:

- Select the <u>face</u> as indicated and open a new sketch.

- Hold the control key and select the circular edge of the round flange <u>and</u> the 4 edges of its mounting holes (arrow).

Sketch face

- Click **Convert Entities**.

Convert 5 edges

- The selected edges are converted and projected onto the sketch face.

- Each sketch entity is linked to the original geometry where it was converted from. A relation called On-Edge is added to maintain their parent and child relationships.

- Click **Extruded Boss-Base**.

- Use the default **Blind** option.

- Enter **.650"** for depth.

- Extrude direction is outward.

- Click **OK**.

16. Adding an Offset-Distance plane:

- Select the <u>Top</u> plane of the part from the FeatureManager tree.

- From the Features tab, click **Reference Geometry / Plane**.

- The Offset Distance option should be selected already, enter **1.625"** for distance, and place the new plane <u>above</u> the Top plane.

- Click **OK**.

17. Adding a circular boss:

- Select the new <u>Plane1</u> and open a new sketch.

- Sketch a **circle** approx. as shown.

- Add the **1.50"** diameter dimension and the **1.00"** locating dimension.

- Add the **horizontal** relation as noted to fully define the sketch.

Horizontal

- Click **Extruded Boss-Base**.

- Use the default **Blind** option.

- Enter: **.875"** for depth.

- Click **OK**.

18. Adding a thermostat valve mount:

- Open a new sketch on the <u>upper face</u> of the boss.

- Sketch the shape of the thermostat shown below.

- Use the mirror function to help maintain the symmetrical relationships of the sketch entities.

- Add the dimensions and the relations as noted in the drawing below.

Sketch face

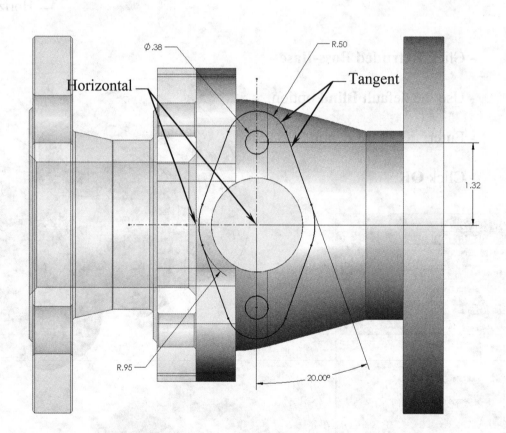

Ø.38

R.50

Horizontal

Tangent

1.32

R.95

20.00°

- The centers of the circles should be vertical with each other.

- If the mirror feature was not used, then be sure to add the symmetric relations to fully define this sketch.

- Click **Extruded Boss-Base**.

- For **Direction 1**: Use **Blind** and the depth of **.250"**.

Direction 2:
Select this Surface

- For **Direction 2**: Use **Up-To-Surface** option and select the <u>planar face</u> of the square mount as indicated.

- Click **OK**.

19. Adding a hole:

- Open a new sketch on the <u>upper face</u> of the thermostat.

- Sketch a **Ø1.00 circle** and add a **concentric** relation to center it.

- Make use of the "Wake up the Entities Snap Mode". With the Circle command selected, hover the mouse cursor over the circular edge of the radius, the appropriate snap-entities will appear to allow snapping to the existing geometry.

Sketch face

- Click **Extruded Cut**.

- Click the **Reverse** direction button.

- Select the option **Up-To-Next** from the list

- Click **OK**.

20. Adding the .080" fillets:

Select 5 edges

- From the Features tab, click **Fillet**.

- Enter **.080"** for radius size.

- Select the **5 edges** as indicated.

- The Tangent Propagation checkbox should be selected.

- Click **OK**.

21. Adding the .032" chamfers:

- Click **Chamfer** below the Fillet command.

- Enter **.032"** for depth.

- Use the default **45deg** angle.

- Select the **edges** of the holes as shown in the preview image. (23 edges total).

- The same result can be achieved by selecting the inner faces of the holes.

- Click **OK**.

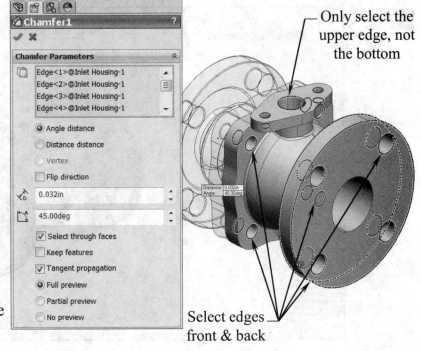

22. Adding the .125" chamfers:

- Click **Chamfer** once again.

- Enter **.125"** for depth.

- Use the same **45deg** angle.

- Select the **2 edges** of the center hole. (Selecting the face of the hole would get the same result).

- Click **OK**.

23. Exiting the Edit Component mode:

- On the Assembly toolbar, click off the **Edit Component** command (arrow).

24. Applying dimension changes:

- Expand the part Outlet Housing and double click on the feature **Revolve1**.

- Change the flange diameter **from 6.00" to 7.00"**

- Click the **Rebuild** (the green traffic light) to execute the change*.

- Notice the dimension change also updates the flange diameter on the right.

Changing this diameter will also change this other diameter

* Press <u>undo</u> to switch the dimension back to its original value, or double click the same dimension, re-enter the previous value, and click Rebuild again.

Double click inside the hole to see its dimensions

- Double click the feature **Cut-Extrude1** of the same part.

- Double the inner face of the small hole would also display its dimensions.

- Locate the dimension **Ø.750**.

- Change the hole diameter **from .750" to .500"**.

- Click the **Rebuild** green traffic light to execute the change*.

Double click the
Ø.750" dimension
and change to .500"

Changing this diameter will also
change the other diameters

- Notice the dimension change also updates the hole diameters on the right.

* Press <u>undo</u> to switch the dimension back to its original value, or double click
the same dimension, re-enter the previous value, and click Rebuild again.

25. Viewing the External Reference Symbols:

- Expand the 2nd part, the **Inlet Housing**.

- Some of the features have the External reference
symbols next to their names. These references
were created automatically when we converted
the entities of the Part1 to create the new sketch
for the Part2. They are called On-Edge relations.

- An external reference is also created when we add
a dimension or a relation between Part1 and Part2.

26. Inserting other components:

- Due to the length of this lesson, we are going to insert and mate the rest of the components that belong to this assembly.

- Go to the Training CD and insert the components as labeled below.

Handle

Cap Screw (2X)

Thermostat Flange

Lock Lever

Hex Bolt (4X)

Ball Valve Sub

Outlet Housing

Inlet Housing

- Create the mates that are appropriate for each component. The non-moving components will get 3 mates, and the moving components will need only two.

27. Optional:

a/. Create a section view to verify how the components were mated.

b/. To center the 2 components, it is best to use the Width mate option.

c/. Change / correct any mates or geometry that would cause the interferences.

- Add the Explode-Line Sketch as shown.

- When adding the explode lines, pay attention to the direction arrows, flip or reverse them before completing each line.

28. Saving your work:

- Click **File / Save As**.

- Enter **Water Control Valve.sldasm** for the name of the file.

- Press **Save**.

Questions for Review

Top Down Assembly

1. In Top Down mode, when a plane is selected to sketch the new part, SolidWorks will create an Inplace mate to reference the new part.
   a. True
   b. False

2. After the plane is selected, SolidWorks will also activate the Edit Component command and the Sketch mode at the same time.
   a. True
   b. False

3. The option Auto-Rotate Normal to the Sketch is not available to set as the default.
   a. True
   b. False

4. The Convert Entities command can only be used when the Sketch pencil is turned off.
   a. True
   b. False

5. The Virtual part is saved / embedded inside an assembly document.
   a. True
   b. False

6. When editing a part in Top Down mode, both the current part and other parts can be filleted at the same time.
   a. True
   b. False

7. The Edit Component command should be left active prior to inserting a new part.
   a. True
   b. False

8. When a dimension is changed, any reference geometry of other parts should also changed.
   a. True
   b. False

7. FALSE 8. TRUE
5. TRUE 6. FALSE
3. FALSE 4. FALSE
1. TRUE 2. TRUE

Top Down Assembly
Using the Lip & Groove Option

Lip & Groove

- You can create lip and groove fastening features to align, mate, and hold together two plastic parts.
    * The Lip option adds material to the part
    * The Groove option removes material from the part

- This session discusses the in-depth details of creating a set of Lip & Groove for the two plastic parts.

Fastening features streamline the creation of common features for plastic and sheet metal parts. You can create: **Lips and Grooves**. Align, mate, and hold together two plastic parts. Lip and groove features support multibodies and assemblies.	
Mounting bosses. Create a variety of mounting bosses. Set the number of fins and choose a hole or a pin.	
Snap hooks and **snap hook grooves**. Customize the snap hook and snap hook groove. You must first create a snap hook before you can create a snap hook groove.	
Vents. Create a variety of vents using a sketch you create. Set the number of ribs and spars. Flow area is calculated automatically.	
(Images Courtesy of the SolidWorks Online Help)	

Using the Lip & Groove option

1. Opening the existing assembly document named:
Lip & Groove Assembly from the Training Files folder.
After opened, right click the file name and <u>Collapse</u> the assembly.

2. Editing Part: Select the part <u>**Housing**</u> and click **Edit Component**.

   - From the **Insert** menu, select **Fastening Feature / Lip /Groove**.

- Select the following from
the FeatureManager tree:

Cap: Lip

Direction: Front

Housing: Groove

Housing: Groove

Cap: Lip

Direction: Front

Select all End Faces

- Under **Groove Selection**, right click and select **all faces** on the left-end of the part Housing as shown.

Groove Selection
Face<5>@housing-1
Face<6>@housing-1
Face<7>@housing-1
Face<8>@housing-1

8 faces for Groove

Tangent propagation

Select Other
OK
Cancel
Clear Selections
Select Tangency
Customize Menu

Select Tangency

(Use Select-Tangency)

- Under **Edges to remove**, select all **outer edges** on the left end of the same part.

Groove Selection
Face<5>@housing-1
Face<6>@housing-1
Face<7>@housing-1
Face<8>@housing-1

Tangent propagation

Edge<13>@housing-1
Edge<14>@housing-1
Edge<15>@housing-1
Edge<16>@housing-1

16 edges to remove

Tangent propagation
Jump gaps

Select all outer edges

(Use Select-Tangency)

- Under **Lip Selection**, right click and pick **Select Tangency** to select **all faces** on the right-end of the part Cap.

Front Plane

Lip Selection
Face<13>@cap-1
Face<14>@cap-1
Face<15>@cap-1
Face<16>@cap-1

8 faces for Lip

Tangent propagation

Select all End Faces

Select Other
OK
Cancel
Clear Selections
Select Tangency
Customize Menu

Select Tangency

(Use Select-Tangency)

- Under **Edges To Add Material**, select all **outer edges** on the right-end of the same part.

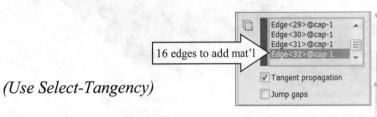

16 edges to add mat'l

(Use Select-Tangency)

Select all outer edges

- Under **Parameters**, set the followings:

  * Groove Width: **.031in.**

  * Spacing :   **0.005in.**

  * Groove Draft: **3.00deg.**

  * Upper Gap: **0.005in.**

  * Lip Height: **.062in.**

  * Lip Width: **.031in.**

  * Lower Gap: **0.005in.**

- Click **OK** 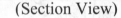.

- Explode the assembly and verify the Lip & Groove features.

(Section View)

3. Saving your work:

- Save your work using the same file name and overwrite the old document.

Top Down Assembly
Using the Mounting Boss Option

Mounting Boss

You can create common mounting features for plastic parts like Mounting Bosses, Snap Hooks, Snap Hook Grooves, Vents, and Lips/Grooves.

The mounting bosses come with a variety of options to help streamline the creation of common Fastening features.

Define/Position the Mounting Boss
Boss diameter
Boss draft angle
Boss height

- Select circular edge (optional). Select a circular edge to position the center axis of the mounting boss.

The projected center of the circular edge must intersect the face where the mounting boss is positioned.

Mounting boss position before selecting circular edge

Position after selecting circular edge

Define the Position for the Pin
Pin
- Pin. Creates a mounting pin.

(Images Courtesy of the SolidWorks Online Help)

Define/Position the Fins
Fin draft angle
Fin height
Fin width
Fin length

No draft   Draft
Fin width sets the thickness at the base of the fin, before applying draft.

Define the Position for the Hole
Hole
- Hole. Creates a mounting hole.

Fin length is measured from the center of the boss.

Using the Mounting Boss option

1. Opening the existing assembly document named:
    Mounting Boss Assembly from the Training Files folder.
    After opened, right click the file name, and <u>Collapse</u> the Assembly.

2. Editing Part: Select the part <u>**Lower Half**</u> and click **Edit Component**

       - From the **Insert** menu, select **Fastening Feature / Mounting Boss**.

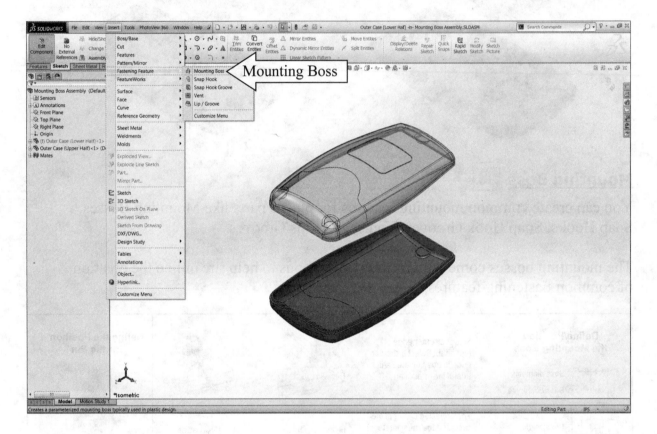

3. Setting the Parameters:

    - The options to set the parameters for the mounting boss appear on the tree.

    - For **Position Face** of the Mounting-Boss, select the **face** as shown.

- For **Position Edge** to line up the Mounting Boss, select the **circular edge** as shown.

(Use the Top plane here for direction only when required)

Position Edge

Select Edge

- Under the **Boss Type** section, select the **Pin Boss** and the **Hole** option.

- Under the Boss section, click the **Enter Boss Height** and **Enter Diameter** options.

- Enter the following dimensions:

> * **A = .200in**.

> * **B = .165in**.

> * **C = 5.00deg**.

> * **D = .093in**.

> * **E = .175in**.

> * **F = 2.00deg**

> * **Clearance = .005in**.

Clearance

- Under the **Fins** section, change the number of fins to **0** (zero).

Change to 0

- Click **OK**.

4. Adding 2 more mounting bosses:

- Repeat the steps above and create two other Mounting Bosses on the opposite side.

- Exit the **Edit Component** when finished.

Mounting Boss 1

Mounting Boss 2 & 3

5. Toggling between the Explode and the Collapse views:

- Right click on the name of the assembly and select **Explode*.**

Explode View

- Rotate the view to verify the details of the 3 mounting bosses.

* Remember to **Collapse** the assembly prior to editing the next component.

6. Creating the Mating Bosses:

- Select the part **Outer-Case (Upper Half)** and click the **Edit Component** command.

- Select **Insert/Fastening Feature/ Mounting Boss**.

- For **Position Face**, select the **Face** as indicated. (To select the hidden face, right click in the area where the surface is under and pick **Select Other** then select the face from the list.

- For **Direction**, select the **Top** plane from the Feature tree (use only if required).

- For **Position Edge**, select the **Edge** as noted to align the center of the mounting boss to the center of the circular edge.

- Under the **Boss Type** section, select the **Pin Boss** option.

- Select the options **Select-Mating Face** and **Enter-Diameter**.

- Select the **upper surface** of the mounting boss as noted.

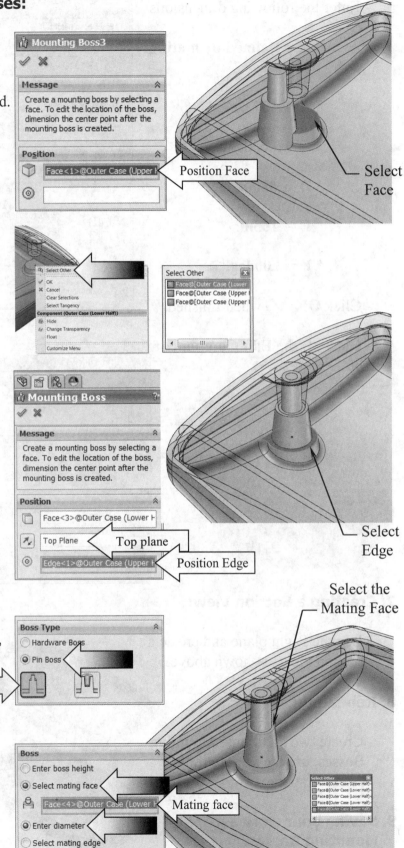

- Enter the following dimensions:

    * **A = Defined by mating face**.

    * **B = .157 in.**

    * **C = 5.00deg.**

    * **D = .080in.**

    * **E = .165in**.

    * **F = 2.00deg.**

- Click **OK** when finished.

- Click off the **Edit Component** button.

Section View

7. Creating a Section View:

- Use the <u>Right</u> plane and create a section view as shown above.

8. Repeating:

- Create two additional Mounting-Bosses, use the same settings as the first one.

9. Saving your work as: Mounting Bosses.

CHAPTER 20

External References & Repair Errors

External References & Repair Errors

An *external reference* is created when one document is dependent on another document for its solution. If the referenced document changes, the dependent document changes also.

In an assembly, you can create an *in-context* feature on one component that references the geometry of another component. This in-context feature has an external reference to the other component. If you change the geometry on the referenced component, the associated in-context feature changes accordingly.

The External Symbols:

-> .... External Reference   **?** .... Out Of Context

(+) .... Over Defined   ***** .... Reference Locked

X .... Reference Broken

a. External Reference ->:
The part itself or some of its entities are depending on the geometry of other parts for their solutions.

b. Out Of Context ?:
The part or its features are not solved, not up-to-date or disconnected from its assembly.

c. Over Defined (+):
The Dimensions or Relations of the sketch are conflicting; redundant dimensions or wrong relations were used.

d. Reference Locked *:
Lock the external references on a part, the existing references no longer update and the part will not accept any new references from that point.

e. Reference Broken X:
The references between the part and the others are broken. Changes done to the part will not affect the others.

External References & Repair Errors

View Orientation Hot Keys:

Ctrl + 1 = Front View
Ctrl + 2 = Back View
Ctrl + 3 = Left View
Ctrl + 4 = Right View
Ctrl + 5 = Top View
Ctrl + 6 = Bottom View
Ctrl + 7 = Isometric View
Ctrl + 8 = Normal To
        Selection

Dimensioning Standards: **ANSI**
Units: **INCHES** – 3 Decimals

External Reference Symbols:

->	External Reference	?	Out of Context
(+)	Over Defined	*	External Reference Locked
X	External Reference Broken	[icon]	Display/Delete Relations

Understanding & Removing External References

1. Opening an existing part: Double Joint

- <u>Go to:</u>

    Training Files folder
    Repair Errors folder.

- Open the part named: **Double Joint**.

- The **What's Wrong** dialog appears displaying the current errors. Close it.

2. Listing the External References:

- Right click on the part's name and select **List External Refs**.

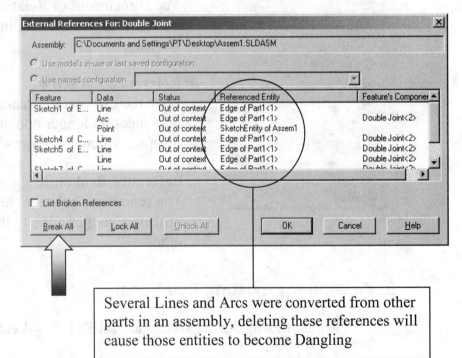

Several Lines and Arcs were converted from other parts in an assembly, deleting these references will cause those entities to become Dangling

3. Removing External References:

- Click **Break All** to remove the external references.

- Click OK [OK].

4. Understanding the External Symbols:

-> .... External Reference
? .... Out Of Context
(+) .... Over Defined
* .... Reference Locked
X .... Reference Broken

> ☀ **Error Colors**
>
> - **Olive Green:** Dangling
>   (Missing references/detached).
> - **Red:** Over Defined
>   (Wrong Relations/Dimension).
> - **Yellow:** Not Solved
>   (Relation is conflicting with
>   dimensions).

(From the Feature-Manager tree, expand the first two features, to see their sketches)

a. External Reference ->:
The part itself or some of its entities are depending on the geometry of other parts for their solutions.

b. Out Of Context ?:
The part or its features are not solved, not up-to-date, Or disconnected from its assembly.

c. Over Defined (+):
The Dimensions or Relations of the sketch are conflicting; Redundant dimensions or wrong relations were used.

d. Reference Locked * :
Lock the external references on a part, the existing references no longer update - and - the part will not accept any new references from that point.

e. Reference Broken X:
The references between the part and the others are broken. Changes done to the part will not affect the others.

5. Viewing the existing Relations:

- Right-click on the 1st sketch and select **Edit-Sketch** .

- Click or select **Tools / Relations / Display/Delete.**

- The Ø.325 is shown in Olive Green color; this indicates either a relation is wrong or the sketch is over dimensioned.

- Change the Relations Filter to **All In This Sketch**

6. Repairing the 1st sketch:

- Click **Display / Delete Relations** and delete the **Coradial** relation (the Circle is Coradial with an entity that is no longer exists).

- Delete all relations that have the External Relations (->X) next to their names.

Delete Coradial
(Wrong Relation)

Delete External
Relations (-> X)

- Add the new Dimensions as noted to fully define the sketch.

Add new dimensions to
fully define the Sketch.

- The sketch is no longer Over Defined.

- Click **OK** .

- **Exit** the sketch. There are still some errors in the part.

7. Repairing the 2nd sketch:

- Right click on the 2nd sketch and select **Edit-Sketch** and click the **Display / Delete Relations** command once again.

- Delete the External Dimensions and Relations that were created in context of other parts.

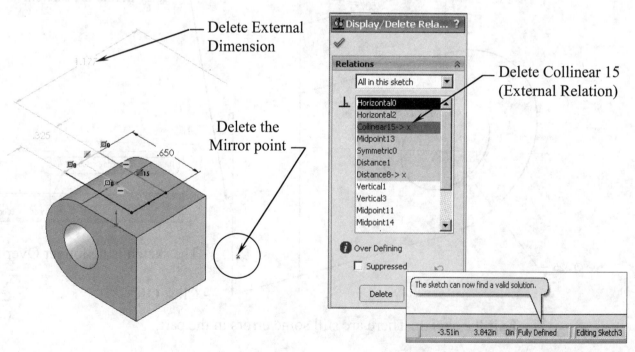

Delete External
Dimension

Delete the
Mirror point

Delete Collinear 15
(External Relation)

8. Rebuilding the model:

- Press Rebuild ⏺ to re-generate the model.

- Verify that the part has no rebuild errors and there should not be any external reference symbols in the FeatureManager tree.

9. Saving your work:

- Select **File / Save As / Breaking External References / Save**.

Questions for Review

External References

1. The symbol -> next to a file name means:
   a. Dangling dimension
   b. External reference
   c. Not solved

2. The symbol ? next to a file name means:
   a. The part cannot be found
   b. Wrong mates
   c. Wrong relations
   d. Out of context

3. The symbol X next to a file or a feature name means:
   a. The part or feature is wrong
   b. The part or feature is deleted
   c. The external references are broken

4. The symbol * next to a file name means:
   a. External references are locked
   b. Select all references
   c. Deselect all references

5. The symbol *X next to a feature name means:
   a. The feature is fully defined
   b. The feature is over defined
   c. The feature is under defined
   d. None of the above

6. The Olive-Green color in a sketch means:
   a. The sketch entity is selected
   b. The sketch entity is being copied.
   c. The sketch has dangling entities, relations or dimensions

7. The dangling dimensions can be "re-attached" simply by dragging its handle point to a sketch line or a model edge.
   a. True
   b. False

7. TRUE
6. C   5. D
4. A   3. C
2. D   1. B

CHAPTER 20 Cont.

Repairing Part Errors

Understanding and Repairing Part Errors

When an error occurs, SolidWorks will try and solve it based on the settings below:

To pre-set the rebuild action:

A. Click **Options** ▦ (Standard toolbar) or **Tools, Options**.

B. Select **Stop**, **Continue**, or **Prompt** for **When rebuild error occurs**, then click **OK**. With **Stop** or **Prompt**, the rebuild action stops for each error so you can fix feature failures one at a time.

Indicates an error with the model. This icon appears on the document name at the top of the FeatureManager design tree, and on the feature that contains the error. The text of the part or feature is in red.

Indicates an error with a feature. This icon appears on the feature name in the FeatureManager design tree. The text of the feature is in red.

Indicates a warning underneath the node indicated. This icon appears on the document name at the top of the FeatureManager design tree and on the parent feature in the FeatureManager design tree whose child feature issued the error. The text of the feature is in Olive Green.

Indicates a warning with a **feature** or **sketch**. This icon appears on the specific feature in the FeatureManager design tree that issued the warning. The text of the feature or sketch is in Olive Green.

1. Opening a part document:

- Insert the Training File folder, browse to the Repair Errors folder, and open the part named: **Repair Errors**.

- When opening
a document
that contains
errors, the
What's Wrong
dialog box
will appear
and display
where the
errors are
located and
suggest some
solutions in
solving them.

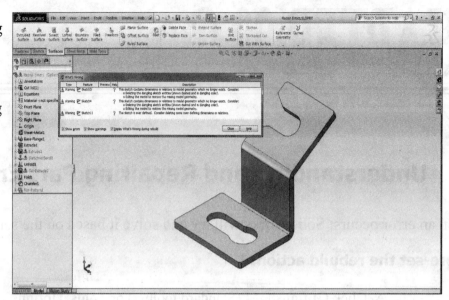

- **Expand** each feature on the FeatureManager tree and hover the pointer over the **Sketch3**.

- An explanation about the error or the warning is displayed in the tooltip. This is the same as right clicking on the error and selecting What's Wrong.

- Another way to see the explanation about the error is to right click on the error and select: **What's Wrong**.

- The What's Wrong dialog box pops up displaying the same explanation about the selected error. Enable the **Show Warnings** checkbox (arrow) to see the warnings after each rebuild.

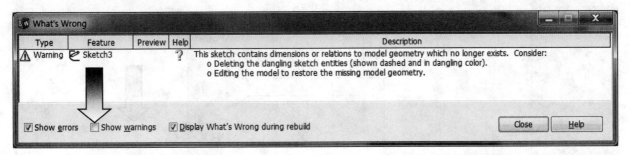

- From the Sketch toolbar click the **Display / Delete-Relations** button.

- The relations or dimensions that contain errors will appeared in different colors, Olive Green in this case.

Tangent8 is missing an entity

- **Select** the relation **Tangent8** from the relation dialog box. An arc and the missing entity are highlighted. The missing entity appears in **Red** along with an **Olive Green** tangent symbol above.

- **Delete** the **Tangent8** relation.

- A message on the bottom right of the screen appears, indicating that: **The sketch can now find a valid solution**.

- To see the status for the rest of the relations and dimensions, change from **Over Defining / Not Solved** to **All In This Sketch**.

- Select the **Coincident3**. An endpoint of the line is coincident to a missing edge. **Delete** this Coincident3.

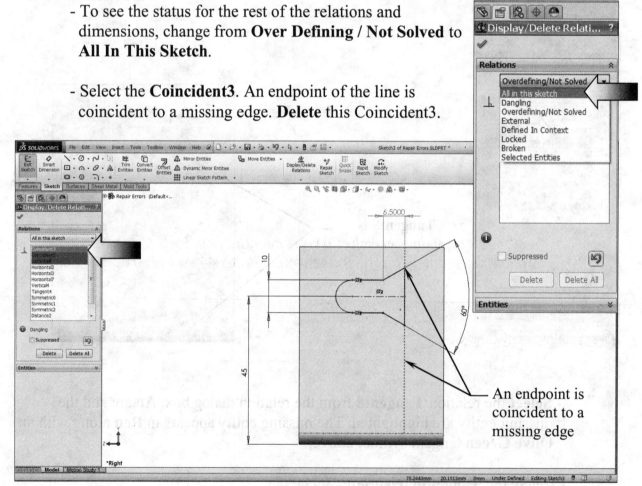

An endpoint is coincident to a missing edge

- **Delete** also the **Coincident5**. It's missing the same edge as the previous relation.

- The dimension **6.500** is dangling. It was also measured to a missing entity, **delete it**.

- **Add** 3 new dimensions as indicated to fully define this sketch. **Exit** the sketch when completed.

Delete this
Dangling dimension ⟶

Add 3 new ⟶
dimensions

- After exiting the sketch, SolidWorks continues to report other errors still remained in the part. The **Sketch4** and **Sketch11** still need to be repaired.

- **Close** the What's Wrong dialog box.

2. Repairing the 2nd error:

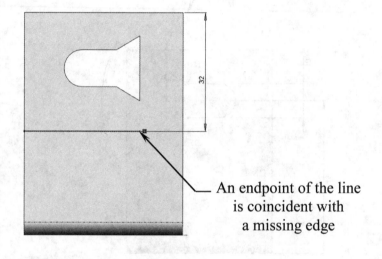

- Right click the **Sketch4** (under the Sketched Bend1 feature) and select **Edit Sketch**.

- Click the **Display / Delete Relations** button once again.

- Change the display relations option to **Dangling** (arrow).

- The **Coincident1** is dangled and has the Olive Green color. **Delete it**.

An endpoint of the line
is coincident with
a missing edge

- The endpoint of the line turns to Blue color. This indicates the sketch is under defined.

- **Drag and drop** the endpoint of the line until it touches the vertical right edge of the part. A coincident relation should be created automatically.

An endpoint of the
line is coincident with
a missing edge

- **Exit** the sketch or press **Control + Q**.

- SolidWorks continues to report the last error in the model. Click the **Continue (Ignore Error)** button to continue.

3. Repairing the 3rd error:

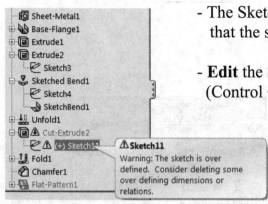

- The Sketch11 has a plus sign next to its name, this indicates that the sketch is Over Defined.

- **Edit** the **Sketch11**. Change to the Top orientation (Control + 5).

- Click the **Display / Delete Relations** button.

- Set the display relations option to: **Over Defining / Not Solved**.

- Select the **Collinear1** from the list. This relation shows a **Magenta** color next to its Collinear symbol.

- Delete the **Collinear1** from the list.

- This last step should bring the sketch back to its Fully Define status.

- **Exit** the sketch or press **Control + Q**.

4. Saving your work:

- Click **File / Save As**.

- Enter **Repair Errors (Completed)** for the name of the file.

- Click **Save**.

- All errors have been repaired. The Feature-Manager tree is now free of errors.

- Close all documents.

Repair Errors & External References

1. Opening an existing part:

- <u>Go to:</u>

 The Training Files folder.
 Repair Errors folder.

- Open the document named:
 Molded Part.

- The **What's Wrong** dialog pops
 up displaying the current errors.

- Click **Close**. We are going to
 take a look at breaking the
 external references first.

 Sketches or Features
 that have the Olive-green
 color indicate Dangling
 entities or dimensions.

2. Breaking all External References:

- Right click on the part's name and select: **List External Refs**.

- All of the Out of Context entities are displayed in the dialog box along with the names of the component parts in which they were related.

- Click **Break All** (Arrow).

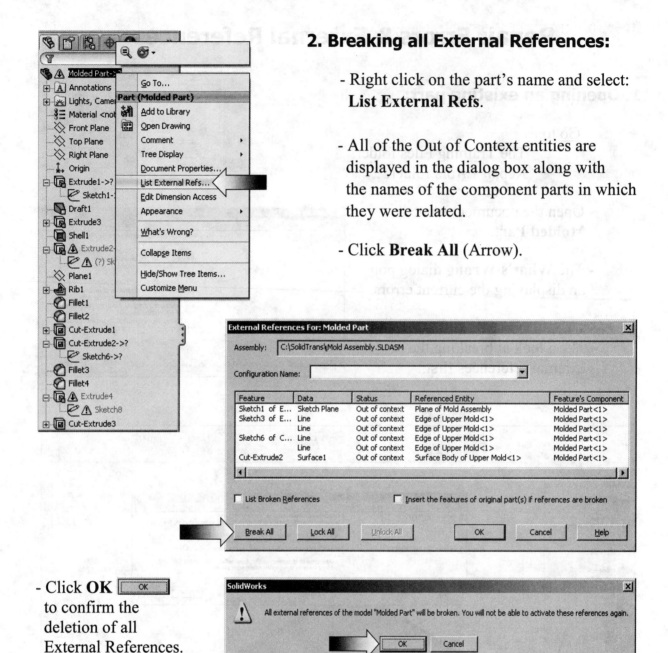

- Click **OK** to confirm the deletion of all External References.

💡 **_TIPS:_** _4 basic steps should be done, in most cases, to repair or replace External References:_

1. Break all External references (Right click on the part's name and select List External Refs.).

2. Replace the sketch Plane or Face (if missing).

3. Delete or replace any Relation with an External Reference symbol next to it (Display/Delete Relations).

4. Repair or replace the extrude type.

3. Replacing the Sketch Plane:

- Expand the **Extrude1** feature to see the **Sketch1** below.

- Right click on **Sketch1** and select **Edit Sketch Plane** .

- The Sketch Plane is missing, its dialog box is empty

- Select the **Front** plane from the Feature tree.

- After replacing the plane, click **OK** ✓.

- The system displays the warning on other errors along with the solutions for repairing.

- Click **Close** Close .

4. Repairing the sketch Relations and Dimensions:

- Right click on **Sketch1** and select **Edit Sketch** .

- Click Display/...
Relations or select **Tools /**
Relations / Display-Delete.

- Delete the 2 geometric relations
  that have the external symbols
  next their names (Arrows).

- The sketch becomes fully-defined.

- Click **OK** ⊘.

- **Exit** the sketch .

The sketch can now find a valid solution.

| -3.51in | 3.842in | 0in | Fully Defined | Editing Sketch3 |

5. Repairing the next sketch errors:

- Right click on **Sketch6** (under Cut-Extrude2) and select:

Edit Sketch .

- Two dimensions are no longer attached to the part (Circled).

Detached

Select the dimension to see the handle points. Drag the handle point of the dimension line (the red dot) to the model edge as shown, to re-attach it.

Re-attach the vertical dimension.

- The sketch becomes fully defined;
  the two dimensions are
  attached to locate the
  center of the circle.

- **Exit** the sketch .

6. Repairing the extrude type:

- Right click on **Cut-Extrude2** and select **Edit Feature**.

Select this face

- The surface that was used as the end condition option is no longer recognized, a new surface has to be selected for replacement.

- Select the **face** as indicated.

- Leave extrude depth as **.100**in.

- Click **OK**.

7. Repairing the errors in the last sketch:

- Right click on the **Sketch8** and select **Edit Sketch**.

- Change to the Bottom orientation, or press Control + 6 to switch to the bottom view.

Drag handle point to an edge to re-attach

- Dimensions created from or to other parts, became Dangling and detached from the model (Olive-green color).

Dangling Dimensions (Olive-Green color) drag to re-attached

- Select one of the dimensions and drag its handle point (the red dot) to a model edge to re-attach.

- Repeat the same step to re-attach all other dimensions.

- The sketch becomes fully defined after all dimensions are re-attached.

- The text color is set to Blue by default.

- **Exit** the sketch

- The reference symbols and the error colors on the FeatureManager tree should now be all removed.

8. Saving your work:

- Select **File / Save As / Repair Errors / Save**.

Level 4: Final Exam

1. Open an existing part document:

<u>Go to:</u>

    Training CD
    Tooling Design folder
    L4 Final Exam.sldprt.

2. Create a **Parting Line** using:

    - Direction of Pull = **TOP plane**.

    - Draft Angle   = **1deg.****

    - Parting Lines   = **All outer edges** as shown.

Parting Lines

** <u>*Important*</u> *- Roll back under the Loft feature and:*

a/ Add 1° drafts to all Yellow faces, including the 4 holes, this change will create some errors in the part.

b/ <u>Re-order</u> or <u>re-create</u> the fillets if necessary, after adding the drafts.

3. Create a **Parting Surface** using:

- **Perpendicular to Pull**.

- Parting Line: **Parting Line1**.

- Parting Surface Length = **.250 in**.

4. Create a new **Offset Distance plane** using:

- The **Top** reference plane and **.375 in**. distance.

- The new plane is placed **above** the Top plane.
(This new plane will also be use to create the Interlock Surfaces)

5. Sketch a **Rectangle** on the new plane (Plane1) and add dimensions* shown.

Adjust the dimensions if needed to center the rectangle around the part.

6. Exit the Sketch and create a **Tooling split** using:
- **1.250in**. (upper block)
- **1.250in**. (lower block)
- Use **Interlock Surface** with **5° Draft**.

7. Re-order or **re-create** the fillets if necessary.

8. Use the **Move/Copy** command to separate the two halves.

** <u>OPTIONAL</u>: Make the upper and lower solid bodies transparent for clarity.

9. Save your work as L4-Final.

Interlock Surfaces

Interlock Surfaces

CHAPTER 21

Using Appearances

A knurled feature would create hundreds of extra faces in the model and will increase file size, bog down their graphical performance. But if it is important to be able to represent a knurl then there are a couple of techniques that can be used to accommodate it.

This first half of the chapter will guide you through the method of modeling the Raised Diamond Knurls where a sketch profile will be swept along a path to create a spiral cut. The spiral cut is patterned and mirrored to repeat the raised diamond shapes of the knurl.

Modeling diamond knurls

1. Opening a part document:

 - Go to the Training Files folder and open a part document named:
   Knurled Handle.

 - This model has a single solid body, a sweep profile, and a sweep path that was previously created.

Before   After

2. Creating a swept cut:

- Select the Features tool tab and click the **Swept Cut** command.

- Select the **Sketch2** as the sweep profile.

- Select the **Helix** as the sweep path.

- Click **OK**.

- Rotate the model and examine the swept cut feature

3. Creating a circular pattern:

- Click the **Circular Pattern** command under the Linear Pattern drop down arrow.

- Select the <u>circular edge</u> on the left end of the model for Pattern Direction.

- Enable the **Equal Spacing** checkbox (arrow).

- Enter **25** for Number of instances.

- Select the **Swept Cut** feature either from the Feature tree or Directly from the graphics area.

- Click **OK**.

- Change to the top orientation (Control+5) to verify the pattern of the swept cut feature.

4. Creating a mirror pattern:

- Click the **Mirror** command from the Features tool tab.

- Expand the Feature tree and select the **Front** plane to use as Mirror Plane.

- For Features to Mirror select both: the **Cut-Swept1** and the **CirPattern1** features.

- Enable the option:
  Geometry Pattern to
  create the pattern using only
  the geometry (faces and edges) of
  the features, rather than patterning and
  solving each instance of the feature.

- Click **OK**.

- Change to the top
  orientation (Control+5)
  to verify the result of the
  mirror pattern.

- **Save** and <u>close</u> the document.

Applying knurl appearance

- Certain appearances required the use of RealView Graphics for more realistic representation, knurled, dimpled, or sandblasted are some examples.

- RealView gives models a realistic and dynamic representation without the need to render. If your graphics card is RealView-compatible, RealView is enabled by default.

1. Opening a part document:

- Open a part document named: **Knurl Appearance**.

- Click the drop down arrow next to View Settings and enable the **RealView Graphics** option (arrow).

2. Applying the knurl appearance:

- Expand the **Task pane** on the right side of the screen and pin it.

- Expand the Metal and Steel folders. Drag and drop the **Stainless Steel Knurled** appearance onto the <u>surface</u> of the handle.

Drag & drop

stainless steel knurled

machined steel

stainless steel treadplate

stainless steel knurled

- Select the **Apply to Face** option in the pop-up menu.

- The default knurled appearance is applied to the selected face.

Face(Revolve1)

- Next, we will modify the settings to make the diamond knurl appearance looks a little more realistic.

3. Modifying the knurl appearance:

- <u>Right click</u> the surface of the handle where the knurled appearance was applied and select: **Appearance > Face** edit option (arrow).

- Select the **Advanced** and **Mapping** tabs (arrow).

- Select **Automatic** under the mapping drop down selection.

- Enter **.125in** for both **Width** and **Height** of the diamonds.

- Click **OK**.

- Rotate the model to verify the result of the knurls.

- Additionally, change the following:

* Mapping Type: **Cylindrical**

* Axis Direction: **ZX**

* Rotation: **90deg**.

- Click **OK**.

- **Save** and <u>close</u> the document.

Applying Wire Mesh appearance

- Similar to diamond knurls, modeling 3D wire mesh is just too time consuming, the rebuild time would be too long, and the amount of memory needed for the task is just simply not practical.

- Appearance once again can offer some acceptable results without sacrificing your computer performance, or the time it takes to create one.

- We will take a look at modifying an existing appearance and make it looks like a wire meshed cable (pictured).

1. Opening a part document:

- Open a part document named: **Wire Mesh.sldpr**

- This model has 8 solid bodies and the sleeve in the middle will be used to apply the wire mesh.

2. Applying the wire mesh:

- Expand the **Task Pane** on the right side of the screen and pin it.

- Expand the following 2 folders: **Plastic** > **Composite** (arrows).

- Drag and drop the **Carbon Fiber Epoxy** appearance to the <u>middle sleeve</u> as noted.

Drag & drop

- Select the **Advanced** and the **Mapping** tabs and set the parameters shown below.

3. Modifying the wire mesh appearance:

- <u>Right click</u> the middle sleeve and select: **Appearance > Edit** (arrow).

- Select the **Advanced** and **Mapping** tabs. Set the Mapping type to Surface, and set the **Width** and **Height** to **.075in**, and the **angle** to **25deg**.

- Click **OK**.

- Alternatively, change the rotation to **90deg** (arrow) to change the angle of the mesh, if desired.

- Click **OK**.

- Save and close the document.

Flatten Surfaces

This new feature is only available in SOLIDWORKS Premium.

You can flatten surfaces and multi-faced surfaces (such as surfaces that are split into multiple faces). Surfaces that have holes or other internal geometries cut out of the middle cannot not be flattened.

1. Opening a part document:

- Open the part document named:
Flatten Surfaces.sldprt

- Click **Insert > Surface > Flatten** .

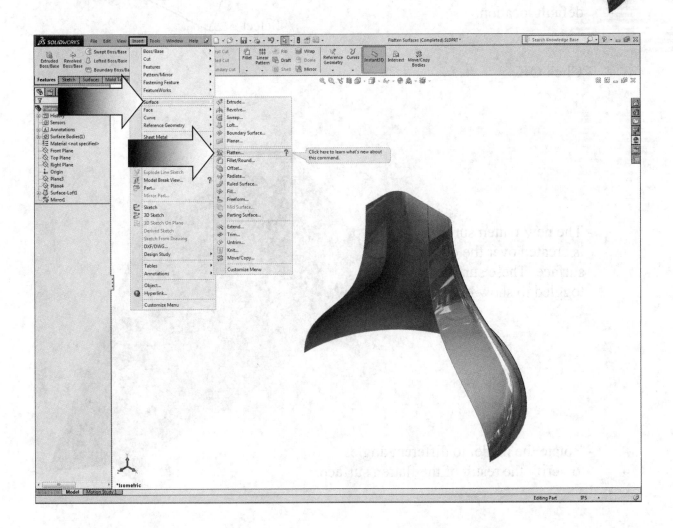

2. Flattening a surface:

- Click in the Face/
  Surface to Flatten
  section and select
  the <u>left and right
  surfaces</u> of the
  model.

- Click in the
  Vertex to Flatten
  From and select
  <u>the vertex</u> as
  indicated.

- Leave the Accuracy slider at its
  default location.

- Click O**K**.

Select vertex

Select 2
surfaces

- The new flatten surface
  is created over the original
  surface. These surfaces can
  toggled to show or hide.

- Rotate the model to different angles
  to verify the result of the flatten surface.

3. Viewing the deformation plot:

- To view a deformation plot of the flattened surface, right-click the surface and click Deformation Plot.

- The deformation plot shows the areas on the flattened surface with the highest levels of stretch and compression. You can mouse over the surface to see the percent of deviation at any given point.

In the graphics area, right-click the flatten surfaces, and click Deformation Plot .

A deformation plot appears in the graphics area showing where the surface is compressed or stretched

- Change to the front orientation and mouse over one of the red areas to see the percentage of the deformation (stretch).

4. Moving the surfaces:

- Click **Insert > Surface > Move/Copy**.

- In the <u>Translate</u> section, select the **Flatten Surface** to move.

- Enter **10.00in** in the <u>Delta X</u> box.

- Click **OK**.

- **Save** and <u>close</u> the document.

SolidWorks 2015

Certified SolidWorks Professional (CSWP)

Certification Practice for the Core Examination

Certified-SolidWorks-Professional program (CSWP)
Certification Practice for the Core-Exam

Challenge I: Part Modeling & Modifications

Complete this challenge within 90 minutes

(The following examples are intended to assist you in familiarizing yourself with the structures of the exams and the method in which the questions are asked).

- Create this part in SolidWorks   - Unit: **Inches, 3 decimals**   - Origin: **Arbitrary**

- Drafting Standards: **ANSI**   - Material: **Cast Alloy Steel**   - Density: **0.264 lb/in^3**

1. Creating the 1st revolve body:

- Using the <u>Front</u> plane, sketch the profile shown below.

- Add the dimensions and relations needed to fully define the sketch.

(Using revolve instead of extrude will help editing the the model much easier in the next few steps).

- Click **OK** .

2. Creating the 2nd revolve body:

- Open a new sketch on the <u>Front</u> plane.

- Sketch a **rectangle** on the left side of the vertical centerline.

- Add the dimensions shown.

8.000

5.000

Horizontal

1.250

3.000

- Add a horizontal relation to fully define the sketch.

- Revolve the sketch **360 degrees**.

- Click **OK** ✔.

Note: Use revolve instead extrude will make editing much easier later.

8.000

5.000

1.250

3.000

3. Linking the dimension values:

- To save time on editing features later on, we will link some of the dimensions together.

- From the FeatureManager tree, right click on Annotations and enable both options:

  * **Display Annotations**

  * **Show Feature Dimensions**

- At this point, we will link the two ID dimensions (Ø1.250), by giving them the exact same name.

- Hold the **Control** key and select both **ID** dimensions (circled), then right click on one of them and select: **Link Values** (arrow).

- Enter **ID Holes** for Name and click OK.

- The linked dimensions now have a red link symbol next to their values.

4. Creating the transition wall:

- Select the <u>Front</u> plane and open a new sketch.

- Sketch the profile as shown.

- Add the dimensions and the relations as indicated.

Temporary Axis

Enable the Temporary Axis from the View pull down menu.

- Extrude the sketch profile using the following parameters:

   * **Mid Plane**

   * **.750 in**.

   * **Merge Result**

- Click **OK** .

5. Creating a recess feature:

- Select the <u>face</u> as indicated and open a new sketch.

Offset 3 entities

Sketch face

.375

.375

- Select the **arc**, the **2 lines**, and click **Offset Entities**.

- Enter **.375"** for offset distance and click OK.

.375

Add 2 lines and trim

- Add 2 more lines as shown and trim them to their nearest intersections.

.375

- Add a sketch fillet of **R.125** to 5 places.

.375

5X R.125

- Enable the Temporary Axis and add the dimensions as shown to fully define this sketch.

1.500   .375   1.875

- Click **Extruded Cut** and use the following parameters:

  * **Blind**

  * **.215 in**.

- Click **OK**

6. Mirroring the recess feature:

- Select the <u>Front</u> plane for use as the Mirror plane and click the **Mirror** Command from the Features toolbar.

- Select the recess feature either from the graphics area or from the FeatureManager tree.

Select Feature to Mirror

- Click **OK** .

- Turn off the temporary axis.

(Section View)

7. Adding Fillets:

- Click the **Fillet** command and enter **.062"** for radius value.

- Select the **6 edges** as shown.

- Click **OK** .

Select 6 edges

8. Changing dimension values:

- The grading scores are based on the mass of the part after certain changes. At this point, we will change several dimensions and see what the final mass may be.

- Double click on the Transition-Wall to see its dimensions.

- Locate the **2.500"** dimension and change it to **3.250"**.

- Change the dimension
  8.000" to **8.750"**

- Click Rebuild
  or **Control + Q**.

8.000

Modify
8.750in

5.000

Ø3.000   Ø1.250

9. Measuring the mass of the part:

- Select **Tools / Mass Properties**.

- Enter the Mass here: _____ pounds.

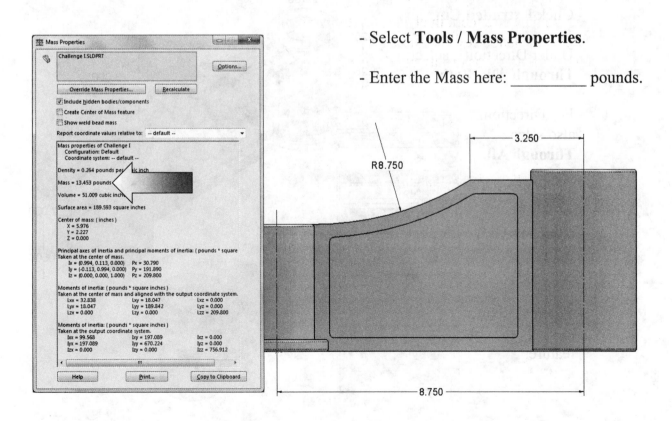

Mass Properties

Challenge I.SLDPRT

Options...

Override Mass Properties...   Recalculate

☑ Include hidden bodies/components
☐ Create Center of Mass feature
☐ Show weld bead mass

Report coordinate values relative to: -- default --

Mass properties of Challenge I
  Configuration: Default
  Coordinate system: -- default --

Density = 0.264 pounds per cubic inch

Mass = 13.453 pounds

Volume = 51.009 cubic inch

Surface area = 189.593 square inches

Center of mass: (inches)
  X = 5.976
  Y = 2.227
  Z = 0.000

Principal axes of inertia and principal moments of inertia: (pounds * square
Taken at the center of mass.
  Ix = (0.994, 0.113, 0.000)   Px = 30.790
  Iy = (-0.113, 0.994, 0.000)   Py = 191.890
  Iz = (0.000, 0.000, 1.000)   Pz = 209.800

Moments of inertia: (pounds * square inches)
Taken at the center of mass and aligned with the output coordinate system.
  Lxx = 32.838   Lxy = 18.047   Lxz = 0.000
  Lyx = 18.047   Lyy = 189.842   Lyz = 0.000
  Lzx = 0.000   Lzy = 0.000   Lzz = 209.800

Moments of inertia: (pounds * square inches)
Taken at the output coordinate system.
  Ixx = 99.568   Ixy = 197.089   Ixz = 0.000
  Iyx = 197.089   Iyy = 670.224   Iyz = 0.000
  Izx = 0.000   Izy = 0.000   Izz = 756.912

Help   Print...   Copy to Clipboard

3.250

R8.750

8.750

10. Adding the cut features:

- Select the Front plane and open a new sketch.

Collinear (both sides)

Front Plane

2.186

3.000

1.250

1.250

2.000

1.500

Not Collinear with edge

- Sketch the 2 rectangles as shown, and add dimensions/relations to fully define the sketch.

- Click **Extruded Cut**.

- Under Direction1, select: **Through All - Both**.

- For Direction2 also select: **Through All**.

- Click **OK**.

- Rotate the part to verify the cut feature.

11. Adding fillets and chamfers:

- Click the **Fillet** command.

- Enter **.093"** for radius value.

- Select the **4 Edges** as noted.

- Click **OK** ✓.

- Click the **Chamfer** command.

- Enter **.080"** for chamfer depth.

- Use the default **45°** angle.

- Select the **8 Edges** as noted.

- Click **OK** ✓.

(By selecting the circular faces of the ID holes, we can reduce the selections to 4 faces, instead of 8 edges)

Select 4 edges

Select 8 ID edges

12. Adding a recess feature:

Offset Entities

Offset Entities

Select Sketch Face

- Select the <u>face</u> as indicated and open a new sketch.

- Create an Offset of **.250"** from the **2 edges** as noted.

- Add **3 lines** approximately as shown.

- Add the dimensions as indicated in the image below.

- Trim the lines to their closest intersections.

- Add the **sketch fillets** of **R.093"** to **5 places**.

- Make sure the sketch is fully defined.

- Click **Extruded Cut**.

- Under Direction1, select:
Through All - Both.

- For Direction2
also select:
Through All.

- Click **OK**.

- Rotate the part
to verify the cut
feature.

13. Adding 2 circular bosses:

- Select the <u>Front</u> plane from the FeatureManager tree and open a new sketch.

- Sketch 2 circles and add the dimensions as shown to fully define them.

- Link the diameter dimensions using the Link Values option. Rename them to:
Cir_Bosses.

- Click **Extruded Boss/Base**.

- Under Direction1, select: **Mid Plane**.

- For extrude depth enter: **2.000in**.

- Click **OK**.

- Change to the Top view (Control + 5) to verify the boss feature.

14. Measuring the mass of the part*:

- Click **Tools / Mass Properties**.

- Locate the mass* (arrow) and enter

  it here _____ lbs.

* *The mass of an object is the amount of material it contains.*
A body with greater mass has more inertia; it needs a greater force to accelerate.
Weight depends on the force of gravity, but mass does not.

15. Modifying the feature dimensions:

- Locate the diameter dimensions for the 2 ID holes (circled) and change them from: Ø1.250 to Ø **1.500"**.

- Click **Rebuild** or press **Control + Q**.

- Locate the OD dimension (Ø3.000) for the Circular boss on the right side (circled) and change it from Ø3.000" to Ø**2.750"**.

- Click **Rebuild** or press **Control + Q.**

- Did the changes caused any rebuild errors? If so, stop and repair them before to moving forward to the next step.

- Locate the OD dimension for the circular boss on the left (circled) and change it from Ø2.250 to **2.500"**.

- Click **Rebuild** or press **Control + Q**.

16. Measuring the mass of the part:

- Click **Tools / Mass Properties**.

- Locate the mass (arrow) and enter it

here: _____ lbs.

17. Creating the Counter-Bores:

- Click the **Hole-Wizard** command from the Features toolbar.

- Select the following:

* Hole Type: **Counterbore**

* Standard: **Ansi Inch**

* Type: **Binding Head Screw**

* Size: **1/4**

* Fit: **Normal**

* End Condition: **Through All**

Both C'bores are centered on the cir_bosses

* Clear the Near-Side-Countersink box

- Change to the **Positions** tab (circled) and place 2 Counter-bores on the same centers as the circular boss features, click **OK** when finished.

- Create a **Section View** similar to the one shown below to verify the 2 counter bores.

18. Adding a side tab:

- Open a new sketch on the <u>Front</u> plane.

Collinear with edge of ID

Ø.250

1.625

Front Plane

R.325

3.000

- Sketch the profile of the tab as show.

- Add the dimensions and relations needed to fully define the sketch.

- Click **Extruded Boss/Base**.

- Under Direction1, select: **Mid Plane**.

- For extrude depth enter: **.425 in**.

Boss-Extrude3

From
Sketch Plane

Direction 1
Mid Plane

D1   0.425in

☑ Merge result

☐ Draft outward

Selected Contours

- Click **OK**.

- Rotate the part and Verify that the tab is centered on the Front plane.

Rotated 180°

19. Modifying the recess feature:

- Locate the spacing dimension of the recess (1.375") and change to **.875"**.

- Click **Rebuild** .

- Find the final mass of the part and enter it here: _____ lbs.

20. Modifying the Revolved feature:

- <u>Edit the sketch</u> of the **Revolved2** feature.

- Add 3 new lines as indicated.

- Add the 3 dimensions (circled) to fully define this sketch.

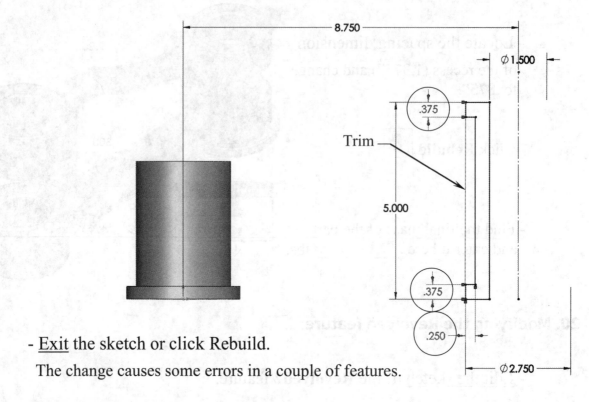

- <u>Exit</u> the sketch or click Rebuild.

The change causes some errors in a couple of features.

- <u>Edit</u> the **Fillet1** feature and select the missing edge as noted.

- Edit the Sketch5 under the Cut-Extrude2. Replace the relation as noted. Click Rebuild.

- Measure the final mass of the part and enter it here: _____ lbs.

21. Saving your work:

- Save your work as **Challenge1** and close the document when done.

- Use the example file from the Training Files to review the construction of the part, if needed.

Certified-SolidWorks-Professional program (CSWP)
Certification Practice for the Core-Exam

Challenge II-A: Part Configurations & Design Tables

Complete both challenges A&B within 40 minutes

(The following examples are intended to assist you in familiarizing yourself with the structures of the exams and the method in which the questions are asked).

- Modify this part in SolidWorks   - Unit: **Millimeter, 2 decimals**   - Origin: **Arbitrary**

- Drafting Standards: **ANSI**   - Material: **Alloy Steel**   - Density: **0.008 /mm^3**

1. Opening a part document:

   - Browse to the Training Files, open the part document: **Challenge II-A**.

2. Setting the options:

   - Change the material to **Alloy Steel**.

   - Change the system options to match the settings above.

3. Switching Configuration:

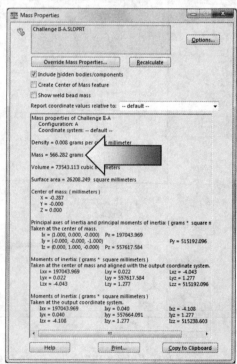

   - Switch to the ConfigurationManager tree, double click to activate **Configuration A**.

4. Measuring the Mass:

   - Select **Tools/ Mass Properties**.

   - Enter the mass in grams:

   _____ grams.

<u>NOTE:</u> *Material must be selected before calculating the mass of the part.*

5. Adding a New Configuration:

- Create a <u>new configuration</u> named **D**, and enter the comment: **Added a 10mm hole**.

- Select the face shown below and open a new sketch.

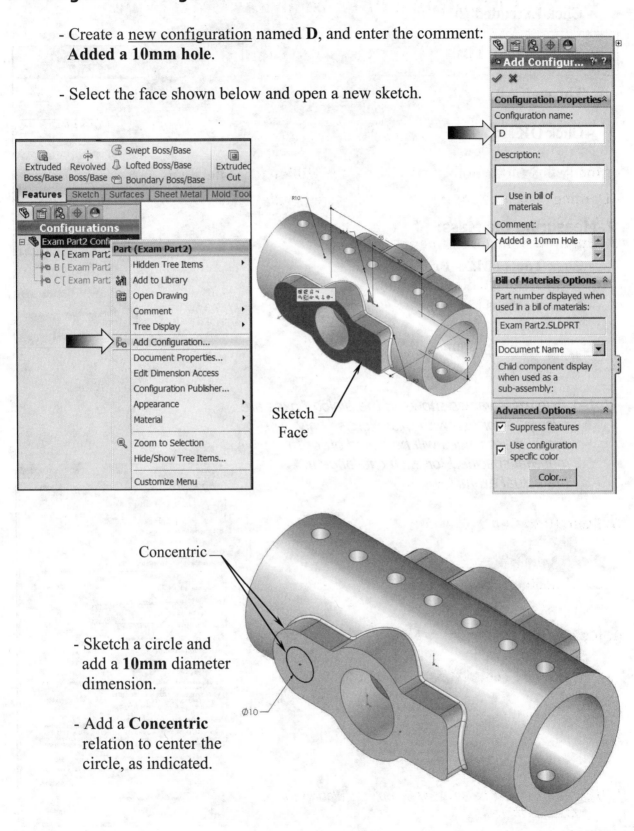

Sketch Face

Concentric

- Sketch a circle and add a **10mm** diameter dimension.

- Add a **Concentric** relation to center the circle, as indicated.

Ø10

6. Extruding a cut:

- Click **Extruded Cut**.

- Set Direction1 to:

Through All.

- Click **OK** .

Ø10

7. Measuring the Mass:

- Click **Tools / Mass Properties**.

- Enter the mass in grams:

_____ grams.

<u>Note:</u> *The mass values shown in the dialog boxes are examples for use with this exercise only. The actual mass values will be based off of the material specified for each challenge in the actual exam.*

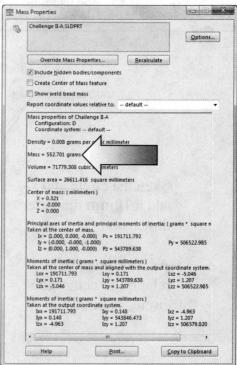

8. Switching configuration:

- Double click on **Configuration B** to make it active.

9. Measuring the Mass:

- Select **Tools/ Mass Properties**.

- Enter the new mass:

_____ grams.

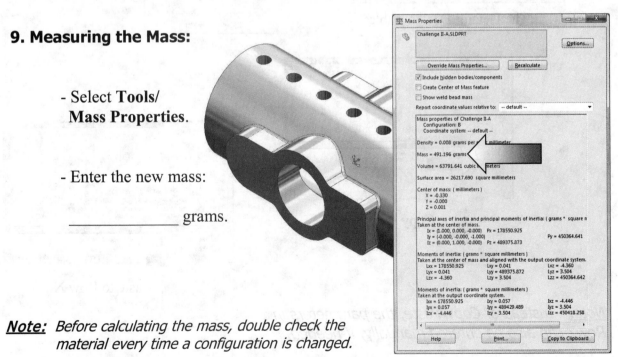

Note: _Before calculating the mass, double check the material every time a configuration is changed._

10. Creating a Design Table:

- Double click the configuration **B** to activate it.

- Go to: **Insert / Tables / Design Tables**.

- Select the **Auto Create** option and leave all other options at their default settings.

11. Adding new Configurations:

- Right click on **Row4** and select **Copy**.

- Right click on **Row7** and select **Paste**.

The Default Design Table

Copy Row No. 4

Paste to Row No. 7

Note: _Instead of Copy/Paste, the parameters in Row7 can also be entered manually, if needed._

12. Modifying the new configurations:

- Change the names of the configuration and description to **E**.

- Change the ID dimension on the body to **24**.

- Change the hole Diameter to **16**.

- Leave the Suppression States at Suppressed (S).

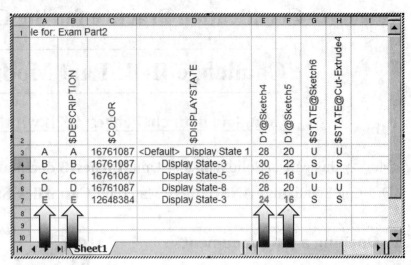

	A	B	C	D	E	F	G	H	I
1	le for: Exam Part2								
2		$DESCRIPTION	$COLOR	$DISPLAYSTATE	D1@Sketch4	D1@Sketch5	$STATE@Sketch6	$STATE@Cut-Extrude4	
3	A	A	16761087	\<Default\> Display State 1	28	20	U	U	
4	B	B	16761087	Display State-3	30	22	S	S	
5	C	C	16761087	Display State-5	26	18	U	U	
6	D	D	16761087	Display State-8	28	20	U	U	
7	E	E	12648384	Display State-3	24	16	S	S	
8									
9									
10									

- Click anywhere in the background to return to SolidWorks.

- Double click on **Configuration E** to activate. *Uncheck the Link to Display State option and click <u>Rebuild</u> to update the color).*

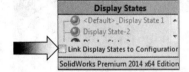

13. Measuring the final Mass:

- Select **Tools/ Mass Properties**.

- Enter the final mass: _____ grams

14. Save your work as Challenge 2-A.

Certified-SolidWorks-Professional program (CSWP)
Certification Practice for the Core-Exam

Challenge II-B: Part Modifications

Complete both challenges A&B within 40 minutes

- Modify this part in SolidWorks
- Unit: **Inches, 3 decimals**
- Origin: **Arbitrary**
- Drafting Standards: **ANSI**
- Material: **Cast Alloy Steel**
- Density: **0.264 / in^3**

1. Opening a part document:

- Browse to the Training Files folder and open the part named **Challenge II-B**.

2. Setting the options:

- Change the material to **Cast Alloy Steel**.

- Change the system options to match the settings above.

3. Adding the 1st cut:

- Select the <u>Top</u> plane and open a new sketch.

- Sketch the profile shown below, it will be used to trim off the material on the top.

- Add the dimensions and relations needed to fully define the sketch.

Glossary

Alloys:
An Alloy is a mixture of two or more metals (and sometimes a non-metal). The mixture is made by heating and melting the substances together.
Example of alloys are Bronze (Copper and Tin), Brass (Copper and Zinc), and Steel (Iron and Carbon).

Gravity and Mass:
Gravity is the force that pulls everything on earth toward the ground and makes things feel heavy. Gravity makes all falling bodies accelerates at a constant 32ft. per second (9.8 m/s). In the earth's atmosphere, air resistance slow acceleration. Only on airless Moon would a feather and a metal block fall to the ground together.
The mass of an object is the amount of material it contains.
A body with greater mass has more inertia; it needs a greater force to accelerate.
Weight depends on the force of gravity, but mass does not.

When an object spins around another (for example: a satellite orbiting the earth) it is pushed outward. Two forces are at work here: Centrifugal (pushing outward) and Centripetal (pulling inward). If you whirl a ball around you on a string, you pull it inward (Centripetal force). The ball seems to pull outward (Centrifugal force) and if released will fly off in a straight line.

Heat:
Heat is a form of energy and can move from one substance to another in one of three ways: by Convection, by Radiation, and by Conduction.

- Convection takes place only in liquids like water (for example: water in a kettle) and gases (for example: air warmed by a heat source such as a fire or radiator). When liquid or gas is heated, it expands and become less dense. Warm air above the radiator rises and cool air moves in to take its place, creating a convection current.
- Radiation is movement of heat through the air. Heat forms a match sets molecules of air moving and rays of heat spread out around the heat source.
- Conduction occurs in solids such as metals. The handle of a metal spoon left in boiling liquid warms up as molecules at the heated end moves faster and collide with their neighbors, setting them moving. The heat travels through the metal, which is a good conductor of heat.

Inertia:
A body with a large mass is harder to start and also to stop. A heavy truck traveling at 50mph needs more power breaks to stop its motion than a smaller car traveling at the same speed.
Inertia is the tendency of an object either to stay still or to move steadily in a straight line, unless another force (such as a brick wall stopping the vehicle) makes it behave differently.

Joules:
The Joules is the SI unit of work or energy.
One Joule of work is done when a force of one Newton moves through a distance of one meter.
The Joule is named after the English scientist James Joule (1818-1889).

Materials:
-   Stainless steel is an alloy of steel with chromium or nickel.

-   Steel is made by the basic oxygen process. The raw material is about three parts melted iron and one part scrap steel. Blowing oxygen into the melted iron raises the temperature and gets rid of impurities.

-   All plastic are chemical compounds called polymers.

-   Glass is made by mixing and heating sand, limestone, and soda ash. When these ingredients melt they turn into glass, which is hardened when it cools. Glass is in fact not a solid but a "supercooled" liquid, it can be shaped by blowing, pressing, drawing, casting into molds, rolling, and floating across molten tin, to make large sheets.

-   Ceramic objects, such as pottery and porcelain, electrical insulators, bricks, and roof tiles are all made from clay. The clay is shaped or molded when wet and soft, and heated in a kiln until it hardens.

Machine Tools:
Are powered tools used for shaping metal or other materials, by drilling holes, chiseling, grinding, pressing or cutting. Often the material (the work piece) is moved while the tool stays still (lathe), or vice versa, the work piece stayed while the tool moves (mill).
Most common machine tools are: Mill, Lathe, Saw, Broach, Punch press, Grind, Bore and Stamp break.

CNC:
Computer Numerical Control is the automation of machine tools that are operated by precisely programmed commands encoded on a storage medium, as opposed to controlled manually via hand wheels or levers, or mechanically automated via cams alone. Most CNC today is computer numerical control in which computers play an integral part of the control.

3D Printing:
All methods work by working in layers, adding material, etc. different to other techniques, which are subtractive. Supports needed because almost all methods could support multi material printing, but it is currently only available in certain top tier machines.

A method of turning digital shape into physical objects. Due to its nature, it allows us to accurately control the shape of the product. The drawback is size restraints and materials often not durable.

While FDM doesn't seem like the best method for instrument manufacturing, it is one of the cheapest and most universally available methods.

EDM
Electric Discharge Machining.

FDM
Fused Deposition Modeling.

SLA
Stereo Lithography.

SLS
Selective Laser Sintering.

SLM
Selective Laser Melting.

J-P
Jetted Photopolymer (or Polyjet)

Newton's Law:
1. Every object remains stopped or goes on moving at a steady rate in a straight line unless acted upon by another force. This is the inertia principle.
2. The amount of force needed to make an object change its speed depends on the mass of the object and the amount of the acceleration or deceleration required.
3. To every action there is an equal and opposite reaction. When a body is pushed on way by a force, another force pushes back with equal strength.

Polymers:
A polymer is made of one or more large molecules formed from thousands of smaller molecules. Rubber and Wood are natural polymers. Plastics are synthetic (artificially made) polymers.

Speed and Velocity:
- Speed is the rate at which a moving object changes position (how far it moves in a fixed time).
- Velocity is speed in a particular direction.
- If either speed or direction is changed, velocity also changed.

Absorbed
A feature, sketch, or annotation that is contained in another item (usually a feature) in the FeatureManager design tree. Examples are the profile sketch and profile path in a base-sweep, or a cosmetic thread annotation in a hole.

Align
Tools that assist in lining up annotations and dimensions (left, right, top, bottom, and so on). For aligning parts in an assembly.

Alternate position view
A drawing view in which one or more views are superimposed in phantom lines on the original view. Alternate position views are often used to show range of motion of an assembly.

Anchor point
The end of a leader that attaches to the note, block, or other annotation. Sheet formats contain anchor points for a bill of materials, a hole table, a revision table, and a weldment cut list.

Annotation
A text note or a symbol that adds specific design intent to a part, assembly, or drawing. Specific types of annotations include note, hole callout, surface finish symbol, datum feature symbol, datum target, geometric tolerance symbol, weld symbol, balloon, and stacked balloon. Annotations that apply only to drawings include center mark, annotation centerline, area hatch, and block.

Appearance callouts
Callouts that display the colors and textures of the face, feature, body, and part under the entity selected and are a shortcut to editing colors and textures.

Area hatch
A crosshatch pattern or fill applied to a selected face or to a closed sketch in a drawing.

Assembly
A document in which parts, features, and other assemblies (sub-assemblies) are mated together. The parts and sub-assemblies exist in documents separate from the assembly.
For example, in an assembly, a piston can be mated to other parts, such as a connecting rod or cylinder. This new assembly can then be used as a sub-assembly in an assembly of an engine. The extension for a SolidWorks assembly file name is .SLDASM.

Attachment point
The end of a leader that attaches to the model (to an edge, vertex, or face, for example) or to a drawing sheet.

Axis
A straight line that can be used to create model geometry, features, or patterns. An axis can be made in a number of different ways, including using the intersection of two planes.

Balloon
Labels parts in an assembly, typically including item numbers and quantity. In drawings, the item numbers are related to rows in a bill of materials.

Base
The first solid feature of a part.

Baseline dimensions
Sets of dimensions measured from the same edge or vertex in a drawing.

Bend
A feature in a sheet metal part. A bend generated from a filleted corner, cylindrical face, or conical face is a round bend; a bend generated from sketched straight lines is a sharp bends.

Bill of materials
A table inserted into a drawing to keep a record of the parts used in an assembly.

Block
A user-defined annotation that you can use in parts, assemblies, and drawings. A block can contain text, sketch entities (except points), and area hatch, and it can be saved in a file for later use as, for example, a custom callout or a company logo.

Bottom-up assembly
An assembly modeling technique where you create parts and then insert them into an assembly.

Broken-out section
A drawing view that exposes inner details of a drawing view by removing material from a closed profile, usually a spline.

Cavity
The mold half that holds the cavity feature of the design part.

Center mark
A cross that marks the center of a circle or arc.

Centerline
A centerline marks, in phantom font, an axis of symmetry in a sketch or drawing.

Chamfer
Bevels a selected edge or vertex. You can apply chamfers to both sketches and features.

Child
A dependent feature related to a previously-built feature. For example, a chamfer on the edge of a hole is a child of the parent hole.

Click-release
As you sketch, if you click and then release the pointer, you are in click-release mode. Move the pointer and click again to define the next point in the sketch sequence.

Click-drag
As you sketch, if you click and drag the pointer, you are in click-drag mode. When you release the pointer, the sketch entity is complete.

Closed profile
Also called a closed contour, it is a sketch or sketch entity with no exposed endpoints; for example, a circle or polygon.

Collapse
The opposite of explode. The collapse action returns an exploded assembly's parts to their normal positions.

Collision Detection

An assembly function that detects collisions between components when components move or rotate. A collision occurs when an entity on one component coincides with any entity on another component.

Component

Any part or sub-assembly within an assembly

Configuration

A variation of a part or assembly within a single document. Variations can include different dimensions, features, and properties. For example, a single part such as a bolt can contain different configurations that vary the diameter and length.

ConfigurationManager

Located on the left side of the SolidWorks window, it is a means to create, select, and view the configurations of parts and assemblies.

Constraint

The relations between sketch entities, or between sketch entities and planes, axes, edges, or vertices.

Construction geometry

The characteristic of a sketch entity that the entity is used in creating other geometry but is not itself used in creating features.

Coordinate system

A system of planes used to assign Cartesian coordinates to features, parts, and assemblies. Part and assembly documents contain default coordinate systems; other coordinate systems can be defined with reference geometry. Coordinate systems can be used with measurement tools and for exporting documents to other file formats.

Cosmetic thread

An annotation that represents threads.

Crosshatch

A pattern (or fill) applied to drawing views such as section views and broken-out sections.

Curvature

Curvature is equal to the inverse of the radius of the curve. The curvature can be displayed in different colors according to the local radius (usually of a surface).

Cut

A feature that removes material from a part by such actions as extrude, revolve, loft, sweep, thicken, cavity, and so on.

Dangling
A dimension, relation, or drawing section view that is unresolved. For example, if a piece of geometry is dimensioned, and that geometry is later deleted, the dimension becomes dangling.

Degrees of freedom
Geometry that is not defined by dimensions or relations is free to move. In 2D sketches, there are three degrees of freedom: movement along the X and Y axes, and rotation about the Z axis (the axis normal to the sketch plane). In 3D sketches and in assemblies, there are six degrees of freedom: movement along the X, Y, and Z axes, and rotation about the X, Y, and Z axes.

Derived part
A derived part is a new base, mirror, or component part created directly from an existing part and linked to the original part such that changes to the original part are reflected in the derived part.

Derived sketch
A copy of a sketch, in either the same part or the same assembly that is connected to the original sketch. Changes in the original sketch are reflected in the derived sketch.

Design Library
Located in the Task Pane, the Design Library provides a central location for reusable elements such as parts, assemblies, and so on.

Design table
An Excel spreadsheet that is used to create multiple configurations in a part or assembly document.

Detached drawing
A drawing format that allows opening and working in a drawing without loading the corresponding models into memory. The models are loaded on an as-needed basis.

Detail view
A portion of a larger view, usually at a larger scale than the original view.

Dimension line
A linear dimension line references the dimension text to extension lines indicating the entity being measured. An angular dimension line references the dimension text directly to the measured object.

DimXpertManager
Located on the left side of the SolidWorks window, it is a means to manage dimensions and tolerances created using DimXpert for parts according to the requirements of the ASME Y.14.41-2003 standard.

DisplayManager

The DisplayManager lists the appearances, decals, lights, scene, and cameras applied to the current model. From the DisplayManager, you can view applied content, and add, edit, or delete items. When PhotoView 360 is added in, the DisplayManager also provides access to PhotoView options.

Document

A file containing a part, assembly, or drawing.

Draft

The degree of taper or angle of a face, usually applied to molds or castings.

Drawing

A 2D representation of a 3D part or assembly. The extension for a SolidWorks drawing file name is .SLDDRW.

Drawing sheet

A page in a drawing document.

Driven dimension

Measurements of the model, but they do not drive the model and their values cannot be changed.

Driving dimension

Also referred to as a model dimension, it sets the value for a sketch entity. It can also control distance, thickness, and feature parameters.

Edge

A single outside boundary of a feature.

Edge flange

A sheet metal feature that combines a bend and a tab in a single operation.

Equation

Creates a mathematical relation between sketch dimensions, using dimension names as variables, or between feature parameters, such as the depth of an extruded feature or the instance count in a pattern.

Exploded view

Shows an assembly with its components separated from one another, usually to show how to assemble the mechanism.

Export

Save a SolidWorks document in another format for use in other CAD/CAM, rapid prototyping, web, or graphics software applications.

Extension line
The line extending from the model indicating the point from which a dimension is measured.

Extrude
A feature that linearly projects a sketch to either add material to a part (in a base or boss) or remove material from a part (in a cut or hole).

Face
A selectable area (planar or otherwise) of a model or surface with boundaries that help define the shape of the model or surface. For example, a rectangular solid has six faces.

Fasteners
A SolidWorks Toolbox library that adds fasteners automatically to holes in an assembly.

Feature
An individual shape that, combined with other features, makes up a part or assembly. Some features, such as bosses and cuts, originate as sketches. Other features, such as shells and fillets, modify a feature's geometry. However, not all features have associated geometry. Features are always listed in the FeatureManager design tree.

FeatureManager design tree
Located on the left side of the SolidWorks window, it provides an outline view of the active part, assembly, or drawing.

Fill
A solid area hatch or crosshatch. Fill also applies to patches on surfaces.

Fillet
An internal rounding of a corner or edge in a sketch, or an edge on a surface or solid.

Forming tool
Dies that bend, stretch, or otherwise form sheet metal to create such form features as louvers, lances, flanges, and ribs.

Fully defined
A sketch where all lines and curves in the sketch, and their positions, are described by dimensions or relations, or both, and cannot be moved. Fully defined sketch entities are shown in black.

Geometric tolerance
A set of standard symbols that specify the geometric characteristics and dimensional requirements of a feature.

Graphics area
The area in the SolidWorks window where the part, assembly, or drawing appears.

Guide curve

A 2D or 3D curve used to guide a sweep or loft.

Handle

An arrow, square, or circle that you can drag to adjust the size or position of an entity (a feature, dimension, or sketch entity, for example).

Helix

A curve defined by pitch, revolutions, and height. A helix can be used, for example, as a path for a swept feature cutting threads in a bolt.

Hem

A sheet metal feature that folds back at the edge of a part. A hem can be open, closed, double, or tear-drop.

HLR

(Hidden lines removed) a view mode in which all edges of the model that are not visible from the current view angle are removed from the display.

HLV

(Hidden lines visible) A view mode in which all edges of the model that are not visible from the current view angle are shown gray or dashed.

Import

Open files from other CAD software applications into a SolidWorks document.

In-context feature

A feature with an external reference to the geometry of another component; the in-context feature changes automatically if the geometry of the referenced model or feature changes.

Inference

The system automatically creates (infers) relations between dragged entities (sketched entities, annotations, and components) and other entities and geometry. This is useful when positioning entities relative to one another.

Instance

An item in a pattern or a component in an assembly that occurs more than once. Blocks are inserted into drawings as instances of block definitions.

Interference detection

A tool that displays any interference between selected components in an assembly.

Jog

A sheet metal feature that adds material to a part by creating two bends from a sketched line.

Knit
A tool that combines two or more faces or surfaces into one. The edges of the surfaces must be adjacent and not overlapping, but they cannot ever be planar. There is no difference in the appearance of the face or the surface after knitting.

Layout sketch
A sketch that contains important sketch entities, dimensions, and relations. You reference the entities in the layout sketch when creating new sketches, building new geometry, or positioning components in an assembly. This allows for easier updating of your model because changes you make to the layout sketch propagate to the entire model.

Leader
A solid line from an annotation (note, dimension, and so on) to the referenced feature.

Library feature
A frequently used feature, or combination of features, that is created once and then saved for future use.

Lightweight
A part in an assembly or a drawing has only a subset of its model data loaded into memory. The remaining model data is loaded on an as-needed basis. This improves performance of large and complex assemblies.

Line
A straight sketch entity with two endpoints. A line can be created by projecting an external entity such as an edge, plane, axis, or sketch curve into the sketch.

Loft
A base, boss, cut, or surface feature created by transitions between profiles.

Lofted bend
A sheet metal feature that produces a roll form or a transitional shape from two open profile sketches. Lofted bends often create funnels and chutes.

Mass properties
A tool that evaluates the characteristics of a part or an assembly such as volume, surface area, centroid, and so on.

Mate
A geometric relationship, such as coincident, perpendicular, tangent, and so on, between parts in an assembly.

Mate reference
Specifies one or more entities of a component to use for automatic mating. When you drag a component with a mate reference into an assembly, the software tries to find other combinations of the same mate reference name and mate type.

Mates folder
A collection of mates that are solved together. The order in which the mates appear within the Mates folder does not matter.

Mirror
(a) A mirror feature is a copy of a selected feature, mirrored about a plane or planar face.
(b) A mirror sketch entity is a copy of a selected sketch entity that is mirrored about a centerline.

Miter flange
A sheet metal feature that joins multiple edge flanges together and miters the corner.

Model
3D solid geometry in a part or assembly document. If a part or assembly document contains multiple configurations, each configuration is a separate model.

Model dimension
A dimension specified in a sketch or a feature in a part or assembly document that defines some entity in a 3D model.

Model item
A characteristic or dimension of feature geometry that can be used in detailing drawings.

Model view
A drawing view of a part or assembly.

Mold
A set of manufacturing tooling used to shape molten plastic or other material into a designed part. You design the mold using a sequence of integrated tools that result in cavity and core blocks that are derived parts of the part to be molded.

Motion Study
Motion Studies are graphical simulations of motion and visual properties with assembly models. Analogous to a configuration, they do not actually change the original assembly model or its properties. They display the model as it changes based on simulation elements you add.

Multibody part
A part with separate solid bodies within the same part document. Unlike the components in an assembly, multibody parts are not dynamic.

Native format
DXF and DWG files remain in their original format (are not converted into SolidWorks format) when viewed in SolidWorks drawing sheets (view only).

Open profile
Also called an open contour, it is a sketch or sketch entity with endpoints exposed. For example, a U-shaped profile is open.

Ordinate dimensions
A chain of dimensions measured from a zero ordinate in a drawing or sketch.

Origin
The model origin appears as three gray arrows and represents the (0,0,0) coordinate of the model. When a sketch is active, a sketch origin appears in red and represents the (0,0,0) coordinate of the sketch. Dimensions and relations can be added to the model origin, but not to a sketch origin.

Out-of-context feature
A feature with an external reference to the geometry of another component that is not open.

Over defined
A sketch is over defined when dimensions or relations are either in conflict or redundant.

Parameter
A value used to define a sketch or feature (often a dimension).

Parent
An existing feature upon which other features depend. For example, in a block with a hole, the block is the parent to the child hole feature.

Part
A single 3D object made up of features. A part can become a component in an assembly, and it can be represented in 2D in a drawing. Examples of parts are bolt, pin, plate, and so on. The extension for a SolidWorks part file name is .SLDPRT.

Path
A sketch, edge, or curve used in creating a sweep or loft.

Pattern
A pattern repeats selected sketch entities, features, or components in an array, which can be linear, circular, or sketch-driven. If the seed entity is changed, the other instances in the pattern update.

Physical Dynamics
An assembly tool that displays the motion of assembly components in a realistic way. When you drag a component, the component applies a force to other components it touches. Components move only within their degrees of freedom.

Pierce relation
Makes a sketch point coincident to the location at which an axis, edge, line, or spline pierces the sketch plane.

Planar
Entities that can lie on one plane. For example, a circle is planar, but a helix is not.

Plane
Flat construction geometry. Planes can be used for a 2D sketch, section view of a model, a neutral plane in a draft feature, and others.

Point
A singular location in a sketch, or a projection into a sketch at a single location of an external entity (origin, vertex, axis, or point in an external sketch).

Predefined view
A drawing view in which the view position, orientation, and so on can be specified before a model is inserted. You can save drawing documents with predefined views as templates.

Profile
A sketch entity used to create a feature (such as a loft) or a drawing view (such as a detail view). A profile can be open (such as a U shape or open spline) or closed (such as a circle or closed spline).

Projected dimension
If you dimension entities in an isometric view, projected dimensions are the flat dimensions in 2D.

Projected view
A drawing view projected orthogonally from an existing view.

PropertyManager
Located on the left side of the SolidWorks window, it is used for dynamic editing of sketch entities and most features.

RealView graphics
A hardware (graphics card) support of advanced shading in real time; the rendering applies to the model and is retained as you move or rotate a part.

Rebuild
Tool that updates (or regenerates) the document with any changes made since the last time the model was rebuilt. Rebuild is typically used after changing a model dimension.

Reference dimension
A dimension in a drawing that shows the measurement of an item, but cannot drive the model and its value cannot be modified. When model dimensions change, reference dimensions update.

Reference geometry
Includes planes, axes, coordinate systems, and 3D curves. Reference geometry is used to assist in creating features such lofts, sweeps, drafts, chamfers, and patterns.

Relation

A geometric constraint between sketch entities or between a sketch entity and a plane, axis, edge, or vertex. Relations can be added automatically or manually.

Relative view

A relative (or relative to model) drawing view is created relative to planar surfaces in a part or assembly.

Reload

Refreshes shared documents. For example, if you open a part file for read-only access while another user makes changes to the same part, you can reload the new version, including the changes.

Reorder

Reordering (changing the order of) items is possible in the FeatureManager design tree. In parts, you can change the order in which features are solved. In assemblies, you can control the order in which components appear in a bill of materials.

Replace

Substitutes one or more open instances of a component in an assembly with a different component.

Resolved

A state of an assembly component (in an assembly or drawing document) in which it is fully loaded in memory. All the component's model data is available, so its entities can be selected, referenced, edited, and used in mates, and so on.

Revolve

A feature that creates a base or boss, a revolved cut, or revolved surface by revolving one or more sketched profiles around a centerline.

Rip

A sheet metal feature that removes material at an edge to allow a bend.

Rollback

Suppresses all items below the rollback bar.

Section

Another term for profile in sweeps.

Section line

A line or centerline sketched in a drawing view to create a section view.

Section scope

Specifies the components to be left uncut when you create an assembly drawing section view.

Section view
A section view (or section cut) is (1) a part or assembly view cut by a plane, or (2) a drawing view created by cutting another drawing view with a section line.

Seed
A sketch or an entity (a feature, face, or body) that is the basis for a pattern. If you edit the seed, the other entities in the pattern are updated.

Shaded
Displays a model as a colored solid.

Shared values
Also called linked values, these are named variables that you assign to set the value of two or more dimensions to be equal.

Sheet format
Includes page size and orientation, standard text, borders, title blocks, and so on. Sheet formats can be customized and saved for future use. Each sheet of a drawing document can have a different format.

Shell
A feature that hollows out a part, leaving open the selected faces and thin walls on the remaining faces. A hollow part is created when no faces are selected to be open.

Sketch
A collection of lines and other 2D objects on a plane or face that forms the basis for a feature such as a base or a boss. A 3D sketch is non-planar and can be used to guide a sweep or loft, for example.

Smart Fasteners
Automatically adds fasteners (bolts and screws) to an assembly using the SolidWorks Toolbox library of fasteners.

SmartMates
An assembly mating relation that is created automatically.

Solid sweep
A cut sweep created by moving a tool body along a path to cut out 3D material from a model.

Spiral
A flat or 2D helix, defined by a circle, pitch, and number of revolutions.

Spline
A sketched 2D or 3D curve defined by a set of control points.

Split line
Projects a sketched curve onto a selected model face, dividing the face into multiple faces so that each can be selected individually. A split line can be used to create draft features, to create face blend fillets, and to radiate surfaces to cut molds.

Stacked balloon
A set of balloons with only one leader. The balloons can be stacked vertically (up or down) or horizontally (left or right).

Standard 3 views
The three orthographic views (front, right, and top) that are often the basis of a drawing.

StereoLithography
The process of creating rapid prototype parts using a faceted mesh representation in STL files.

Sub-assembly
An assembly document that is part of a larger assembly. For example, the steering mechanism of a car is a sub-assembly of the car.

Suppress
Removes an entity from the display and from any calculations in which it is involved. You can suppress features, assembly components, and so on. Suppressing an entity does not delete the entity; you can unsuppressed the entity to restore it.

Surface
A zero-thickness planar or 3D entity with edge boundaries. Surfaces are often used to create solid features. Reference surfaces can be used to modify solid features.

Sweep
Creates a base, boss, cut, or surface feature by moving a profile (section) along a path. For cut-sweeps, you can create solid sweeps by moving a tool body along a path.

Tangent arc
An arc that is tangent to another entity, such as a line.

Tangent edge
The transition edge between rounded or filleted faces in hidden lines visible or hidden lines removed modes in drawings.

Task Pane
Located on the right-side of the SolidWorks window, the Task Pane contains SolidWorks Resources, the Design Library, and the File Explorer.

Template
A document (part, assembly, or drawing) that forms the basis of a new document. It can include user-defined parameters, annotations, predefined views, geometry, and so on.

Temporary axis
An axis created implicitly for every conical or cylindrical face in a model.

Thin feature
An extruded or revolved feature with constant wall thickness. Sheet metal parts are typically created from thin features.

TolAnalyst
A tolerance analysis application that determines the effects that dimensions and tolerances have on parts and assemblies.

Top-down design
An assembly modeling technique where you create parts in the context of an assembly by referencing the geometry of other components. Changes to the referenced components propagate to the parts that you create in context.

Triad
Three axes with arrows defining the X, Y, and Z directions. A reference triad appears in part and assembly documents to assist in orienting the viewing of models. Triads also assist when moving or rotating components in assemblies.

Under defined
A sketch is under defined when there are not enough dimensions and relations to prevent entities from moving or changing size.

Vertex
A point at which two or more lines or edges intersect. Vertices can be selected for sketching, dimensioning, and many other operations.

Viewports
Windows that display views of models. You can specify one, two, or four viewports. Viewports with orthogonal views can be linked, which links orientation and rotation.

Virtual sharp
A sketch point at the intersection of two entities after the intersection itself has been removed by a feature such as a fillet or chamfer. Dimensions and relations to the virtual sharp are retained even though the actual intersection no longer exists.

Weldment
A multibody part with structural members.

Weldment cut list
A table that tabulates the bodies in a weldment along with descriptions and lengths.

Wireframe
A view mode in which all edges of the part or assembly are displayed.

Zebra stripes

Simulate the reflection of long strips of light on a very shiny surface. They allow you to see small changes in a surface that may be hard to see with a standard display.

Zoom

To simulate movement toward or away from a part or an assembly.

Index

Designed and Rendered with Solidworks 2015

SolidWorks® Quick-Guide

Quick Reference Guide To SolidWorks® Command Icons & Toolbars

The STANDARD Toolbar

- Creates a new document.
- Opens an existing document.
- Saves an active document.
- Make Drawing from Part/Assembly
- Make Assembly from Part/Assembly
- Prints the active document.
- Displays full pages as they are printed.
- Cuts the selection & puts it on the clipboard.
- Copies the selection & puts it on the clipboard.
- Inserts the clipboard contents.
- Deletes the selection.
- Reverses the last action.
- Redo the last action that was undone.
- Rebuilds the part / assembly / drawing.
- Saves all documents.
- Changes the color of the current selection(s).
- Edits material.
- Closes an existing document
- Shows or hides the Selection Filter toolbar.
- Shows or hides the Web toolbar.
- Displays Help topics for SolidWorks.
- Displays full pages as they will be printed.

The STANDARD Toolbar (Cont.)

- Loads or unloads the 3D instant website add-in
- Select tool.
- Reloads the current document from disk.
- Places an online order for a rapid prototype part.
- Checks read-only files for write access.
- Show/Edit the properties of the current selection.
- Changes options settings for SolidWorks.
- Tiles windows vertically, as non-overlapping.
- Tiles windows horizontally, as non-overlapping.
- Opens another window for the active document.

The SKETCH TOOLS Toolbar

- Sketches a rectangle from the center.
- Sketches a centerpoint arc slot.
- Sketches a 3-point arc slot.
- Sketches a straight slot.
- Sketches a centerpoint straight slot.
- Stretches sketch entities and annotations.
- Inserts an Equation Driven Curve.
- Sketches a 3-point arc.
- Inserts a picture into the sketch background.
- Creates sketched ellipses.

The SKETCH TOOLS Toolbar

Selects items for commands to act on.

Sets up Grid parameters.

Creates a sketch on a selected plane or face.

Creates a 3D sketch.

Scales/Translates/Rotates the current sketch.

Moves or copies sketch entities and annotations.

Scales sketch entities and annotations.

Sketches an angle rectangle from the center.

Sketches a parallelogram.

Sketches a line.

Creates a center point arc: center, start, end.

Creates an arc tangent to a line.

Sketches splines on a surface or face.

Sketches a circle.

Sketches a circle by its perimeter.

Sketches a partial ellipse.

Makes a path of sketch entities.

Mirrors entities dynamically about a

Insert a plane into the 3D sketch.

Rotates sketch entities and

Copies sketch entities and

Sketches on a plane in a 3D sketch.

Moves sketch entities without solving dimensions or relations.

The SKETCH TOOLS Toolbar (Cont.)

Partial ellipses.

Adds a Parabola.

Creates sketched splines.

Sketches a polygon.

Sketches a rectangle.

Sketches a parallelogram.

Creates points.

Creates sketched centerlines.

Adds text to sketch.

Converts selected model edges or sketch entities to sketch segments.

Creates a sketch along the intersection of multiple bodies.

Converts face curves on the selected face into 3D sketch entities.

Mirrors selected segments about a centerline.

Fillets the corner of two lines.

Creates a chamfer between two sketch entities.

Creates a sketch curve by offsetting model edges or sketch entities at a specified distance.

Fits a spline to selected entities.

Trims a sketch segment.

Extends a sketch segment.

Splits a sketch segment.

Construction Geometry.

Creates linear steps and repeat of sketch entities.

Creates circular steps and repeat of sketch entities.

Quick Reference Guide To SolidWorks® Command Icons & Toolbars

The SHEET METAL

Inserts a FlattenBends & a ProcessBends feature, A sheet metal feature will be added.

Shows flat pattern for this sheet metal part.

Shows part without inserting any bends.

Inserts a rip feature to a sheet metal part.

Inserts a Sheet Metal Base Flange or a Tab feature.

Inserts a Sheet Metal Miter Flange feature.

Folds selected bends.

Unfolds selected bends.

Inserts bends using a sketch line.

Inserts a flange by pulling an edge.

Inserts a sheet metal corner feature.

Inserts a Hem feature by selecting edges.

Breaks a corner by filleting/chamfering it.

Inserts a Jog feature using a sketch line.

Inserts a lofted bend feature using 2 sketches.

Creates inverse dent on a sheet metal part.

Trims out material from a corner, in a sheet metal

Inserts a fillet weld bead.

Converts a solid/surface into a sheet metal part.

Adds a Cross Break feature into a selected face.

The SURFACES Toolbar

Deletes a face or a set of faces.

Creates mid surfaces between offset face pairs.

Patches surface holes and external edges.

The SURFACES Toolbar (cont.)

Creates an extruded surface.

Creates a revolved surface.

Creates a swept surface.

Creates a lofted surface.

Creates an offset surface.

Radiates a surface originating from a curve, parallel to a plane.

Knits surfaces together.

Creates a planar surface from a sketch or A set of edges.

Creates a surface by importing data from a file.

Extends a surface.

Trims a surface.

Generating MidSurface(s).

Surface Flatten.

Replaces Face with Surface.

Patches surface holes and external edges by extending the surfaces.

Creates parting surfaces between core & cavity surfaces.

Inserts ruled surfaces from edges.

The WELDMENTS Toolbar

Creates a weldment feature.

Creates a structure member feature.

Adds a gusset feature between 2 planar adjoining faces.

Creates an end cap feature.

Adds a fillet weld bead feature.

Trims or extends structure members.

The DIMENSIONS/RELATIONS Toolbar

Inserts dimension between two lines.

Creates a horizontal dimension between selected entities.

Creates a vertical dimension between selected entities.

Creates a reference dimension between selected entities.

Creates a set of ordinate dimensions.

Creates a set of Horizontal ordinate dimensions.

Creates a set of Vertical ordinate dimensions.

Creates a chamfer dimension.

Adds a geometric relation.

Automatically Adds Dimensions to the current sketch.

Displays and deletes geometric relations.

Fully defines a sketch.

Scans a sketch for elements of equal length or radius.

Automatically recognize tolerance features.

Creates linked, unlinked, or collection pattern feature.

Paints faces of toleranced features in different colors.

Adds DimXpert location dimension.

Adds DimXpert datum.

Copies existing tolerance scheme to current configuration.

Adds DimXpert size dimension.

Adds DimXpert geometric tolerance.

Deletes all tolerance data base.

Adds new TolAnalyst.

The STANDARD VIEWS

Front view.

Back view.

Left view.

Right view.

Top view.

Bottom view.

Isometric view.

Trimetric view.

Dimetric view.

Normal to view.

Links all views in the viewport together.

Displays viewport with front & right views

Displays a 4 view viewport with 1st or 3rd Angle of projection.

Displays viewport with front & top

Displays viewport with a single

The Block Toolbar

Makes a new block.

Edits the selected block.

Inserts a new block to a sketch or drawing.

Adds/Removes sketch entities to/from blocks.

Updates parent sketches effected by this block.

Saves the block to a file.

Explodes the selected block.

Inserts a belt.

Did you know??

* Ctrl+Q will force a rebuild on all features of a part.
* Ctrl+B will rebuild the feature being worked on and its dependants.

The FEATURES Toolbar

Creates a boss feature by extruding a sketched profile.

Creates a revolved feature based on profile and angle parameter.

Creates a cut feature by extruding a sketched profile.

Creates a cut feature by revolving a sketched profile.

Creates a sweep feature by sweeping a profile along a path curve.

Creates a cut by sweeping a closed profile along an open or closed path.

Creates a cut by removing material between two or more profiles

Creates a cut by thickening one or more adjacent surfaces.

Adds a deformed surface by push or pull on

Creates a lofted feature between two or more profiles.

Creates a solid feature by thickening one or more adjacent surfaces.

Creates a filled feature.

Chamfers an edge or a chain of tangent edges.

Inserts a rib feature.

Scales model by a specified factor.

Creates a shell feature.

Applies draft to a selected surface.

Creates a cylindrical hole.

Inserts a hole with a pre-defined cross section.

Puts a dome surface on a face.

Puts a shape feature on a face.

Applies global deformation to solid or surface bodies.

Wraps closed sketch contour(s) onto a face.

Moves / Sizes features.

Suppresses the selected feature or component.

Un-suppresses the selected feature or component.

Flexes solid and surface bodies

Creates a linear pattern using the selected feature(s).

Creates a circular pattern using the selected feature(s).

Mirrors a feature about a plane.

Creates a Curve Driven Pattern.

Creates a Sketch Driven pattern.

Creates a Table Driven Pattern.

Inserts a split Feature.

Combines two or more solid bodies.

Joins bodies from one or more parts into a single part in the context of an assembly.

Deletes a solid or a surface.

Inserts solid(s) or surface(s) into an existing open document.

Inserts a part from file into the active part document.

Moves/Copies solid and surface bodies or moves graphics bodies.

Merges short edges on faces

Pushes solid / surface model by another solid / surface model

Moves face(s) of a solid

Area fills faces or bodies into one or more contours.

Inserts holes into a series of parts.

Returns suppressed items with dependents to the model.

Cuts a solid model with a surface.

Adds material between profiles in two directions to create a solid feature.

Cuts a solid model by removing material between profiles in two directions.

Did you know??

* Right-mouse drag a component in an assembly rotates it.
* Left- mouse drag a component in an assembly moves it.

Extracts core(s) from existing tooling split

 Constructs a surface patch

 Moves face(s) of a solid

 Finds & creates mold shut-off surfaces

 Inserts cavity into a base part.

 Scales a model by a specified factor.

 Applies draft to a selected surface.

 Inserts a split line feature.

 Creates an offset surface.

 Creates parting lines to separate core & cavity surfaces

 Creates a planar surface from a sketch or A set of edges.

 Knits surfaces together.

 Analyzes draft angles of faces, based on a mold pull direction.

 Inserts ruled surfaces from edges.

 Creates parting surfaces between core & cavity surfaces

 Creates multiple bodies from a single body.

 Inserts a tooling split feature.

 Identifies faces that form undercuts.

 Creates parting surfaces between the core & cavity.

 Inserts surface body folders for mold operation.

The **SELECTION** FILTERS

 Turns selection filters on and off.

 Clears all filters.

 Selects all filters.

 Inverts current selection.

 Allows selection of edges only.

 Allows selection of faces only.

 Adds filter for Surface Bodies.

 Adds filter for Solid Bodies.

 Adds filter for Axes.

 Adds filter for Planes.

 Adds filter for Sketch Points.

 Adds filter for Sketch Segments.

 Adds filter for Midpoints.

 Adds filter for Center Marks.

 Adds filter for Centerline.

 Adds filter for Dimensions and Hole Callouts.

 Adds filter for Surface Finish Symbols.

 Adds filter for Geometric Tolerances.

 Adds filter for Notes / Balloons.

 Adds filter for Weld Symbols.

 Adds filter for Datum Targets.

 Adds filter for Cosmetic Threads.

 Adds filter for blocks.

 Adds filter for Dowel pin symbols.

 Adds filter for connection points.

 Allows selection filter for vertices only.

 Allows selection of weld symbols only.

 Allows selection of blocks only.

 Adds filter for routing points.

The **FLYOUT** Toolbar

 2D to 3D.

 Align.

 Annotation.

 Assemblies.

 Curves.

 Dimensions / Relation.

 Drawings.

 Features.

 Fonts.

 Line Formats.

 Macros.

 Molds.

 Reference Geometry.

 Quick snap filters.

 Selection Filters.

 Sheet Metal.

 Simulation.

 Sketch.

 SolidWorks Office.

 Splines.

 Standard.

 Standard Views.

 Surfaces.

 Tools.

 View.

 Web.

 Weldments.

 Block commands.

 Explode sketch commands.

 Table commands.

 Fastening feature commands.

 Creates a rounded internal or external fillet.

 Linear Patterns Features, Faces and Bodies.

 Creates various corner treatments.

 Displays Deletes geometric relations.

 Creates dimensions for one or more entities.

 Adds an existing part or assembly.

 Linear Patterns components in assembly.

 Moves components in assembly.

 Adds section view with a section line.

 Creates various assembly features.

 Toggles various view settings.

The **SCREEN CAPTURE** Toolbar

 Copies the current graphics window to the clipboard.

 Records the current graphics window to an AVI file.

 Stops recording the current graphics window to an AVI file.

The **Explode Line Sketch** Toolbar

 Adds a route line that connect entities.

 Adds a jog to the route lines.

The LINE FORMAT Toolbar

Changes layer properties.

Changes line color.

Changes line thickness.

Changes line style.

Hides a visible edge.

Shows a hidden edge.

Changes line display mode.

The 2D-To-3D Toolbar

Makes a Front sketch from the selected entities.

Makes a Top sketch from the selected entities.

Makes a Right sketch from the selected entities.

Makes a Left sketch from the selected entities.

Makes a Bottom sketch from the selected entities.

Makes a Back sketch from the selected entities.

Makes an Auxiliary sketch from the selected entities.

Creates a new sketch from the selected entities.

Repairs the selected sketch.

Aligns a sketch to the selected point.

Creates an extrusion from the selected sketch segments, starting at the selected sketch point.

Creates a cut from the selected sketch segments, optionally starting at the selected sketch point.

The ALIGN Toolbar

Aligns the left side of the selected annotations with the leftmost annotation.

Aligns the right side of the selected annotations with the rightmost annotation.

Aligns the top side of the selected annotations with the topmost annotation.

Aligns the bottom side of the selected annotations with the lowermost annotation.

Evenly spaces the selected annotations horizontally.

Evenly spaces the selected annotations vertically.

Centrally aligns the selected annotations horizontally.

Centrally aligns the selected annotations vertically.

Compacts the selected annotations horizontally.

Compacts the selected annotations vertically.

Aligns the center of the selected annotations between

Creates a group from the selected items

Deletes the grouping between these items

Aligns & groups selected dimensions along a line or an arc

Aligns & groups dimensions at a uniform distances

The SIMULATION Toolbar

Stops Record or Playback.

Records Simulation.

Replays Simulation.

Resets Components.

Adds Linear Motor.

Adds Rotary Motor.

Adds Spring.

Adds Gravity.

The MACRO Toolbar

Runs a Macro.

Stops Macro recorder.

Records (or pauses recording of) actions to create a Macro.

Launches the Macro Editor and begins editing a new macro.

Opens a Macro file for editing.

Creates a custom macro.

The **TABLE** Toolbar

 Adds a hole table of selected holes from a specified origin datum.

 Adds a Bill of Materials.

 Adds a revision table.

 Displays a Design table in a drawing.

 Adds a weldments cuts list table.

 Adds a Excel based of Bill of Materials

 Adds a general table to a drawing sheet.

The **REFERENCE GEOMETRY**

 Adds a reference plane

 Creates an axis.

 Creates a coordinate system.

 Adds a reference point

 Specifies entities to use as references using SmartMates.

The **SPLINE TOOLS** Toolbar

 Adds a point to a spline.

 Displays points where the concavity of selected spline changes.

 Displays minimum radius of selected spline.

 Displays curvature combs of selected spline.

 Reduces numbers of points in a selected spline.

 Adds a tangency control.

 Adds a curvature control.

 Adds a spline based on selected sketch entities & edges.

 Displays all handles of selected splines.

 Displays the spline control polygon.

The **ANNOTATIONS** Toolbar

 Inserts a note.

 Inserts a surface finish symbol.

 Inserts a new geometric tolerancing symbol.

 Attaches a balloon to the selected edge or face.

 Adds balloons for all components in selected view.

 Inserts a stacked balloon.

 Attaches a datum feature symbol to a selected edge / detail.

 Inserts a weld symbol on the selected edge / face / vertex.

 Inserts a datum target symbol and / or point attached to a selected edge / line.

 Selects and inserts block.

 Inserts annotations & reference geometry from the part / assembly into the selected.

 Adds center marks to circles on model.

 Inserts a Centerline.

 Inserts a hole callout.

 Adds a cosmetic thread to the selected cylindrical feature.

 Inserts a Multi-Jog leader.

 Selects a circular edge or and arc for Dowel pin symbol insertion.

 Toggles the visibility of annotations & dimensions.

 Inserts latest version symbol.

 Adds a cross hatch patterns or solid fill.

 Adds a weld symbol on a selected entity.

 Adds a weld bead caterpillar on an edge.

The "Feathers"

 Lightweight component.

 Out-of-Date component.

 Hidden Lightweight component.

 Hidden, Out-of-Date and Lightweight.

The DRAWINGS Toolbar

Updates the selected view to the model's current stage.

Creates a detail view.

Creates a section view.

Inserts an aligned section using the selected line or section line.

Unfolds a new view from an existing view.

Generates a standard 3-view drawing (1st or 3rd angle).

Inserts an auxiliary view of an inclined surface.

Adds an Orthogonal or Named view based on an existing part or assembly.

Adds a Relative view by two orthogonal faces or planes.

Adds a Predefined orthogonal projected or Named view with a model.

Adds an empty view.

Adds vertical break lines to selected view.

Crops a view.

Creates a Broken-out section.

Inserts an Alternate Position view.

The QUICK SNAP Toolbar

Snap to points.

Snap to center points.

Snap to midpoints.

Snap to quadrant points.

Snap to intersection of 2 curves.

Snap to nearest curve.

Snap tangent to curve.

Snap perpendicular to curve.

Snap parallel to line.

Snap horizontally / vertically.

Snap horizontally / vertically to points.

Snap to discrete line lengths.

Snap to grid points.

Snap to angle.

The LAYOUT Toolbar

Creates the assembly layout sketch.

Sketches a line.

Sketches a rectangle.

Sketches a circle.

Sketches a 3 point arc.

Rounds a corner.

Trims or extends a sketch.

Adds sketch entities by offsetting faces, Edges curves.

Mirrors selected entities about a centerline.

Adds a relation.

Creates a dimension.

Displays / Deletes geometric relations.

Makes a new block.

Edits the selected block.

Inserts a new block to the sketch or drawing.

Adds / Removes sketch entities to / from a block.

Saves the block to a file.

Explodes the selected block.

Creates a new part from a layout sketch block.

Positions 2 components relative to one another.

Moves a component within the degrees of freedom defined by its mates.

The CURVES Toolbar

Projects sketch onto selected surface.

Inserts a split line feature.

Creates a composite curve from selected edges, curves and sketches.

Creates a curve through free points.

Creates a 3D curve through reference points.

Helical curve defined by a base sketch and shape parameters.

The VIEW Toolbar

Displays a view in the selected orientation.

Reverts to previous view.

Zooms out to see entire model.

Zooms in by dragging a bounding box.

Zooms in or out by dragging up or down.

Zooms to fit all selected entities.

Dynamic view rotation.

Scrolls view by dragging.

Displays image in wireframe mode.

Displays hidden edges in gray.

Displays image with hidden lines removed.

Controls the visibility of planes.

Controls the visibility of axis.

Controls the visibility of parting lines.

Controls the visibility of temporary axis.

Controls the visibility of origins.

Controls the visibility of coordinate systems.

Controls the visibility of reference curves.

Controls the visibility of sketches.

Controls the visibility of 3D sketch planes.

Controls the visibility of 3D sketch

Controls the visibility of all annotations.

Controls the visibility of reference points.

Controls the visibility of routing points.

Controls the visibility of lights.

Controls the visibility of cameras.

Controls the visibility of sketch relations.

Redraws the current window.

Rolls the model view.

Turns the orientation of the model view.

Dynamically manipulate the model view in 3D to make selection.

Changes the display style for the active view.

Displays a shade view of the model with its edges.

Displays a shade view of the model.

Toggles between draft quality & high quality HLV.

Cycles through or applies a specific scene.

Views the models through one of the model's cameras.

Displays a part or assembly w/different colors according to the local radius of curvature.

Displays zebra stripes.

Displays a model with hardware accelerated shades.

Edits the real view appearance of entities in the model.

Applies a texture to entities in a model.

Changes the visibility of items in the graphics area.

Controls visibility of the sketch grid.

The **TOOLS** Toolbar

 Calculates the distance between selected items.

 Adds or edits equation.

 Calculates the mass properties of the model.

 Checks the model for geometry errors.

 Inserts or edits a Design Table.

 Evaluates section properties for faces and sketches that lie in parallel planes.

 Reports Statistics for this Part/Assembly.

 Deviation Analysis.

 Runs the SimulationXpress analysis wizard Powered by SolidWorks Simulation.

 Checks the spelling.

 Import diagnostics.

 Runs the DFMXpress analysis wizard.

 Runs the DriveWorkXpress wizard.

 Runs the SolidWorksFloXpress analysis wizard.

The **ASSEMBLY** Toolbar

 Creates a new part & inserts it into the assembly.

 Adds an existing part or sub-assembly to the assembly.

 Creates a new assembly & inserts it into the assembly.

 Turns on/off large assembly mode for this document.

 Hides / shows model(s) associated with the selected model(s).

 Toggles the transparency of components.

 Changes the selected components to suppressed or resolved.

 Toggles between editing part and assembly.

 Inserts a belt.

 Inserts a new part into an assembly.

 Smart Fasteners.

 Positions two components relative to one.

 External references will not be created.

 Moves a component.

 Rotates an un-mated component around its center point.

 Replaces selected components.

 Replaces mate entities of mates of the selected components on the selected Mategroup.

 Creates a New Exploded view.

 Creates or edits explode line sketch.

 Interference detection.

 Changes assembly transparency.

 Shows or Hides the Simulation toolbar.

 Patterns components in one or two linear directions.

 Patterns components around an axis.

 Toggles the transparency of components Between 0 and 75 percent.

 Toggles between editing a Part and Assembly.

 Adds fasteners to the assembly using Toolbox.

 Displays statistics and check the health of The current assembly.

 Patterns components relative to an existing Pattern in a part.

 Shows hidden components.

 Toggles large assembly mode for this document.

 Checks assembly hole alignments.

 Mirrors subassemblies and parts.

To add or remove an icon
to or from the toolbar, first select:

Tools/Customize/Commands

Next select a **Category**, click a button to see its description and then drag / drop the command icon into any toolbar.

Standard Keyboard Shortcuts

Rotate the model

* Horizontally or Vertically: _____ Arrow keys

* Horizontally or Vertically 90°: _____ Shift + Arrow keys

* Clockwise or Counterclockwise: _____ Alt + left or right Arrow

* Pan the model: _____ Ctrl + Arrow keys

* Zoom in: _____ Z (shift + Z or capital Z)

* Zoom out: _____ z (lower case z)

* Zoom to fit: _____ F

* Previous view: _____ Ctrl+Shift+Z

View Orientation

* View Orientation Menu: _____ Space bar

* Front: _____ Ctrl+1

* Back: _____ Ctrl+2

* Left: _____ Ctrl+3

* Right: _____ Ctrl+4

* Top: _____ Ctrl+5

* Bottom: _____ Ctrl+6

* Isometric: _____ Ctrl+7

Selection Filter & Misc.

* Filter Edges: _____ e

* Filter Vertices: _____ v

* Filter Faces: _____ x

* Toggle Selection filter toolbar: _____ F5

* Toggle Selection Filter toolbar (on/off): _____ F6

* New SolidWorks document: _____ F1

* Open Document: _____ Ctrl+O

* Open from Web folder: _____ Ctrl+W

* Save: _____ Ctrl+S

* Print: _____ Ctrl+P

* Magnifying Glass Zoom _____ g

* Switch between the SolidWorks documents _____ Ctrl + Tab

Double click the **SW-2015 Sample Settings** to install the sample keyboard shortcuts and use the **Sample Part Template** (included) to try out the hot keys (below).

Function Keys

F1	SW-Help
F2	2D Sketch
F3	3D Sketch
F4	Modify Sketch
F5	Selection Filters
F6	Move (2D Sketch)
F7	Rotate (2D Sketch)
F8	Measure
F9	Extrude
F10	Revolve
F11	Sweep
F12	Loft

Sketch

C	Circle
P	Polygon
E	Ellipse
O	Offset Entities
R	Corner Rectangle
Alt + C	Convert Entities
M	Mirror
Alt + M	Dynamic Mirror
Alt + F	Sketch Fillet
T	Trim
Alt + X	Extend
D	Smart Dimension
Alt + R	Add Relation
Alt + P	Plane
Control + F	Fully Define Sketch